How to access the supplemental web resource

We are pleased to provide access to a web resource that supplements your textbook, *Teaching Fundamental Motor Skills, Third Edition.* This resource offers partner skill check assessments and troubleshooting charts that can be printed out or used on mobile devices. Online animations bring the critical elements of each motor skill to life. Cue sets with the critical elements illustrated are also included.

Accessing the web resource is easy!

1. Visit www.HumanKinetics.com/TeachingFundamentalMotorSkills.

2. Click the <u>third</u> edition link next to the corresponding third edition book cover.

3. Click the Sign In link on the left or top of the page. If you do not have an account with Human Kinetics, you will be prompted to create one.

4. If the online product you purchased does not appear in the Ancillary Items box on the left of the page, click the Enter Key Code option in that box. Enter the key code that is printed at the right, including all hyphens. Click the Submit button to unlock your online product.

5. After you have entered your key code the first time, you will never have to enter it again to access this product. Once unlocked, a link to your product will permanently appear in the menu on the left. For future visits, all you need to do is sign in to the textbook's website and follow the link that appears in the left menu!

→ Click the Need Help? button on the textbook's website if you need assistance along the way.

For technical support, send an e-mail to:
support@hkusa.com . . . . U.S. and international customers
info@hkcanada.com . . . . Canadian customers
academic@hkeurope.com . . . . European customers
keycodesupport@hkaustralia.com . . . . . Australian and New Zealand customers

D0927554

HUMAN KINETICS
The Information Leader in Physical Activity & Health

02-2016

Product: Teaching Fundamental Motor Skills, Third Edition, web resource

Key code: COLVIN-ACC7FK-OSG

This unique code allows you access to the web resource.

Access is provided if you have purchased a new book. Once submitted, the code may not be entered for any other user.

THIRD EDITION

TEACHING FUNDAMENTAL MOTOR SKILLS

A. Vonnie Colvin, EdD

Longwood University, Farmville, Virginia

Nancy J. Egner Markos, MEd

Physical education presenter and consultant,
Earlysville, Virginia

Pamela J. Walker, MEd

Red Hill Elementary School,
North Garden, Virginia

SHAPE America SOCIETY OF HEALTH AND PHYSICAL EDUCATORS®

health. moves. minds.

Human Kinetics

Library of Congress Cataloging-in-Publication Data

Names: Colvin, A. Vonnie, 1951- author. | Markos, Nancy J. Egner, 1949-
author. | Walker, Pamela J., 1953- author.
Title: Teaching fundamental motor skills / A. Vonnie Colvin, Nancy J. Egner
Markos, Pamela J. Walker.
Other titles: Teaching the nuts and bolts of physical education
Description: Third edition. | Champaign, IL : Human Kinetics, 2016. | This
book is a revised edition of Teaching the Nuts and Bolts of Physical
Education published in 2008. | Includes bibliographical references.
Identifiers: LCCN 2015028892 | ISBN: 978-1-4925-2126-6 (print)
Subjects: LCSH: Physical education for children. | Movement education.

Classification: LCC GV443 .C59 2016 | DDC 372.86--dc23 LC record available at http://lccn.loc.gov/2015028892

ISBN: 978-1-4925-2126-6 (print)

The web addresses cited in this text were current as of November 2015, unless otherwise noted.

Acquisitions Editor: Scott Wikgren; **SHAPE America Editor:** Joe McGavin; **Developmental Editor:** Melissa Feld; **Managing Editor:** Anne E. Mrozek; **Copyeditor:** Shannon Foreman; **Proofreader:** Jan Feeney; **Permissions Manager:** Dalene Reeder; **Senior Graphic Designers:** Fred Starbird and Joe Buck; **Cover Designer:** Keith Blomberg; **Photograph (cover):** © Human Kinetics; **Photographs (interior):** © Human Kinetics, unless otherwise noted; **Photo Asset Manager:** Laura Fitch; **Photo Production Manager:** Jason Allen; **Art Manager:** Kelly Hendren; **Associate Art Manager:** Alan L. Wilborn; **Illustrations:** © Human Kinetics; **Printer:** Sheridan Books

The animation contents of this product are licensed for educational public performance for viewing by a traditional (live) audience, via closed circuit television, or via computerized local area networks within a single building or geographically unified campus. To request a license to broadcast these contents to a wider audience—for example, throughout a school district or state, or on a television station—please contact your sales representative (www.HumanKinetics.com/SalesRepresentatives).

SHAPE America — Society of Health and Physical Educators
1900 Association Drive
Reston, VA 20191
800-213-7193
www.shapeamerica.org

Printed in the United States of America

10 9 8 7 6 5 4 3 2 1

The paper in this book is certified under a sustainable forestry program.

Human Kinetics
Website: www.HumanKinetics.com

United States: Human Kinetics
P.O. Box 5076
Champaign, IL 61825-5076
800-747-4457
e-mail: info@hkusa.com

Canada: Human Kinetics
475 Devonshire Road Unit 100
Windsor, ON N8Y 2L5
800-465-7301 (in Canada only)
e-mail: info@hkcanada.com

Europe: Human Kinetics
107 Bradford Road
Stanningley
Leeds LS28 6AT, United Kingdom
+44 (0) 113 255 5665
e-mail: hk@hkeurope.com

Australia: Human Kinetics
57A Price Avenue
Lower Mitcham, South Australia 5062
08 8372 0999
e-mail: info@hkaustralia.com

New Zealand: Human Kinetics
P.O. Box 80
Mitcham Shopping Centre, South Australia 5062
0800 222 062
e-mail: info@hknewzealand.com

E6698

We dedicate this book to the many students we have been privileged to teach. Students of all ages have helped us become better teachers and enabled us to write this book. As we near the end of our teaching careers, we also dedicate this text to the professionals in our field and hope they fall in love with teaching as much as we have.

Contents

Preface

As educators, we should strive to create developmentally appropriate learning environments for our students in which they can practice in noncompetitive situations with a focus on personal growth (SHAPE America, 2014). While the main goal of all areas of education is improving skills, we believe that instruction can be presented so that it is motivating and enjoyable. Although fun is not the goal of education, it can be a very motivating by-product. When children are motivated and they receive sound instruction, they are more focused on learning. In physical education, this learning can help students continue to be physically active throughout their lives.

There are peak times for children to learn to read, learn a foreign language, and learn fundamental movements, and these times occur when children are young. The ages between three and nine are a critical time for children to learn physical skills (Pangrazi, Chomokos, & Massoney, 1981). In the early grades, children are able to master basic movement skills with less difficulty than at any other time in their lives. Locomotor and manipulative skills are the essential building blocks that enable students to cross the proficiency barrier to be successful movers (Seefeldt, 1979). High-quality instruction and practice, however, are necessary for mastering the proper mechanics of all motor skills. These experiences can translate into skill acquisition and a physically active lifestyle.

In the past, many programs focused on playing games that had no instructional focus. The games of Red Rover and Duck, Duck, Goose are enjoyable, but they do nothing to develop basic skills. Yet for more than two decades, reports from the National Association for Sport and Physical Education (NASPE)—now known as SHAPE America—have stressed instruction in basic skills. As NASPE's outcomes of quality physical education programs (1992) reported, "the greatest emphasis during the preschool and early elementary grades should be upon movement skill acquisition" (p. 9).

NASPE's outcomes project was the forerunner for the development of the National Standards for Physical Education (NASPE, 1995), which were revised in 2003 and again in 2013. The current edition of the National Standards sets the goal of creating "physically literate individuals" who have "learned the skills necessary to participate in a variety of physical activities" (SHAPE America, 2014, p. 11). SHAPE America elaborates: "Because elementary school is the foundation for the development of fundamental motor skills, it is imperative that the focus of physical education be on skill acquisition. . . . Emerging skills become mature skills only with deliberate practice and quality instruction. The fundamental motor skills of elementary school form the building blocks for game play, physical activity and fitness activities that follow in middle and high school" (pp. 15-16). The challenge for those who teach elementary-age children is clear: Basic skills should be the heart of the physical education curriculum. Yet, while the current literature clearly indicates *what* should be taught, few resources are available to explain *how* those skills should be taught. This book provides those who work with elementary-age children with a sequence of information and activities that serve as the building blocks for successful movement experiences for children. These building blocks include mastering the critical elements of the basic locomotor and manipulative skills. This book presents standards-based information in ways that students will find motivating. These enjoyable activities will ensure more practice and improved skill acquisition. After all, when you enjoy what you do, you want to continue.

ORGANIZATION

To help you build this foundation, we have organized this book in a user-friendly way, with similar ideas and skills combined. We begin by providing an overview of how to best use this book. Chapter 1 is perhaps the most crucial chapter; it introduces nine activities that stress learning the essential parts of each skill. Any or all of the activities will help students master the critical elements of the 8 locomotor skills (chapter 2) and the 17 manipulative skills (chapters 3-10) that are detailed in this book.

Chapter 2 addresses eight locomotor skills: hopping, galloping, sliding, running, skipping, jumping in the vertical plane, jumping in the horizontal plane, and leaping. Although locomotor skills are an integral part of sport participation, they are often overlooked when planning a complete physical education experience for all students. Chapter 2 describes each locomotor skill in detail and includes assessments.

Chapters 3 through 10 are devoted to the manipulative skills. While chapter 3 addresses just one manipulative skill, underhand rolling, the remaining chapters address multiple skills that are similar. For example, chapter 4 explores underhand throwing, overhand throwing, and two-hand overhead throwing, which are distinct skills that all involve throwing an object. Chapter 5 is devoted to catching above the waist and below the waist. Chapter 6, Passing, covers bounce passing and chest passing. Chapter 7, Striking, covers underhand striking, sidearm striking, and two-hand sidearm striking. Chapter 8, Volleying, covers forearm passing and overhead volleying. Chapter 9 is devoted to using the feet for kicking and punting. Chapter 10 involves dribbling, which is unique because it combines locomotor and manipulative skills; both dribbling with the hands and dribbling with the feet are addressed in detail.

Our curriculum focus as physical educators should be on skill mastery and lifetime fitness. While there are many sport-specific manipulative skills, the ones we have selected provide a foundation for the acquisition of other skills. For example, a skillful tennis serve requires many of the same skill components as the overhand throw, and an underhand serve in volleyball is composed of many components needed for mastery of the underhand throw. The list is endless, but the outcome is the same: When students are able to master fundamental manipulative skills, they can apply that knowledge to other skills that use similar actions.

ORGANIZATION OF SKILL CHAPTERS

In chapter 2, Locomotor Skills, and in each of the chapters on manipulative skills (3-10), we progress through each skill in the following order:

1. A general introduction to the skill is provided.

2. Critical elements of each skill are explained and line drawings are provided. Each skill is broken down into the critical elements that are necessary for the skill to be performed correctly.

3. Alignment of the skill with *National Standards & Grade-Level Outcomes for K-12 Physical Education* (SHAPE America, 2014) is emphasized in narrative and chart forms for all skills that this text and the outcomes share.

4. Cue words are included to assist students in remembering each critical element of the skill, and the cue words are interwoven throughout the chapter.

5. Partner assessments are included for each skill to help students master the information about the critical elements of that skill. Two types of assessments are included: one for children who can read and one for nonreaders.

6. To reinforce the critical elements of each skill, a variety of activities are included. Numerous individual, partner, and group activities are included to reinforce the *entire* skill, not just isolated elements.

7. Troubleshooting charts for each skill highlight typical problem areas and provide suggestions for remedying identified problems.

8. Each of the manipulative skill chapters (3-10) also contains a sample lesson plan. This scripted plan is designed to be used when introducing the skill.

NEW FEATURES IN THIS EDITION

All of the features of the original *Teaching the Nuts and Bolts of Physical Education* have returned in this *Teaching Fundamental Motor Skills* text. However, there are two major changes. The most obvious new feature is the addition of a web resource. The reproducible partner skill check assessments, troubleshooting charts, and cue sets included in the text are available on the web resource as full-size PDFs, which will enable you to easily make copies of them for classroom use. In addition, you can find animations of each skill on the web resource.

A second major addition is the embedding of SHAPE America's Grade-Level Outcomes, which also appear in *National Standards & Grade-Level Outcomes for K-12 Physical Education* (SHAPE America, 2014) within the text and in chart form for most of the skills included in this book. The alignment of critical elements with the appropriate grade level for mastery is an important feature. Although each child is unique, the added information included from SHAPE America will be very beneficial as you plan your lesson sequences. Children who attempt skills too early become frustrated, and delaying the introduction of other skills can also be problematic. The information from SHAPE America is incredibly helpful and we have aligned our content with it.

We believe that the skills covered in this book represent the fundamentals of building a successful physical education curriculum for children. This book is a collection of teaching strategies and ideas that we have developed throughout our combined 100 years of teaching experience. The activities contained in our book are kid tested, and they have been very successful in our elementary schools. We hope that you will use our ideas, create some of your own, and, most of all, enjoy what you do.

50 MILLION STRONG BY 2029

Approximately 50 million students are currently enrolled in America's elementary and secondary schools (grades pre-K to 12). SHAPE America is leading the effort to ensure that by the time today's preschoolers graduate from high school in 2029, all of America's students will have developed the skills, knowledge and confidence to enjoy healthy, meaningful physical activity.

Acknowledgments

Many thanks to the wonderful faculty and staff at Scottsville Elementary School in Albemarle County, Virginia, for providing us with a place to work on this third edition. We are also very appreciative of our students in elementary schools and college classrooms. You are our motivation and our passion. Thank you.

Vonnie Colvin

I would like to thank my family for their encouragement, love, and support. Professionally, I have been fortunate to work with such outstanding mentors as Barb Call and Jim Nance from the University of Kentucky, Ann Boyce from the University of Virginia, and Sarah Bingham from Longwood University. But the people who keep me going are the students, from pre-K to grad school. Thank you.

Nancy Markos

I would like to thank my husband, Artie, for the love and support he has given me over the years. To my children, Lance and Wendy, thank you for making my life complete. A special thanks to my parents, Bob and Betty Egner, for their constant love and support. They taught me that anything in life is possible. I would like to thank my sister, Barbara Stansfield, who is always there when I need a laugh. Finally, a big thank-you to my students for making my job the best one anyone can have!

Pam Walker

I would like to thank my parents, Sue and Jim Walker, for their constant love and support and for teaching me that anything is possible. A big thank-you to Deb, Kim, Howard, and the kids for keeping me from taking myself or life too seriously. I would also like to thank my many friends for their encouragement, humor, and support. Finally, I would like to thank all of the students I have taught through the years. Their willingness to try new activities and games I have created and their ingenuity in creating their own activities and games have contributed to the writing of this book.

SHAPE America acknowledges and thanks Shirley Holt/Hale, PhD, for reviewing some of the content for this book. Shirley, who retired recently after teaching physical education at Linden Elementary School in Oak Ridge, Tennessee, for 38 years, served on the team that developed and wrote *National Standards & Grade-Level Outcomes for K-12 Physical Education* (SHAPE America, 2014).

How to Use This Resource

Elementary-age children bring an excitement to the physical education environment that is contagious. This book capitalizes on that student excitement by presenting motivating methods to promote successful learning experiences that enable children to demonstrate competency in motor skills and movement patterns. When children are motivated to learn, when they want to keep practicing because they enjoy it, and when they are provided sound, sequential instruction, then success and achievement will follow.

Although motivation and success are important components of the teaching and learning process, high-quality instruction requires that detailed lesson plans be developed and implemented to meet the needs of all children, regardless of skill level. This book provides those resources.

The foundational knowledge required for being a skillful mover is found in mastery of the locomotor movements and basic manipulative skills. Within this text, we address the locomotor skills of hopping, galloping, sliding, running, skipping, jumping in the vertical plane, jumping in the horizontal plane, and leaping. The manipulative skills essential for later sport participation are also included: underhand rolling, throwing (underhand, overhand, and two-hand), catching, passing (bounce and chest), striking (underhand, sidearm, and two-hand sidearm), volleying (forearm and overhead), kicking, punting, and dribbling with the hands and the feet.

The primary objective of this edition of the book is to align this text with the *National Standards & Grade-Level Outcomes for K-12 Physical Education* (SHAPE America, 2014). As table 1 indicates, all eight of the basic locomotor skills are included and aligned with the new outcomes.

Table 1 Alignment of This Text With Grade-Level Outcomes for Locomotor Skills

Locomotor skills detailed in this text	Locomotor skills detailed in this text and in the Grade-Level Outcomes
Hopping (S1.E1)	
Galloping (S1.E1)	
Sliding (S1.E1)	
Skipping (S1.E1)	
Leaping (S1.E1)	
	Running (S1.E2)
	Jumping in the horizontal plane (S1.E3)
	Jumping in the vertical plane (S1.E4)

Standards reprinted, by permission, from SHAPE America – Society of Health and Physical Educators, 2014, *National standards & grade-level outcomes for K-12 physical education* (Champaign, IL: Human Kinetics).

Manipulative skills (i.e., those that involve controlling an object) are not as easily aligned to the outcomes. The progression of a basic manipulative skill to a sport skill can be very unique. The outcomes and this book both contain 17 manipulative skills, but the alignment is not exact; however, every effort for alignment has been made (see table 2).

Table 2 Alignment of Text With Grade-Level Outcomes for Manipulative Skills

Manipulative skills exclusive to this text	Manipulative skills detailed in this text and in the Grade-Level Outcomes	Manipulative skills included in this text and in the Grade-Level Outcomes (slight variations exist between this text and the outcomes)
Underhand rolling		
	Underhand throwing (S1.E13)	
	Overhead throwing (S1.E1 4)	
Two-hand overhead throwing		
	Catching above the waist (S1.E16)	
	Catching below the waist (S1.E16)	
Bounce passing		Passing with hands is addressed (S1.E15), but not specific to bounce passing
Chest passing		Passing with hands is addressed (S1.E15), but not specific to chest passing
	Underhand striking (S1.E22)	
Sidearm striking		Striking with short-handled implements (S1.E24), but very similar to sidearm striking
Two-hand sidearm striking		Striking with long-handled implements (S1.E25), but very similar to two-hand sidearm striking
Forearm passing		
	Overhead volleying (S1.E23)	
	Kicking (S1.E21)	
Punting		Addressed in grades 4 and 5 under Outcomes for kicking (S1.E21)
	Dribbling with hands (S1.E17)	
	Dribbling with feet (S1.E18)	

Standards reprinted, by permission, from SHAPE America – Society of Health and Physical Educators, 2014, *National standards & grade-level outcomes for K-12 physical education* (Champaign, IL: Human Kinetics).

WEB RESOURCE

The third edition of this text is similar to previous editions, but the inclusion of a web resource is a major advancement. Full-size, reproducible partner skill assessments are available on the web resource; these are shown at a smaller size in the book. In addition, you can find troubleshooting charts, cue sets, and animations of the skills on the web. Instructions for accessing the web resource appear at the front of the book.

MORE ABOUT THE GRADE-LEVEL OUTCOMES AND NATIONAL STANDARDS

As you read the information pertaining to the Grade-Level Outcomes, you will notice letters and numbers included within parentheses. The S indicates which National Standard is being addressed. In this text, we will primarily address Standard 1 (S1), which relates to demonstrating competency in a variety of motor skills and movement patterns. We also briefly address Standard 2 (S2), which involves applying knowledge of concepts, principles, strategies, and tactics related to movement and performance.

After the S1 or S2, you will see a letter. Because this text is designed for teachers of the elementary grades, we use only the outcomes that are related to those grades. The E means the outcome is specific to elementary-age children, and the grade levels addressed are kindergarten through grade 5. The number to the right of the E indicates the number of the outcome. When specific grade levels are included, that information is also noted. For example, S1.E13 refers to Standard 1 and Outcome 13, the underhand throw. Within each outcome, grade-level information is delineated. For second grade, the information for the underhand throw reads, "Throws underhand using a mature pattern" (S1.E13.2). This information ties the grade level to the specific outcome.

ORGANIZATION

We have attempted to provide a variety of materials for teaching the 8 locomotor and the 17 manipulative skills addressed in this book. Our goal is for you to be able to easily locate and implement multiple activities that will enhance instruction and promote student learning. Regardless of the topic, all skill chapters are organized in the following manner:

1. *Introduction:* Depending on the skill, this general introduction may include teaching suggestions, safety precautions, and equipment modifications. In addition, suggested ages at which the skill or a part of the skill should be mastered are included and, whenever possible, this is aligned with the Grade-Level Outcomes (SHAPE America, 2014). A narrative and charts about the outcomes and skills are included to make this information easier to use.

2. *Critical elements:* Next, we identify the three to six critical elements that are necessary for the skill to be performed correctly. The critical elements are aligned with the Grade-Level Outcomes whenever possible.

3. *Cue words:* To assist the students in remembering each element, cue words are emphasized and interwoven throughout instruction. The cue words are part of a start phase (ready position), an action phase (which may have two or three parts), and an ending phase (stop). Your choice of cue words will depend on your areas of emphasis and the developmental levels of the students you are teaching. Younger students should be given cues that are short and descriptive of the action they are to perform; older students may be able to use longer, more specific cues. You should be sure that the cues you use contain only a few words and don't become long sentences. When introducing a skill for the first time, you should emphasize just one or two parts of the skill.

It may be necessary to adapt cues for children with disabilities. For example, when teaching underhand rolling to a child in a wheelchair, you might omit the *step* cue, but maintain the other cues (*ready, arm back, roll,* and *follow through*).

4. *Partner skill check assessments:* To help your students master each skill's critical elements, partner skill check assessments are included for each of the 25 skills. The partner skill check assessments allow partners to evaluate each other's progress in

learning the selected skill. You may also use these as formative or summative assessments. In addition, they can be provided to parents to document student progress.

We have designed two versions of the skill check assessments so that all children can benefit from their use. The first version contains drawings that relate to the designated cue words. Use this version with young children who do not read or those who do not speak English. The second version contains written descriptions of the skill's critical elements as well as drawings and appropriate boxes to check. Use this version with older children who are able to read. Both versions are included in the web resource to make duplication easier. These assessments may be imported into electronic devices.

5. *Success builders:* In the manipulative skills chapters (3 through 10) we have included sections on success-building activities. If the partner skill check assessment reveals that a student is experiencing difficulty with one or more elements of the skill, specific activities are explained in the success builders section to help the student correct the problem.

At each success builder station, regardless of the skill being taught, we suggest having an unbreakable mirror and a poster showing each critical element. The mirror is particularly helpful because it allows the children to see what they are doing. You can make the posters by photocopying and enlarging the partner skill check assessment drawings from this book (or from the web resource). Laminating each poster will ensure its use for many years. These drawings may be imported into electronic devices.

6. *Activities:* To reinforce the *entire* skill, we have included numerous activities for individuals, partners, and groups. Each activity contains extensions to add variety to the lesson or to make the tasks easier or more difficult. Whenever possible, we have integrated other academic areas (e.g., language arts, math) into the performance of physical skills in the practice activities. For example, the Color Targets activity suggests using colors, shapes, numbers, or words, depending on the ages and abilities of the students. In Create-a-Word, students use letter targets to spell words. After students have achieved mastery of a particular skill, the activities in these sections may be used again during recess.

7. *Troubleshooting charts:* We have included troubleshooting charts that describe typical problem areas and suggest remedies. The partner skill check assessments and success builder activities examine how students perform the skills. The troubleshooting charts describe problem areas in overall student performance (e.g., what happened, the result).

Each chart includes two headings. The first heading, *If you see this,* details common problem areas. The second heading, *Then try this,* offers solutions. For example, in a lateral slide, you may see the student's body turned in such a way that his side does not lead the slide. In this situation, a possible solution would be to have the student stand with his back to a wall and slide along the wall at a slow speed. Once he understands the movement, the speed of the skill can be increased and the student can practice away from the wall.

8. *Lesson plans:* For each of the manipulative skills, we have included a sample 30-minute lesson plan. This plan focuses on an aspect of the skill that can be the most challenging to teach and the most difficult for children to learn. To guide you through the instructional sequence, each lesson is deliberately overplanned and described in detail. Within each scripted lesson plan are instant activities and detailed directions for the entire lesson, as well as instructions on exactly what to watch for when the students are practicing.

CHANGE IS GOOD

Since movements are never the same every time they are executed, we encourage you to combine skills with other activities as soon as possible. This method is embedded in chapter 2, where we use the various movement concepts (e.g., pathways, levels) throughout instruction for each locomotor skill. We also include challenges in chapters 3 through 10 that encourage students to combine each manipulative skill with other movements. These challenges include the use of space, force, level, speed, direction, and pathways. Using the movement concepts will not only add to the challenge of the activity, but it will also make the practice sessions more exciting for your students.

ASSESSMENT

Assessment is an essential part of the teaching and learning process. The information obtained through assessment can help you modify instructional strategies and identify areas of student strength or weakness. Assessments can also serve as motivational tools.

Assessments may be done by students, teachers, or both. They might be informal, such as when the teacher observes the students to determine what part of the skill the students need to continue practicing or whether they are ready for an increased challenge, or they might be more formal, where there is a specific evaluation tool (e.g., the partner skill check assessment) used and the evaluation results become part of the grading process. *How* you choose to assess your students will depend on many factors, including time, resources, personal philosophy, and expectations. Whether you use informal or formal assessments, it is important to evaluate the skill development of your students. These assessments will help you focus on student needs and develop your lesson plans to better meet the instructional challenges of your students.

This book provides several activities that can assist you and your students with assessment. Sections devoted to specific skill elements, skill check assessments, success builder activities, and troubleshooting charts are included for each skill. Each of these activities can be used as they are or adapted to fit your specific assessment needs.

We strongly recommend using ongoing peer observations in which the students are asked to examine one another's skills. Learning can be enhanced when students use the partner skill check assessments. A student can also observe a partner without these tools to determine whether she has mastered one or more specific elements of the skill. In either situation, a student can tell his partner what parts of the skill are being performed correctly and what elements need improvement. This specific feedback will improve students' understanding of the skill.

You may also use the partner skill check assessments to highlight individual students' strengths or weaknesses or as a method of student evaluation to be shared with parents. When used as pretests and later as posttests, the assessments can clearly show specific areas of student improvement and skill acquisition.

Information from this book will help you in planning future lessons. The partner skill check assessments and troubleshooting charts will help identify potential problem areas and suggest ways to correct them. Once you have a clear idea of what needs to be emphasized or corrected, a lesson plan can be specifically designed to meet the needs of your students. Skill mastery will be enhanced with this procedure.

ORGANIZATIONAL TIPS

Becoming a successful teacher requires training in sound pedagogical practices. While this book is designed as a resource for teachers (physical education and classroom), it is not a replacement for professional preparation. As you use the ideas in this book, we recommend that you maximize practice or activity time and keep class organizational time to a minimum. Following are two lists of strategies we have used to reduce organizational time and maximize activity time.

Management Tips

- Have students help you create appropriate rules for the gymnasium, then implement and consistently enforce these rules.
- Have an instant activity ready when students enter the gymnasium; post it on the gymnasium door or wall.
- Use clear protocols for obtaining equipment, selecting partners, lining up, what to do with equipment when the teacher is speaking, and so forth.
- Have predetermined start and stop signals.
- Maximize student participation by avoiding any activity that eliminates a child from participation or requires students to stand in line.
- Minimize student wait time by having equipment for every child, if possible.
- Students should be involved in moderate to vigorous physical activity at least 50 percent of the class time. However, longer time in correctly executed sessions is even better.

Instructional Tips

- Make sure your day's lesson is well planned, and follow it.
- Minimize the time you talk or give instructions and transitions from one part of the lesson to the next. If you are a novice, this can take hours of preparation time, but it will ensure that lessons go well.
- Have equipment set up and ready for use.
- Use a remote for your music player to make lessons flow easier.
- Use visual cues such as pictures, photos, and a dry-erase board listing the elements of a skill. Take photos of your students performing skills correctly and post them or use them to make skill posters.
- Use technology in the class; for example, show videos of the skill and use iPads for viewing, recording, and assessing.

We hope you will find this book to be a valuable tool in helping you to create rewarding and successful movement programs for your students. Have fun!

1

Building Skills for Success

Children in the primary grades are very easy to motivate in physical education. For these children, everything physical is fun. Moving, galloping, kicking, throwing, and catching are exciting. Furthermore, making a basket, knocking down a bowling pin, and jumping over a rope are notable accomplishments for inexperienced movers.

Unfortunately, young children often become so motivated by *what* they are able to do that they don't learn *how* to correctly perform a skill. For example, a kindergartner may be able to roll a ball and hit a target even if he steps with the wrong foot. Without correction, this poor motor pattern becomes a habit that is very difficult to correct. When the target or task becomes more difficult, the student will not have the techniques necessary for success. The tennis serve will be inefficient, and throwing a ball in from the outfield will be very challenging. The poor habits the child learned in the primary grades will severely affect athletic competencies in adulthood.

SUCCESS STARTS HERE

The college basketball player who has to shoot two foul shots when her team is down by one point with no time on the clock is under a great deal of pressure. If she misses that first shot, she knows instantly that the ball did not go in the basket. This is the result, or *what happened*. What she really needs to know is how to fix the shot so that the next one will go in. Because of the years of practice and coaching that this athlete has received, she has some knowledge base to work from to improve the next foul shot.

Young children, however, must be provided with such experiences. Unfortunately, once a child discovers that he can hit the target, make a basket, or kick the ball, it is difficult to then go back and have him work on the critical elements of the skill.

The elementary physical educator should stress the technique, or the *how-to,* first. Tying the cues to the critical elements as the child practices is essential. Learning the critical elements—such as an arm extension, a step in opposition, or a follow-through—will increase the likelihood that the child will develop skillful movement.

This chapter offers activities that emphasize how to perform particular skills. We recommend using any or all of these activities with each of the locomotor and manipulative skills. The examples given in each activity are generic. The only adaptation necessary will be to change the cues and elements to fit the skill being taught.

SUGGESTED ACTIVITIES FOR REINFORCING
THE CRITICAL ELEMENTS

Statues/Movement

Objective

To evaluate students' understanding of a specific skill element.

Equipment

Music (it is helpful to have a remote).

Activity

1. Students move around the gymnasium in their own personal spaces while listening to music.
2. When the music stops, say a cue word that indicates a particular critical element of the skill.
3. Students freeze in the critical element position indicated by the cue word.
4. The activity continues, with students freezing in a critical element position each time you say a cue word. For example, for the underhand roll skill you would say, *ready, arm back, step and roll,* and *follow through.*

Extensions

- Use the previous activity without the music.
- Create your own stop signal, such as clapping your hands in a pattern and having the students clap the same pattern back to you or using a musical instrument.
- Assign each critical element a number. Roll dice to select the element to be demonstrated. You can also use playing cards, other numbered cards, or a spinner number card.
- Partners may select the critical element to be demonstrated.

I'll Bet You Know; Here We Go

Objective

To check for students' understanding of the critical elements of the skill while creating a cooperative environment.

Equipment

None.

Activity

1. Call a student by name and say, "I'll bet you know; here we go."
2. Ask the student a question about some part of the skill. For example, when teaching the underhand throw, you might ask, "Where is our hand on the follow-through for the underhand throw?"
3. If the student is able to answer, terrific! If not, rephrase the question. If after you've provided sufficient thinking time the student is unable to answer, select a student who knows the answer.
4. The student who knows the answer tells the answer to the first student you called on.
5. The first student communicates the answer to you.
6. This activity can be repeated five or more times throughout the class session with different students.

Extensions

- Teach this activity to other school personnel. It is a great way to review information in all academic areas.
- Because you see your students only once or twice a week, you can use this technique to determine how much they remember from your class. You can use it at the start of a class as a review or when you observe the class in another setting, such as when students are waiting to go to the lunchroom.

Teach the Teacher

Objective

To assess students' knowledge of how a specific skill is performed. You can also use it as a lesson closure.

Equipment

None.

Activity

1. Select a student to explain how to perform a skill, such as catching.
2. Perform the skill exactly as the student described the skill.
3. The other students determine whether you are performing the skill correctly.
4. If you perform the skill incorrectly, the students offer solutions to the problem.

Extensions

- Have a different student teach each element of the skill.
- When the classroom teacher arrives to take the children back to their room (or you return the students to their room), have a student teach the classroom teacher how to perform the skill correctly.

Everybody's It

Objective

To combine cardiorespiratory fitness and the acquisition of a specific locomotor or manipulative skill.

Equipment

None.

Activity

1. Tell students that everybody is It.
2. Have students spread out within the play area. On command, students begin moving in the play area and try to tag each other.
3. When a student is tagged, he moves to a designated practice area. In this area, he demonstrates for you the specified skill by going through each critical element slowly and saying the cue words out loud.

Extensions

- Have peers evaluate the critical elements of the skill. You may select a student to go to the designated area as the first "watcher" when the game begins. After the first student is tagged, the watcher observes that student performing the skill while saying the cue words out loud. Then, the first watcher returns to the game, and the student who was tagged first stays in the area and becomes the new watcher. This rotation continues as long as the game is played.

- Once the students learn the skills, they can become more independent. When an error occurs, the student moves to the designated area by herself and performs the skill while repeating the cues and referring to a chart of the critical elements. The student then returns to the game.

- Add appropriate equipment to the designated practice areas, such as softballs, tennis balls, or playground balls.

Orbits

Objective

To demonstrate proper execution of the skill.

Equipment

None.

Activity

1. A rotation (relay) formation is used.

2. Taking turns, each student runs to the opposite end of the play area and demonstrates one critical element of a skill. For example, a student may be asked to demonstrate the ready position for the underhand roll.

3. The student returns to his group and tags a group member, and that student runs and demonstrates the same element.

4. The activity continues until you select another element of the skill to be performed. You may stop the students while running and ask them to demonstrate a different critical element; then the activity continues. By stopping the activity while the students are moving to change tasks, you eliminate the incidence of competition that often occurs in relays.

Extensions

- Use each of the critical elements of a skill.

- Use a variety of locomotor skills in place of running (e.g., skipping, sliding, galloping).

- Have the student demonstrate the critical element for the next student in line before running (walking, skipping, hopping) to the other end of the play area and back.

- Add appropriate equipment. The equipment may be used by each student in line.

Scratch and Match

Objective

To match the critical element cards with the cue word cards.

Equipment

Make one set of cue word cards and one set of critical element description cards for each group in the class. Use separate colors for the cue words and the critical elements.

Activity

1. Arrange each group of four or five students in a rotation (relay) formation.

2. On a signal, group members take turns running to the opposite end of the play area to pick up one cue word at a time.

3. Once the group has picked up the cue words, the students must place them in the proper order.

4. Then the group members take turns running to the opposite end of the play area to pick up one of the cards with a critical element written on it.

5. The activity is completed when the group members have correctly matched the critical elements with the cue words.

Extensions

- Use pictures for the critical elements.
- Have neighboring groups check each other's answers.
- Have students pick up a cue word card and its matching critical element description card, run back to their groups, and then put the two cards in the proper sequence.

Cookie Jar

Objective

To demonstrate critical elements of the specified skill.

Equipment

Cookie jar (large container) and laminated cards with the cue words of the skill written on them. You should have several sets of cards so that every student has the opportunity to pick from the cookie jar.

Activity

1. One student draws a critical element card out of the cookie jar.
2. The class demonstrates that critical element to you.
3. A different student picks the next critical element card.

Extensions

- The student demonstrates the critical element to a peer.
- Place students in groups with a "cookie jar" for each group.
- Use different containers and pieces of paper. Die-cutting machines are useful in creating a variety of shapes. For example, we have used the following:
  - A volcano as the container and cut-out dinosaurs for the elements
  - Cut-out school buses in September
  - A plastic pumpkin with cut-out ghosts in October
  - A roasting pan with cut-out turkeys in November
  - A gingerbread house with cut-out gingerbread men and women in December
  - Cut-out snowflakes in January
  - A heart tin with cut-out hearts in February
  - Cut-out kites in March
  - Cut-out umbrellas in April
  - Cut-out flowers in May

Jigsaw Puzzle

Objective

To complete a skill element puzzle with a partner.

Equipment

One complete puzzle per student pair. To make a skill element jigsaw puzzle, do the following:

1. On a sheet of paper, write or type the critical elements and the descriptions of the skill.

2. Photocopy the words onto heavyweight paper. You will want to have enough copies to allow the students to work in pairs. You may also want to use different colors of paper for the puzzles.

3. Cut each paper into 10 or more pieces, like a jigsaw puzzle. No two puzzles need to be cut the same.

4. Store the puzzle pieces in small plastic bags so different puzzles do not get mixed together.

5. You may want to include the pictures from the picture partner skill check sheets on your puzzle.

Activity

1. Partners are given one skill element puzzle in a bag.

2. On the start signal, partners will empty the puzzle pieces from the bag and begin to put the puzzle together.

3. Once the students have completed the puzzle, they will take turns demonstrating each element of the skill.

4. This is a great activity if space is an issue.

Extensions

- If you have a metal surface or door, or dry-erase board, put magnetic tape on the back of each puzzle piece and have the students put the puzzles together there.

- Have the students work in groups of three or four to put the puzzle together.

- In their groups, they take turns running (or any other locomotor skill) to an area where they pick up one piece to their puzzle and bring it back to the group. As the puzzle pieces are brought back, the group begins to put the puzzle together. Students continue to take turns retrieving one puzzle piece at a time until all the pieces have been collected.

Pizza Game

Objective

To have students correctly demonstrate a specified skill, such as the overhand throw, underhand roll, catch, or kick, while building an eight-piece pizza.

Equipment

The type of equipment will depend on the skill being practiced (e.g., foam balls, tennis balls, or playground balls). You should have one piece of equipment per student pair.

Activity

1. Students work with partners while performing the skill. Students take turns as the thrower (or roller, or dribbler) and as the watcher (or catcher).

2. The thrower earns an imaginary piece of pizza for each successful attempt at the skill. A successful attempt is one in which the thrower demonstrates all of the critical elements of the skill.

3. The watcher determines whether the critical elements were demonstrated. If the skill is correct, the thrower is awarded the pizza slice. If not, then the watcher must tell the thrower what she needs to correct.

Extensions

- Have the pairs record their number of pizza slices. Later, the class uses math skills to calculate how many total pizza slices were obtained (addition) or how many pies were made (addition and division).

- Have the pairs record their number of correct throws, and determine a total for the class. In a follow-up lesson, challenge the class to increase the total number of correct throws. You may choose to chart these numbers to motivate the students and reinforce the skill.

SUMMARY

Learning how to perform a skill is necessary for eventual mastery. It involves really thinking about *how* the skill is performed. Successful completion of this cognitive phase is an essential first step toward correctly performing the skill later. When students understand the critical elements of a skill and can use cue words as a mental checklist for performing the skill, they can begin to correct their own performance. This ability becomes very important when students participate in sport activities.

The nine activities we described in this chapter are just the beginning. Now that you have tried some of our ideas, you and your students can create appropriate activities of your own. Whether you use ours, create your own, or modify the activities from class to class or year to year is entirely up to you. Just remember that thinking activities are the foundation, and they should be used when teaching all of the basic locomotor and manipulative skills.

2

Locomotor Skills

Children begin performing locomotor skills at a young age. They learn to creep, then they learn to crawl, and finally, with much family excitement, they learn to walk. In this chapter, we examine eight other methods of movement: hopping, galloping, sliding, running, skipping, jumping in the vertical plane, jumping in the horizontal plane, and leaping. Some of these locomotor movements (e.g., running, jumping, and sliding) relate directly to sport skills. Others assist students with dance skills (e.g., galloping and skipping) and in becoming skillful movers.

National Standards & Grade-Level Outcomes for K-12 Physical Education (SHAPE America, 2014) addresses locomotor skills at all grade levels. In kindergarten, children should be able to perform hopping, galloping, running, sliding, and skipping while maintaining balance (S1.E1.K). The mature patterns for galloping, jogging, and sliding should occur in grade 1 (S1.E1.1). In grade 2, the mature pattern for skipping should emerge (S1.E1.2), and students should demonstrate the mature pattern for leaping in grade 3. By grades 4 and 5, students should be able to use locomotor skills with other tasks (see table 2.1.).

ABOUT THIS CHAPTER

This chapter is divided into eight sections, one for each locomotor movement previously mentioned. In each section we include a brief description of the locomotor skill, its critical elements or parts of the movement, and selected cue words to use when teaching that particular skill. We include at least two cue sets for each skill. You may use each set individually or mix and match the cue words as needed. We have found it beneficial to have the students say the cue words out loud as they practice.

 Say to teach

In addition, to facilitate your students' skill mastery, we include partner skill check sheets and specific troubleshooting charts in each section. The partner skill check activities allow partners to assess each other's progress in learning the locomotor skills. For students who cannot read or do not speak English, use the picture versions of the partner skill check sheets.

Partner skill check assessments are used as follows:

1. One partner observes the other to see if she has the correct form for the first area of concern, such as the eyes and body position.

2. If the eyes and body position are correct, then the partner places a *Y* in the first box. If the eyes and body position are incorrect, the partner places an *N* in the first box. Nonreaders can put a smiling face if the eyes and body position are correct or a frowning face if the eyes and body position are incorrect.

Table 2.1　Standard 1 Grade-Level Outcomes for Six Basic Locomotor Skills (S1.E1)

	Kindergarten	Grade 1	Grade 2	Grade 3	Grade 4	Grade 5
S1.E1 **Hopping, galloping, running, sliding, skipping, leaping**	Performs locomotor skills (hopping, galloping, running, sliding, skipping) while maintaining balance. (S1.E1.K)	Hops, gallops, jogs and slides using a mature pattern. (S1.E1.1)	Skips using a mature pattern. (S1.E1.2)	Leaps using a mature pattern. (S1.E1.3)	Uses various locomotor skills in a variety of small-sided practice tasks, dance and educational gymnastics experiences. (S1.E1.4)	Demonstrates mature patterns of locomotor skills in dynamic small-sided practice tasks, gymnastics and dance. (S1.E1.5a) Combines locomotor and manipulative skills in a variety of small-sided practice tasks in game environments. (S1.E1.5b) Combines traveling with manipulative skills for execution to a target (e.g., scoring in soccer, hockey and basketball). (S1.E1.5c)

Reprinted, by permission, from SHAPE America – Society of Health and Physical Educators, 2014, *National standards & grade-level outcomes for K-12 physical education* (Champaign, IL: Human Kinetics).

3. This evaluation continues until each of the critical elements has been assessed five times.

4. A partner skill check sheet is used for each student.

You may elect to use the partner skill check sheet yourself to assess the skill development of each student. In addition, to keep parents informed of student progress, you may elect to send these sheets home with report cards or after individual students master specific skills.

While we highly recommend using the movement concept approach (Graham, Holt-Hale, & Parker, 2013) to teach the locomotor skills, we have included a few specific ideas to reinforce the acquisition of selected locomotor skills.

The final section of this chapter describes activities that you can use to reinforce any of the locomotor movements. These may serve as culminating activities or warm-up ideas.

HOW TO TEACH LOCOMOTOR SKILLS

We highly recommend that you begin each school year by teaching or reviewing the basic movement concepts (space, pathways, levels, speed, direction, and force). Their mastery will provide variety to the skill performance and thus promote skillful movement. You should plan to devote at least one class period to each concept and to revisit these concepts often throughout the year. These movement concepts lay the foundation for future skills. The Grade-Level Outcomes under Standard 2 address the concepts of space (S2.E1) (see table 2.2), pathways, shapes, and levels (S2.E2) and speed, direction, and force (S2.E3).

According to the Grade-Level Outcomes, space refers to self-space and general space (S2.E1.Ka). The outcomes expand to recognizing open spaces in the third grade (2.E1.3) and then closing spaces in game situations in the fourth grade (S2.E1.4).

Within the Grade-Level Outcomes, pathways are addressed in kindergarten (S2.E2.K). Levels (low, middle, high) are addressed in first grade (S2.E2.1a), as are relationships (over, under, around, through) (S2.E2.1b). Students should be able to combine shapes, levels, and pathways into a variety of sequences by second grade (S2.E2.2) (table 2.3).

Table 2.2 Standard 2 Grade-Level Outcomes for Moving in Space (S2.E1)

	Kindergarten	Grade 1	Grade 2	Grade 3	Grade 4	Grade 5
S2.E1 Space	Differentiates between movement in personal space (self-space) and general space. (S2.E1.Ka) Moves in personal space to a rhythm. (S.E1.Kb)	Moves in self-space and general space in response to designated beats or rhythms. (S2.E1.1)	Combines locomotor skills in general space to a rhythm. (S2.E1.2)	Recognizes the concept of open spaces in a movement context. (S2.E1.3)	Applies the concept of open spaces to combination skills involving traveling (e.g., dribbling and traveling). (S2.E1.4a) Applies the concept of closing spaces in small-sided practice tasks. (S2.E1.4b) Dribbles in general space with changes in direction and speed. (S2.E1.4c)	Combines spatial concepts with locomotor and nonlocomotor movements for small groups in gymnastics, dance and game environments. (S2.E1.5)

Reprinted, by permission, from SHAPE America – Society of Health and Physical Educators, 2014, *National standards & grade-level outcomes for K-12 physical education* (Champaign, IL: Human Kinetics).

Table 2.3 Standard 2 Outcomes for Pathways, Shapes, and Levels (S2.E2)

	Kindergarten	Grade 1	Grade 2	Grade 3	Grade 4	Grade 5
S2.E2 Pathways, shapes, levels	Travels in 3 different pathways. (S2.E2.K)	Travels demonstrating low, middle and high levels. (S2.E2.1a) Travels demonstrating a variety of relationships with objects (e.g., over, under, around, through). (S2.E2.1b)	Combines shapes, levels and pathways into simple travel, dance and gymnastics sequences. (S2.E2.2)	Recognizes locomotor skills specific to a wide variety of physical activities. (S2.E2.3)	Combines movement concept with skills in small-sided practice tasks, gymnastics and dance environments. (S2.E2.4)	Combines movement concepts with skills in small-sided practice tasks in game environments, gymnastics and dance with self-direction. (S2.E2.5)

Reprinted, by permission, from SHAPE America – Society of Health and Physical Educators, 2014, *National standards & grade-level outcomes for K-12 physical education* (Champaign, IL: Human Kinetics).

Using different speeds should be mastered in kindergarten (S2.E3.K), and first graders should be able to differentiate between fast and slow (S2.E3.1a). First graders should be able to differentiate between strong and light force (S2.E3.1b), and second graders should be able to vary time and force with gradual increases and decreases in speed (S2.E3.2). Third graders should be able to combine movement concepts (direction, levels, force, time) with skills as directed by the teacher (S2.E3.3) (table 2.4).

Table 2.5 is a brief list of the basic movement concepts and possible ways to describe the skills to your students.

Once the foundation of movement concepts is established, you can begin to reinforce specific locomotor skills by integrating the concepts into your lessons. You might, for example, challenge the children to practice jumping, running, and skipping in pathways.

Linking the concept of pathways with another concept, such as force, allows for a more complex combination. For example, you might challenge your students to run along a curvy pathway with light force or along a straight pathway with strong force. Adding a third movement concept further increases complexity and variety. For example, you might add relationships to the combination and challenge your students to run along a curvy pathway with light force while leading (or following) a partner. Table 2.6 organizes these movement concepts to clarify possible combinations (Graham et al., 2013).

Table 2.4 Standard 2 Grade-Level Outcomes for Speed, Direction, and Force (S2.E3)

	Kindergarten	Grade 1	Grade 2	Grade 3	Grade 4	Grade 5
S2.E3 Speed, direction, force	Travels in general space with different speeds. (S2.E3.K)	Differentiates between fast and slow speeds. (S2.E3.1a) Differentiates between strong and light force. (S2.E3.1b)	Varies time and force with gradual increases and decreases. (S2.E3.2)	Combines movement concepts (direction, levels, force, time) with skills as directed by the teacher. (S2.E3.3)	Applies the movement concepts of speed, endurance, and pacing for running. (S2.E3.4a) Applies the concepts of direction and force when striking an object with a short-handled implement, sending it toward a designated target. (S2.E3.4b)	Applies movement concepts to strategy in game situations. (S2.E3.5a) Applies the concepts of direction and force to strike an object with a long-handled implement. (S2.E3.5b) Analyzes movement situations and applies movement concepts (e.g., force, direction, speed, pathways, extensions) in small-sided practice tasks in game environments, dance and gymnastics. (S2.E3.5c)

Table 2.5 Basic Movement Concepts and Suggested Ways to Describe the Skill

Location

Self-space—an area where you can move and not touch anyone else.

General space—the overall play area.

Direction

In place—stay where you are.

Forward—walk the direction your toes point.

Backward—walk the direction your heels point.

Sideways (left and right)—face forward and move so the side of your body takes the lead. You can move to the left or right.

Clockwise—move in the same direction that the hands of a clock move.

Counterclockwise—move in the opposite direction that the hands of a clock move.

Pathways

Straight—move in a straight line.

Curvy—move in a line that curves.

Zigzag—move in a pathway that has many turns with obvious "points." There are no rounded turns.

Relationships

With people:

Leading—be in front of a partner.

Following—be behind a partner.

Mirroring—face your partner and pretend you are looking in a mirror. When he raises his right hand, you raise your left hand; when he moves his right leg, you move your left leg.

Matching—move together with a partner so that when she raises an arm, you raise an arm; when she is on tiptoes, you are on tiptoes. You move together. It usually works better to practice at a slow speed.

With partners—two people together.

With groups—three or more people.

With objects:

Over—move so you are above the object.

Under—move so you are beneath the object.

On—being directly on top of something.

Off—leaving a place.

Near—being close to something.

Far—being away from something.

In front—being ahead of something.

Behind—something is in front of you.

Alongside—being next to something.

Around—move so you are circling an object.

Force

Light—move like a mouse.

Strong—move like an elephant (or T. Rex)

Levels

Low—move in the area closest to the floor, like a snake or a turtle.

Middle—move at your normal walking height.

High—pretend you are a giraffe and be as tall as you can when you move.

Time

Slow—move like a turtle.

Fast—move fast like the wind.

Table 2.6   Components of Basic Movement Concepts

Location	Pathways	Force	Levels	Time	Directions	Relationships with people	Relationships with objects and people
Self-space and general space	Straight, curved, and zigzag	Strong and light	Low, middle, and high	Fast and slow	In place Forward and backward Sideways (right and left) Clockwise and counterclockwise	Leading and following Mirroring and matching Solo, partners, groups	Over and under On and off Near and far In front, behind, and alongside Around

Once they have learned the basic movement concepts and a specific locomotor skill, you can provide limitless challenges to your students by selecting a challenge from one, two, or even three columns of the movement concept chart (table 2.6). This variety of combinations will provide countless opportunities to reinforce each of the locomotor skills.

You may elect to make a bulletin board or poster display of the movement concepts. With either visual aid you can try the following:

1. Allow students to select the movement concept to use with the locomotor skill being taught.

2. Place students in small groups and challenge them to find ways to combine the targeted locomotor skill with two or three movement concepts. These skills may be demonstrated to a nearby group or to the remainder of the class.

3. Place the descriptions of the movement concepts (e.g., light force, low level) in a container and have students randomly select one, two, or even three concepts. Students then perform the locomotor skill as the selected movement concepts indicate.

Students in kindergarten through second grade will be very successful with one or two concepts. Combining three or more concepts with a locomotor skill should be reserved for older children or for those extra-special classes that seem to be able to do anything.

Plan ahead for movement concept combinations that may be very difficult or even impossible to perform. For example, if a student draws the combination of skipping at a low level with strong force, you may decide to change the challenge to skipping at a high level with light force in order to make it an achievable task.

HOPPING

Proper performance of hopping involves taking off from one foot, having a brief period of nonsupport, and landing on the same foot. While hopping is an integral part of many children's games (e.g., hopscotch), it is also crucial to such advanced skills as the layup in basketball.

Unfortunately, the term *hop* is often used to describe a jump. For this reason, some children may be confused when you first begin instruction in the proper hopping technique. You may need to solicit their help in enlightening their teachers about proper terminology. After all, that very popular kindergarten song and dance should really be called the "Bunny Jump."

Learning the hop involves an orderly progression. Before a child can begin to hop, she must be able to balance on one foot. Once the child can balance, she may proceed to the skill of hopping by holding on to a support. The child can then advance to hopping without assistance. According to *National Standards & Grade-Level Outcomes for K-12 Physical Education* (SHAPE America, 2014), kindergarteners should be able to maintain their balance while hopping (S1.E1.K) and should be able to demonstrate a mature pattern by first grade (S1.E1.1). See table 2.7 for the hopping outcomes.

Besides using the movement concepts to reinforce the correct hopping technique, we have found the following ideas to be helpful:

• When teaching hopping, it is helpful to make 10 or more learning stations. These stations are composed of nonparallel lines that are at least 6 feet (1.8 m) long and are positioned 1 inch (2.5 cm) apart at the closest point and 2 feet (0.6 m) apart at the widest point (see figure 2.1). The lines may be taped to the floor, or jump ropes may be used.

Table 2.7   Grade-Level Outcomes for Hopping (S1.E1)

	Kindergarten	Grade 1
S1.E1 **Hopping, galloping, running, sliding, skipping, leaping**	Performs locomotor skills (hopping, galloping, running, sliding, skipping) while maintaining balance. (S1.E1.K)	Hops, gallops, jogs and slides using a mature pattern. (S1.E1.1)

Reprinted, by permission, from SHAPE America – Society of Health and Physical Educators, 2014, *National standards & grade-level outcomes for K-12 physical education* (Champaign, IL: Human Kinetics).

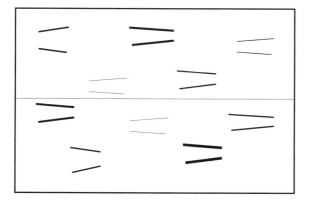

Figure 2.1   Learning stations for hopping.

- Challenge students to hop across these imaginary streams (the lines on the floor). Challenge them further by asking them to go to the widest part and hop across without getting their feet wet. Place small stepping stones (taped lines or floor spots) within wider creeks to assist in hopping.

- Encourage your students to play hopscotch. A variety of hopscotch designs can be found in many activity books; they can be traditional (straight) or spirals or circles (curvy), or you can make up your own (zigzag is a possibility). All you really need are connecting shapes with spaces large enough for a child's foot. The type of pattern is limited only by the imagination!

Extensions

- Provide sidewalk chalk for small groups of students. After showing them the traditional hopscotch design, allow them to make up their own designs. The students can practice hopping on each other's diagrams.

- Make copies of these diagrams and use sidewalk chalk to mark them during recess. When the hopscotch diagrams are made smaller and include numbers, they can become math lessons. Challenge the students to hop on only even numbers or to hop on the answer to 2 + 1.

Critical Elements

Eyes and Body	Foot and Takeoff Leg	Swing Knee	Arms	Glide
The eyes look forward in the direction of travel, and the body moves in an upright position.	Take off and land on the same foot, bending the knee on landing.	The swing knee is bent and swings forward.	The elbows are bent, and the arm opposite the swing leg moves forward.	The body moves with a smooth, rhythmic motion.

Albemarle County Physical Education Curriculum Revision Committee, 2008.

Cue Words

Spring—take off and land on the same foot; knees bend on landing.

Swing—the swing knee is bent and swings forward.

Up—the eyes look forward in the direction of travel, the body moves in an upright position, the swing knee is bent and swings forward, and the student takes off and lands on the same foot.

Down—the knee bends on landing, and preparation begins immediately to take off again.

Step and swing—step forward on the hopping foot, bend the other knee, and swing that knee up and forward. There is a brief period of nonsupport, and then the body moves with a smooth, rhythmic motion.

Cue set 1: spring, swing

Cue set 2: up, down

Cue set 3: step and swing, step and swing

Hopping Troubleshooting Chart

If you see this	Then try this
1. Hopping foot not coming up off the floor or landing knee not bending	• Using floor spots (or carpet squares if outside), have the student hop over the spots (squares). The student will need to bend the knee on the hopping leg to generate more force. • Record the student performing the skill. Show the student the recording, using a remote to start and stop the action.
2. Two feet touching the floor	• Use a wall or partner for support. • Using a scarf, pinny, jump rope, or other item, have the student hold the nonhopping foot up off the ground. The student tries to hop while holding the foot. The student has control of when she can put the nonhopping foot down.
3. Swing knee not moving	• Have the student stand stationary next to a wall. The student is standing with her side to the wall with the hopping foot away from the wall. The hand opposite the hopping-leg side holds the wall for balance. The student swings the swing knee while swinging the arm opposite the swing knee.
4. Arms not swinging during the hop	• Once the student can hop holding on to the wall, have him practice without the wall, swinging the arms in opposition to the legs.
5. Student not hopping with a smooth pattern	• Review the critical elements of the skill. Being able to perform any locomotor skill smoothly requires the student to use the critical elements of the skill correctly. • Select appropriate music or use a percussion instrument. Have the student hop to the beat of the music.

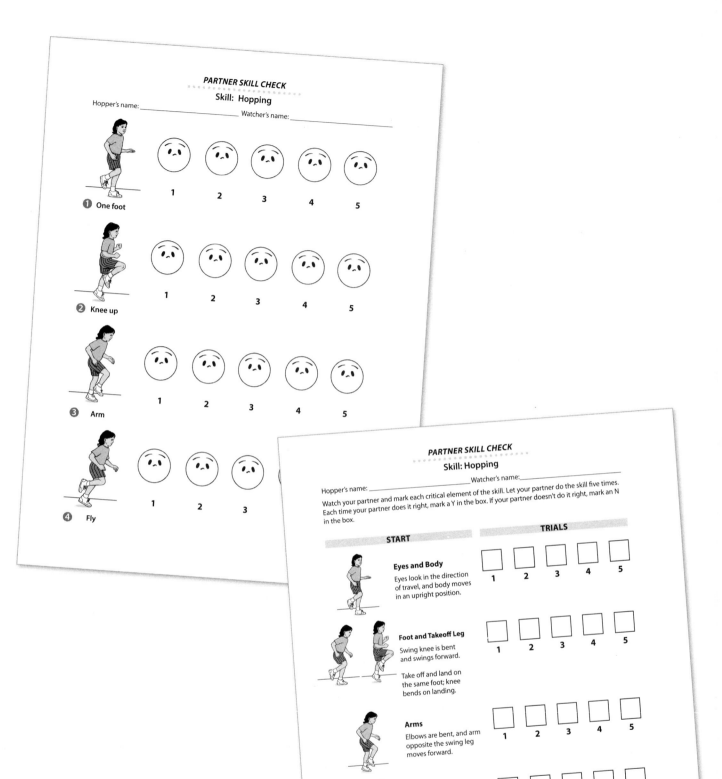

GALLOPING

Galloping is a fairly complicated skill with an uneven rhythm. It is a combination of two other locomotor movements, walking and leaping. Unlike sliding, galloping moves the child forward (and backward for the skilled performer), not to the side. In galloping, the lead leg is propelled forward, while the rear foot quickly closes behind the lead foot. The same foot will take the lead when several gallops are combined.

Galloping is used with dance patterns, but it does not have an obvious connection to traditional sport skills. Unfortunately, it is a movement that children rarely observe on the playground. Since very few children enter elementary school knowing how to gallop, you should be prepared to provide all of the instruction. *National Standards & Grade-Level Outcomes for K-12 Physical Education* (SHAPE America, 2014) indicates that kindergarteners should be able to gallop while maintaining balance (S1. E1.K), and a mature pattern should be evident in grade 1 (S1.E1.1). See table 2.8 for outcomes regarding galloping.

Table 2.8   Grade-Level Outcomes for Galloping (S1.E1)

	Kindergarten	Grade 1
S1.E1 **Hopping, galloping, running, sliding, skipping, leaping**	Performs locomotor skills (hopping, galloping, running, sliding, skipping) while maintaining balance. (S1.E1.K)	Hops, gallops, jogs and slides using a mature pattern. (S1.E1.1)

Reprinted, by permission, from SHAPE America – Society of Health and Physical Educators, 2014, *National standards & grade-level outcomes for K-12 physical education* (Champaign, IL: Human Kinetics).

Critical Elements

Eyes and Body	**Flight**	**Arms**	**Glide**
The eyes look in direction of travel, and the body moves in an upright position with a slight forward lean.	Step forward with the lead foot and close with the back foot. Both feet are temporarily off the ground.	Arms are bent and swinging forward and back.	The body moves with a smooth, rhythmic motion.

Cue Words

Giddy—the eyes look in the direction of travel, and the body moves in an upright position with a slight forward lean. Arms may be bent and in front of the body as the child holds an imaginary pair of reins. The lead foot moves forward.

Step—the lead foot moves forward.

Up—both feet are temporarily off the ground, and the back foot quickly closes.

> *Cue set 1:* giddy, up
> *Cue set 2:* step, up

Galloping Troubleshooting Chart

If you see this	Then try this
1. No forward body lean	• Use a mirror or flashlight (reflection or shadow) to let the student see her body position. The student should have her side to the mirror or wall. • Record the student performing the skill. Show the student the recording, using a remote to start and stop the action.
2. Feet not coming up off the ground during the flight phase or the back foot passing the front foot	• Using floor spots, have the student gallop over the floor spot. This will encourage the student to take a longer forward stride while galloping. • Place spots or "landing pads" down on the floor. The student must land on the spot with the lead foot and bring the back foot to the edge of the spot, not touching the spot. Space the spots far enough apart that the student must take a longer forward stride while galloping.
3. Arms kept straight or not swinging with the movement	• Have the student stand with his back to the wall, about 1 inch (2.5 cm) away. The student bends the elbows and swings the arms with light force back toward the wall so that only the elbows touch the wall. The arms will have some limited movement. • The student works with a partner. The partner stands in front of the student with the hands up at waist level, palms open facing the student. The student swings arms to touch the partner's palms with the fists or hands.
4. Student not galloping with a smooth pattern	• Review the critical elements of the skill. Being able to perform any locomotor skill smoothly requires the student to use the elements of the skill correctly. • Select appropriate music or use a percussion instrument. Music with horses galloping would work well. Have the student gallop to the beat of the music.

PARTNER SKILL CHECK

Skill: Galloping

Galloper's name: _____ Watcher's name: _____

1. Body lean   1   2   3   4   5

2. Fly   1   2   3   4   5

3. Arms   1   2   3   4   5

4. Glide   1   2   3   4

PARTNER SKILL CHECK

Skill: Galloping

Galloper's name: _____ Watcher's name: _____

Watch your partner and mark each critical element of the skill. Let your partner do the skill five times. Each time your partner does it right, mark a Y in the box. If your partner doesn't do it right, mark an N in the box.

START	TRIALS

Eyes and Body

Eyes look in the direction of travel. There is a slight forward lean of the body.

1   2   3   4   5

Flight

Step forward with the lead foot and close with the back foot. Both feet are temporarily off the ground.

1   2   3   4   5

Arms

Arms are bent and swing with the body.

1   2   3   4   5

Glide

Body moves with a smooth, rhythmic motion.

1   2   3   4   5

27

SLIDING

Sliding is the easiest way to move in a sideways direction. When sliding to the right, the right foot takes the lead and there is a brief period of nonsupport as the left leg quickly follows. Children are often motivated to learn how to slide because of this unique sideways movement and the obvious connection between sliding and sports. Children see basketball players sliding while using a person-to-person defense and they see many athletes sliding into the proper positions (e.g., baseball/softball short-stops, tennis players returning a serve).

Once children are successful with the skill of galloping, they are ready to begin learning sliding. The uneven rhythm of sliding and the fact that the child is moving laterally may produce some initial difficulty in learning this locomotor skill. Decreasing the sliding speed and proper instruction in the critical elements should minimize problems. *National Standards & Grade-Level Outcomes for K-12 Physical Education* (SHAPE America, 2014) (table 2.9) indicates that kindergarteners should be able to perform the slide while maintaining balance (S1.E1.K), and a mature pattern should be evident in first grade (S1.E1.1).

Table 2.9 Grade-Level Outcomes for Sliding (S1.E1)

	Kindergarten	Grade 1
S1.E1 **Hopping, galloping, running, sliding, skipping, leaping**	Performs locomotor skills (hopping, galloping, running, sliding, skipping) while maintaining balance. (S1.E1.K)	Hops, gallops, jogs, and slides using a mature pattern. (S1.E1.1)

Reprinted, by permission, from SHAPE America – Society of Health and Physical Educators, 2014, *National standards & grade-level outcomes for K-12 physical education* (Champaign, IL: Human Kinetics).

Critical Elements

Chin, Eyes, and Body	Feet	Flight	Glide
The chin is placed over the lead shoulder, the eyes focus in the direction of travel, and the body maintains an upright position.	Feet stay parallel to each other throughout the entire movement as the body moves either to the right or to the left.	Both feet are temporarily off the ground.	The body moves with a smooth, rhythmic motion.

Cue Words

Chin over shoulder—the chin is placed over the lead shoulder, the eyes focus in the direction of travel, and the body maintains an upright position.

Feet parallel—feet stay parallel to each other throughout the entire movement, even during the flight phase.

Move to the side—the body moves with a smooth and rhythmic motion to the right or to the left.

Step-together—the lead foot moves to the side and the following foot meets the lead foot during the flight phase. This continuous action creates a smooth and rhythmic motion to the right or to the left.

> *Cue set 1:* chin over shoulder, feet parallel, move to the side
>
> *Cue set 2:* chin, step-together, step-together

Sliding Troubleshooting Chart

If you see this	Then try this
1. Chin not near the lead shoulder or feet not parallel	• Use a mirror or flashlight (reflection or shadow) to let the student see her body position. The student should have her side to the mirror or wall. • Record the student performing the skill. Show the student the recording, using a remote to start and stop the action.
2. Feet not coming up off the ground during the flight phase	• Standing with his back to the wall, the student slides along the wall using a slow speed. Once he has the idea, he may increase the speed. • Using floor spots, have the student slide over the spot without touching it.
3. Body turned so the side is not leading the slide	• Standing with her back to the wall, the student slides along the wall using a slow speed. Once she has the idea, she may increase the speed. • Put a rope through a 2-foot (0.6 m) length of PVC pipe. Suspend the rope and pipe between two game standards. The student holds the pipe in both hands and slides along the length of the rope. Have the student repeat this activity several times.
4. Student crosses feet during the slide	• Standing with his back to the wall, the student places his elbows on the wall. Using a slow speed, the student slides along the wall, maintaining contact with the wall. • Once he has the idea, he may increase his speed.
5. Student not sliding with a smooth pattern	• Review the critical elements of the skill. Being able to perform any locomotor skill smoothly requires the student to use the elements of the skill correctly. To create a smooth, rhythmic motion, you will need to review the elements of the skill. • Select appropriate music or use a percussion instrument. Have students slide to the beat of the music.

PARTNER SKILL CHECK

Skill: Sliding

Slider's name: _____

Watcher's name: _____

1 Chin

1   2   3   4   5

2 Feet

1   2   3   4   5

3 Fly

1   2   3   4   5

4 Glide

1   2   3   4

PARTNER SKILL CHECK

Skill: Sliding

Slider's name: _____

Watcher's name: _____

Watch your partner and mark each critical element of the skill. Let your partner do the skill five times. Each time your partner does it right, mark a Y in the box. If your partner doesn't do it right, mark an N in the box.

START		TRIALS

Chin and Eyes

Chin is placed over lead shoulder, eyes look in the direction of travel.

1   2   3   4   5

Body

Body position remains upright.

1   2   3   4   5

Feet

Feet stay parallel to each other.

1   2   3   4   5

Flight

Both feet are temporarily off the ground.

1   2   3   4   5

Glide

Body moves with a smooth, rhythmic motion.

1   2   3   4   5

RUNNING

After a child learns to walk, he wants to move faster, and that naturally progresses to the run. The young child will move intuitively in a way that maintains balance but still allows him to move more quickly. To keep from falling, the young runner may have his arms outstretched and use a much wider running stance than an adult. This is a natural adaptation that occurs as the child tries to maintain balance. Unfortunately, many of these extra movements become permanent motor patterns unless instruction is provided.

Correct skill performance can be established at an early age with proper instruction. While *National Standards & Grade-Level Outcomes for K-12 Physical Education* (SHAPE America, 2014) indicates that mastery of all of the critical elements of the run does not occur until second grade (S1.E2.2), children should be able to run while maintaining balance beginning in kindergarten (S1.E1.K). Within the Grade-Level Outcomes, running is divided into three speeds: jogging, running, and sprinting. Second graders should be able to distinguish between jogging and sprinting (S1.E2.2b), and third graders should be able to differentiate between sprinting and running (S1.E2.3). See table 2.10 for outcomes concerning jogging and running.

Table 2.10   Grade-Level Outcomes for Jogging and Running (S1.E2)

	Kindergarten	Grade 1	Grade 2	Grade 3	Grade 4	Grade 5
S1.E2 Jogging, running	Developmentally appropriate and emerging outcomes first appear in grade 2	Developmentally appropriate and emerging outcomes first appear in grade 2	Runs with a mature pattern. (S1.E2.2a) Travels showing differentiation between jogging and sprinting. (S1.E2.2b)	Travels showing differentiation between sprinting and running. (S1.E2.3)	Runs for distance using a mature pattern. (S1.E2.4)	Uses appropriate pacing for a variety of running distances. (S1.E2.5)

Reprinted, by permission, from SHAPE America – Society of Health and Physical Educators, 2014, *National standards & grade-level outcomes for K-12 physical education* (Champaign, IL: Human Kinetics).

Critical Elements

Eyes and Body	**Flight**	**Arms**	**Knees**
The eyes focus in the direction of travel, and the body moves in an upright position with a slight forward lean and toes pointed forward.	Both feet are temporarily off the ground in a stride position. The foot lands heel to toe.	Arms are bent at about a 90-degree angle and move in a forward and backward direction without crossing the midline of the body.	Knee is bent to bring the heel up behind the body and parallel to the ground.

Cue Words

Eyes forward—eyes focus in the direction of travel.

Pump your arms and **arms bent**—arms are bent at about a 90-degree angle and move in a forward and backward direction without crossing the midline of the body.

Big stride—legs extend farther than they would in a walking step, and there is a temporary flight phase.

Feet straight—feet are parallel to each other throughout the running motion.

> *Cue set 1:* eyes forward, pump your arms, big stride
>
> *Cue set 2:* arms bent, feet straight

Running Troubleshooting Chart

If you see this	Then try this
1. No forward body lean	• Use a mirror or flashlight (reflection or shadow) to let the student see his body position. The student should have his side to the mirror or wall. • Record the student performing the skill. Show the student the recording, using a remote to start and stop the action.
2. No flight phase	• Encourage the student to run at a faster speed. • Place footprints or tape along a straight pathway approximately 40 feet (~12 m) long. The footprints or tape should be far enough apart to create a comfortable stride length for the student. As the student increases the stride length and speed of the run, periods of flight will result.
3. Arms crossing the midline of the body or not swinging with the run	• Have the student work with a partner. The partner must stand about 30 feet (~9 m) in front of the student. The student does a fast walk toward the partner, demonstrating the arm swing. The partner tells the student whether the arm swing is correct and lets the student know if the arms crossed the midline of the body. • Record the student performing the skill. Show the student the recording, using a remote to start and stop the action.
4. Foot not coming up behind the body	• Have the student run in place and try to kick her heel up near her buttocks. • Have the student work with a partner. The partner watches the student run 30 feet (~9 m) and counts the number of times the student's foot does not come up near her bottom. The object is to score a zero.

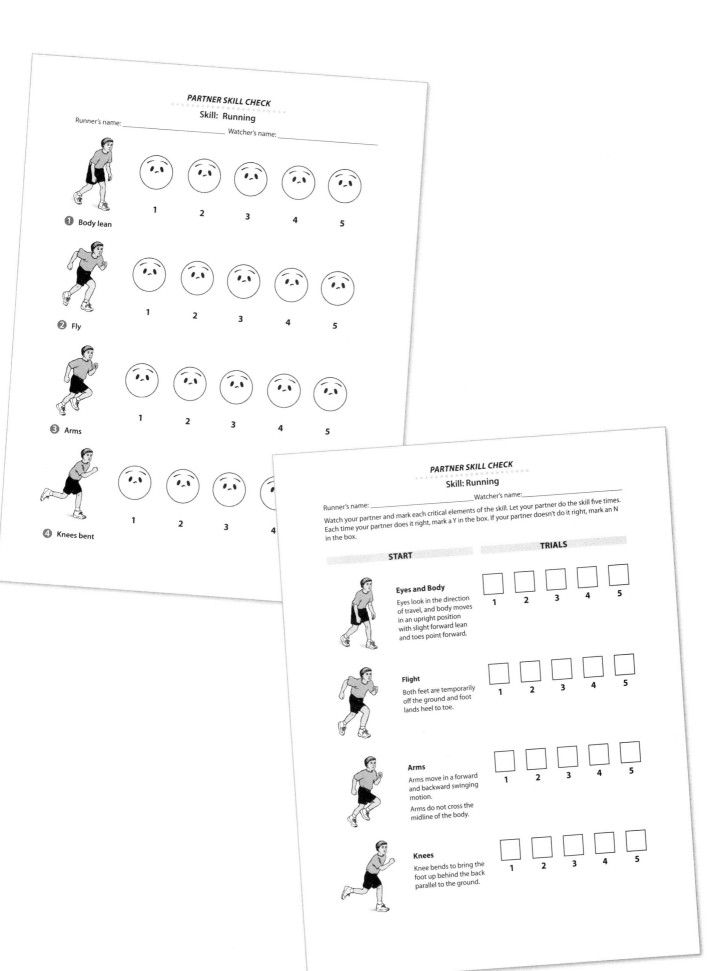

PARTNER SKILL CHECK
Skill: Running

Runner's name: _____   Watcher's name: _____

1. Body lean

   1 2 3 4 5

2. Fly

   1 2 3 4 5

3. Arms

   1 2 3 4 5

4. Knees bent

   1 2 3 4

PARTNER SKILL CHECK
Skill: Running

Runner's name: _____   Watcher's name: _____

Watch your partner and mark each critical elements of the skill. Let your partner do the skill five times. Each time your partner does it right, mark a Y in the box. If your partner doesn't do it right, mark an N in the box.

START   **TRIALS**

Eyes and Body
Eyes look in the direction of travel, and body moves in an upright position with slight forward lean and toes point forward.

   1 2 3 4 5

Flight
Both feet are temporarily off the ground and foot lands heel to toe.

   1 2 3 4 5

Arms
Arms move in a forward and backward swinging motion.
Arms do not cross the midline of the body.

   1 2 3 4 5

Knees
Knee bends to bring the foot up behind the back parallel to the ground.

   1 2 3 4 5

SKIPPING

Skipping is a rhythmic combination of two other locomotor skills, walking and hopping. Once children experience success with hopping, the skill of skipping can be introduced.

Although skipping does not have an obvious connection to other sport skills, many children observe other youngsters performing this skill on the playground and are motivated to learn it.

According to *National Standards & Grade-Level Outcomes for K-12 Physical Education* (SHAPE America, 2014) (table 2.11), kindergarteners should be able to skip while maintaining balance (S1.E1.K). A mature skipping pattern should emerge in grade 2 (S1.E1.2).

Table 2.11   Outcomes for Skipping

	Kindergarten	Grade 1	Grade 2
S1.E1 **Hopping, galloping, running, sliding, skipping, leaping**	Performs locomotor skills (hopping, galloping, running, sliding, skipping) while maintaining balance. (S1.E1.K)	Not addressed	Skips using a mature pattern. (S1.E1.2)

Reprinted, by permission, from SHAPE America – Society of Health and Physical Educators, 2014, *National standards & grade-level outcomes for K-12 physical education* (Champaign, IL: Human Kinetics).

Critical Elements

Eyes and Body	**Step and Hop**	**Arms**	**Flight**	**Glide**
The eyes focus in the direction of travel, and the body maintains an upright position.	Step and hop on the same foot.	Arms move in opposition.	Both feet are temporarily off the ground. The nonsupport leg is bent as the hopping leg leaves the ground.	The body moves with a smooth, rhythmic motion.

Cue Words

Arms bent—arms are bent at a 90-degree angle and swing in opposition to the legs.

Step-hop and **one and, two and**—step forward with the lead leg and immediately hop on that same foot, then step forward with the other foot and immediately hop on that foot. Continue this alternating action, creating a smooth and rhythmic motion.

> *Cue set 1:* arms bent, step-hop, step-hop
> *Cue set 2:* one and, two and; one and, two and

Skipping Troubleshooting Chart

If you see this	Then try this
1. No step-hop or student is using a gallop pattern	• Use colored floor tape to mark where the feet should be during the movement. Use a different color of tape for each foot. The same-color tape pieces should be approximately 5 inches (13 cm) apart, and the opposite color tape marks should indicate a stride of about 12 inches (30 cm). The student must step-hop on the first color and then switch to step-hop on the other color. • Record the student performing the skill. Show the student the recording, using a remote to start and stop the action.
2. Arms crossing the midline of the body or not swinging during skip	• Have the student work with a partner. The partner watches the student skip 30 feet (~9 m) and counts the number of times the arms either cross the midline of the body or do not swing. The object is to score a zero. • Have the student perform a step-hop and pose. The student does the step-hop and then freezes with the arm opposite the swing leg forward and the arm opposite the hop leg back.
3. Foot doesn't come up off the ground	• Use several small rubber (nonskid) bugs for the student to hop on and squash. The student skips with one foot squashing a bug on the hop, then skips with the other foot squashing the next bug on the next hop. • Place 10 to 12 ropes in a line parallel to each other and about 1 foot (0.3 m) apart on the floor. The student is perpendicular to the line of ropes. The student must step-hop over each rope. Have the student do this several times to practice skipping.
4. Student not hopping with a smooth pattern	• Review the critical elements of skipping. Being able to perform any locomotor skill smoothly requires the student to use the elements of the skill correctly. • Select appropriate music or use a percussion instrument. Have the student skip to the beat of the music.

PARTNER SKILL CHECK

Skill: Skipping

Skipper's name: _____ Watcher's name: _____

① Step

1   2   3   4   5

② Hop

1   2   3   4   5

③ Fly

1   2   3   4   5

④ Glide

1   2   3   4

PARTNER SKILL CHECK

Skill: Skipping

Skipper's name: _____ Watcher's name: _____

Watch your partner and mark each critical element of the skill. Let your partner do the skill five times. Each time your partner does it right, mark a Y in the box. If your partner doesn't do it right, mark an N in the box.

START	TRIALS

Eyes and Body
Eyes look in the direction of travel, and the body maintains an upright position.

1   2   3   4   5

Step and Hop
Step and hop on the same foot.

1   2   3   4   5

Arms
Arm opposite skipping leg swings forward.

1   2   3   4   5

Flight
Both feet are temporarily off the ground.

1   2   3   4   5

Glide
Body moves with a smooth, rhythmic motion.

1   2   3   4   5

JUMPING

The locomotor skill of jumping is fairly complex. A jump may technically involve a one- or two-foot takeoff with a two-foot landing. A jump may also involve a two-foot takeoff with a one-foot landing. Technically, leaping and hopping are both variations of jumping, but we have found these explanations to be very confusing for children. Therefore, when teaching the critical elements of both jumping in the horizontal plane and jumping in the vertical plane, we will take the more universal approach of defining jumping as taking off from two feet and landing on two feet.

National Standards & Grade-Level Outcomes for K-12 Physical Education (SHAPE America, 2014) addresses both vertical jumping and horizontal jumping in detail.

JUMPING IN THE VERTICAL PLANE

A rebound in basketball and a spike in volleyball are two obvious examples of jumping in the vertical plan. Children enjoy learning to jump because it is measurable, meaning they can see a result from their movement. For example, being able to touch the net on a basketball rim (even on an 8-foot goal) is a major accomplishment for many elementary school students.

While children generally enjoy jumping, several safety concerns must be addressed. Jumping up to touch a spot on a wall can cause injuries if it is not done properly. The preliminary run may provide too much momentum and the child may run into the wall. Children perform more safely when an object is suspended from an overhead structure. However, students should be taught to touch the object, not pull it. Pulling down on an overhead object may cause injuries.

In addition, you should be sure to clearly mark the starting point for the running approach to a jump. Often children believe that if a 10-foot (3 m) approach is good, a 100-foot (30 m) approach is *much* better. If a student moves back too far, the run becomes more important to him than the jump. This can cause the student to be out of control on his takeoff, thus interfering with mastery of the skill. Carefully marking the starting point for each practice will eliminate this problem. Challenge your students to touch objects suspended from an overhead structure at varying heights and to work with a partner to execute a proper high-five jump. These activities, in addition to using the movement concepts, will help reinforce jumping in the vertical plane.

Jumping instruction can begin in kindergarten. *National Standards and Grade-Level Outcomes for K-12 Physical Education* (SHAPE America, 2014) states that kindergarteners should be able to perform jumping and landing actions with balance (S1.E4.K), and in grade 1, students should be able to demonstrate two of the five critical elements for jumping and landing in a vertical plane (S1.E4.1). The quality of the performance should increase as students demonstrate four of the five critical elements in grade 2 (S1.E4.2), and they should be able to display a mature pattern by grade 3 (S1.E4.3). In grades 4 and 5, students should be able to use the vertical jump in gymnastics, dance, and small-sided games (S1.E4.4 and S1.E4.5). See table 2.12 for the outcomes for jumping in the vertical plane.

Table 2.12   Grade-Level Outcomes for Jumping in the Vertical Plane (S1.E4)

	Kindergarten	Grade 1	Grade 2	Grade 3	Grade 4	Grade 5
S1.E4 Jumping and landing, vertical	Performs jumping and landing actions with balance. (S1.E4.K)	Demonstrates 2 of the 5 critical elements for jumping and landing in a vertical plane. (S1.E4.1)	Demonstrates 4 of the 5 critical elements for jumping and landing in a vertical plane. (S1.E4.2)	Jumps and lands in the vertical plane using a mature pattern. (S1.E4.3)	Uses spring-and-step take-offs and landings specific to gymnastics. (S1.E4.4)	Combines jumping and landing patterns with locomotor and manipulative skills in dance, gymnastics and small-sided practice tasks in game environments. (S1.E4.5)

Reprinted, by permission, from SHAPE America – Society of Health and Physical Educators, 2014, *National standards & grade-level outcomes for K-12 physical education* (Champaign, IL: Human Kinetics).

Critical Elements

Knees and Arms

Knees are bent and arms are back to begin the jump.

Feet

Feet are shoulder-width apart.

Arms

Arms begin to swing forward and up toward the sky.

Legs

Legs forcefully thrust the body upward.

Landing

Knees are bent and shoulder-width apart.

Albemarle County Physical Education Curriculum Revision Committee, 2008.

Cue Words

Swing—knees are bent and arms are back to begin jump, feet are shoulder-width apart, and arms swing forward and up toward the sky.

Explode—forcefully thrust body upward and land with knees bent and feet shoulder-width apart.

Swing high—knees are bent and arms are back to begin the jump. Feet are shoulder-width apart.

Touch the sky—arms swing forward and up toward the sky, legs forcefully thrust body upward, and the student lands with knees bent and feet shoulder-width apart.

Cue set 1: swing, explode
Cue set 2: swing high, touch the sky

Jumping in the Vertical Plane Troubleshooting Chart

If you see this	Then try this
1. Poor body position, such as these: • Knees not bent • Arms not back • Feet not shoulder-width apart • Body upright	• Use a mirror (reflection) or flashlight (shadow) to show the student her body position. The student should have her side to the mirror or wall. • Record the student performing the skill. Show the student the recording, using a remote to start and stop the action.
2. Arms not swinging	• Have the student practice swinging the arms and bringing the body upward so the weight shifts to the toes. • Suspend a rope between two game standards. Hang objects (e.g., aluminum pie plates, wind chimes, Wiffle balls) from the rope so the student can touch them if he stands on his toes. The student must swing the arms upward to try to touch the objects while bringing his body weight up onto the toes.
3. Student not forcefully and extending the body upward during flight	• Attach a sheet of paper to the wall. Have a student stand with her side to the wall, holding a marker in the hand closest to the wall. The student must jump and make a mark on the paper. • Suspend a rope between two game standards. Hang objects (e.g., aluminum pie plates, wind chimes, Wiffle balls) from the rope so the student cannot touch them from a standing position. The student must swing the arms upward and jump to try to touch the objects.
4. Poor landing position, such as these: • Legs straight • Feet together • Arms behind body	• Have the student start on his toes and do a half squat while keeping the feet shoulder-width apart. • Use a mirror (reflection) or flashlight (shadow) to show the student his body position. The student should have his side to the mirror or wall. • Record the student performing the skill. Show the student the recording, using a remote to start and stop the action.

Skill: Jumping in the Vertical Plane

Jumper's name: _____

Watcher's name: _____

1 Knees and Feet

1   2   3   4   5

2 Arms

1   2   3   4   5

3 Legs

1   2   3   4   5

4 Landing

1   2   3   4

PARTNER SKILL CHECK

Skill: Jumping in the Vertical Plane

Jumper's name: _____

Watcher's name: _____

Watch your partner and mark each critical element of the skill. Let your partner do the skill five times. Each time your partner does it right, mark a Y in the box. If your partner doesn't do it right, mark an N in the box.

START

TRIALS

Knees and Arms
Knees are bent and arms are back to begin skill.

1   2   3   4   5

Feet
Feet are shoulder-width apart.

1   2   3   4   5

Arms
Arms swing forward and up toward the sky.

1   2   3   4   5

Legs Push
Legs forcefully thrust the body upward.

1   2   3   4   5

Landing
Knees are bent with feet shoulder-width apart.

1   2   3   4   5

JUMPING IN THE HORIZONTAL PLANE

The standing long jump is the most obvious example of jumping in the horizontal plane. As with jumping in the vertical plane, children enjoy learning to jump in the horizontal plane because they can see results from their movement.

While children generally enjoy jumping, several safety concerns must be addressed. Bending the knees on landing is crucial for student safety. The force of the landing can increase dramatically when children want to jump *down* from a height. The jumping task should be well defined, and the landing surface should be appropriate. We recommend that students perform all jumping on a level plane until they master bending the knees. When jumping from a height (e.g., from several stacked mats), providing an appropriate landing surface (e.g., a gymnastics crash mat) is essential.

Jumping instruction can begin in kindergarten. *National Standards & Grade-Level Outcomes for K-12 Physical Education* (SHAPE America, 2014) states that kindergarteners should be able to perform jumping and landing actions with balance (S1. E3.K), and in grade 1, students should be able to demonstrate two of the five critical elements for jumping and landing in a horizontal plane using two-foot takeoffs and landings (S1.E3.1). The quality of the skill should increase as the students demonstrate four of the five critical elements in grade 2 (S1.E3.2), and they should be able to display a mature pattern by grade 3 (S1.E3.3). In grades 4 and 5, students should be able to use the horizontal jump in gymnastics, dance, and small-sided games (S1.E3.4 and S1.E3.5). See table 2.13 for outcomes regarding jumping in the horizontal plane.

Table 2.13   Grade-Level Outcomes for Jumping in the Horizontal Plane (S1.E3)

	Kindergarten	Grade 1	Grade 2	Grade 3	Grade 4	Grade 5
S1.E3 Jumping and landing, horizontal	Performs jumping and landing actions with balance. (S1.E3.K)	Demonstrates 2 of the 5 critical elements for jumping and landing in a horizontal plane using 2-foot takeoffs and landings. (S1.E3.1)	Demonstrates 4 of the 5 critical elements for jumping and landing in a horizontal plane using a variety of 1- and 2-foot takeoffs and landings. (S1.E3.2)	Jumps and lands in the horizontal plane using a mature pattern. (S1.E3.3)	Uses spring-and-step take-offs and landings specific to gymnastics. (S1.E3.4)	Combines jumping and landing patterns with locomotor and manipulative skills in dance, gymnastics and small-sided practice tasks in game environments. (S1.E3.5)

Reprinted, by permission, from SHAPE America – Society of Health and Physical Educators, 2014, *National standards & grade-level outcomes for K-12 physical education* (Champaign, IL: Human Kinetics).

Besides using the movement concepts to reinforce jumping in the horizontal plane, we have found the following ideas to be helpful:

- Record how far a child is able to jump.
- Use tumbling mats that are several colors. Challenge students to jump to the red area or to the second blue line.
- Make 10 or more learning stations. They should be composed of nonparallel lines that are at least 6 feet (1.8 m) long and positioned 6 inches (15 cm) apart at the closest point and 5 feet (1.5 m) apart at the widest point. Challenge students to jump across the imaginary river. Challenge them further by asking them to go to the widest part and jump across the river without getting their feet wet.

Critical Elements

Knees and Arms	**Arms**	**Feet and Body**	**Legs**	**Landing**
Knees are bent and arms are back to begin the jump.	Arms swing forward and up in the direction of travel.	Feet are shoulder-width apart, and the body has a slight forward lean.	Legs forcefully thrust the body forward in a stretched position.	Knees are bent, feet are shoulder-width apart, and arms are in front of the body for balance.

Albemarle County Physical Education Curriculum Revision Committee, 2008.

Cue Words

Swing—knees are bent and arms are back to begin the jump. Feet are shoulder-width apart.

Explode—arms swing forward and up toward the sky. Forcefully thrust the body upward and forward, landing with knees bent and feet shoulder-width apart.

Up—arms swing forward forcefully and thrust the body up and forward.

Out—land with arms out in front, knees bent, and feet shoulder-width apart.

> *Cue set 1:* swing, explode
> *Cue set 2:* swing, up, out

Jumping in the Horizontal Plane Troubleshooting Chart

If you see this	Then try this
1. Poor body position, such as these: • Knees not bent • Arms not back • Feet not shoulder-width apart • Body upright	• Use a mirror or flashlight (reflection or shadow) to let the student see his body position. Student should have his side to the mirror or wall. • Record the student performing the skill. Show the student the recording, using a remote to start and stop the action.
2. Arms not swinging	• Have the student practice swinging the arms and bringing the body forward so the weight shifts to the toes. • The student works with a partner. Have the partner stand about 18 to 24 inches (45-70 cm) in front of the student. The partner holds up an object (e.g., hoop, picture, pinny) for the student to touch. The partner should hold the object at a sufficient height so that the student needs to reach out and up to touch it. The student must swing the arms forward without completing the jump.
3. Student not forcefully pushing with legs and extending the body during flight	• Have the student practice jumping over a hoop. • The student works with a partner. Have the partner stand about 3 to 4 feet (1-1.2 m) in front of the student (far enough in front so the partner is not touched). The partner holds up an object (e.g., hoop, picture, pinny.) for the student to touch. The partner should hold the object at a sufficient height so that the student needs to reach out and up to touch it. The student must swing the arms forward as she jumps and tries to touch, not grab, the object.
4. Poor landing position, such as these: • Legs straight • Feet together • Arms behind or to side of body	• Have the student do a half squat, keeping the feet shoulder-width apart and arms extended out in front of the body. • Have the student touch his bottom to the edge of a chair and return to a standing position. Repeat this activity several times.

Jumper's name: _____

Watcher's name: _____

1 **Knees and feet**

1   2   3   4   5

2 **Body lean**

1   2   3   4   5

3 **Legs push**

1   2   3   4   5

4 **Landing**

1   2   3   4

Jumper's name: _____

Watcher's name: _____

Watch your partner and mark each critical element of the skill. Let your partner do the skill five times. Each time your partner does it right, mark a Y in the box. If your partner doesn't do it right, mark an N in the box.

START		TRIALS				

START

Knees and Arms
Knees are bent and arms are back to begin skill.

TRIALS
1   2   3   4   5

Feet and Body
Feet are shoulder-width apart with a slight forward lean of the body.

1   2   3   4   5

Arms
Arms swing forward and out in the direction of travel.

1   2   3   4   5

Legs Push
Legs forcefully thrust the body forward in a stretched position.

1   2   3   4   5

Landing
Knees are bent, feet are shoulder-width apart, and arms are in front for balance.

1   2   3   4   5

LEAPING

Leaping is often described as an exaggerated run. The student takes off on one foot and lands on the other, just like in running. The flight phase, however, is longer and more obvious. Leaping is very difficult to teach in isolation. Students will have to begin their leaps with a running approach.

As with jumping vertically, it is helpful to clearly define where students will begin the approach. Again, children believe that if a 20-foot (6 m) approach is good, a 100-foot (30 m) approach is better. Marking the starting point for each practice session will eliminate this problem.

Besides using the movement concepts to reinforce leaping, we have found the following idea to be helpful. Make 10 or more learning stations. These stations are composed of nonparallel lines that are 6 inches (15 cm) apart at the closest point and 5 feet (1.5 m) apart at the widest point. The lines should be at least 6 feet (1.8 m) long. Challenge students to run and leap across the imaginary river. Challenge them further by asking them to go to the widest part and leap across the river without getting their feet wet.

According to *National Standards & Grade-Level Outcomes for K-12 Physical Education* (SHAPE America, 2014) (table 2.14), third graders should be able to leap using a mature pattern (S1.E1.3). In second grade, children should have developed a mature running pattern (S1.E2.2), which is essential for leaping.

Table 2.14 Grade-Level Outcomes for Leaping (S1.E1)

	Kindergarten	Grade 1	Grade 2	Grade 3
S1.E1 **Hopping, galloping, running, sliding, skipping, leaping**	Leaping not addressed before grade 3			Leaps using a mature pattern (S1.E1.3)

Critical Elements

Run
Take several running steps before starting to leap.

Takeoff
Push off the ground with one foot.

Flight
Both feet are temporarily off the ground in a stride position, and the arm opposite the lead foot reaches forward.

Landing
Land on the opposite foot from the takeoff foot; knee is bent to absorb force.

Run
Run a few steps after landing.

Cue Words

Go—take several running steps before starting to leap.

Push—push off the ground with one foot.

Run and **take off on one foot**—take several running steps before starting to leap. Push off the ground with one foot.

Fly and **get airborne**—both feet are temporarily off the ground, legs are in a stride position, and the arm opposite the lead foot reaches forward.

Land on the other foot—land on the opposite foot from the takeoff foot; knee is bent to absorb force.

Run again—run a few steps after landing.

> *Cue set 1:* take off on one foot, get airborne, land on the other foot
> *Cue set 2:* run, fly, run again
> *Cue set 3:* go, push, fly, land

Leaping Troubleshooting Chart

If you see this	Then try this
1. Student not getting the legs into a good stride position	• Have the student practice walking with very large steps. • Use a mirror or flashlight (reflection or shadow) to let the student see his body position. The student should have his side to the mirror or wall. • Place two ropes parallel in the play area and have the student walk over the ropes. Be sure that the ropes are placed a little wider than the widest stride of the student. This will provide an opportunity for the student to leap over the ropes.
2. Student using two feet to initiate the leap or not getting enough height on the leap	• Record the student performing the skill. Show the student the recording, using a remote to start and stop the action. • Make a hurdle that the student can leap over: Using a noodle, one noodle connector, and an 18-inch (45 cm) cone, cut the noodle in half and put one half in each end of the connector. Then place the center hole of the connector over the top of the cone. The student will have to push off using one foot to do this activity.
3. Arms not involved in the action	• Find a picture of a hurdler. Show the student the picture and then ask her to try to look like the picture. You can use the noodle hurdles described previously. • Have the student practice walking with very large giant steps and swinging the stepping leg forward and up. The arm opposite the stepping leg should also swing forward so that the arm and leg are parallel.
4. Student landing on both feet	• Have the student run several steps, take a giant step while swinging the opposite arm forward, and begin to run again. Encourage the student to come up off the ground during the giant step. • Set up two ropes parallel to each other and approximately 2 feet (0.6 m) apart. Place a landing spot on the far side of the ropes for the landing foot to touch.

PARTNER SKILL CHECK

Skill: Leaping

Leaper's name: _____

Watcher's name: _____

① Run
1 2 3 4 5

② Take off
1 2 3 4 5

③ Fly
1 2 3 4 5

④ Land
1 2 3 4

PARTNER SKILL CHECK

Skill: Leaping

Leaper's name: _____

Watcher's name: _____

Watch your partner and mark each critical element of the skill. Let your partner do the skill five times. Each time your partner does it right, mark a Y in the box. If your partner doesn't do it right, mark an N in the box.

START		TRIALS

Run
Take several running steps before starting to leap.
1 2 3 4 5

Takeoff
Push off the ground with one foot.
1 2 3 4 5

Flight
Both feet are temporarily off the ground.
1 2 3 4 5

Landing
Land on the opposite foot from the takeoff foot; knee is bent.
1 2 3 4 5

Run
Run a few steps after the landing.
1 2 3 4 5

ADDITIONAL LOCOMOTOR MOVEMENTS

LOCOMOTOR TAG

Objective

To practice a variety of locomotor skills within a tag game situation.

Equipment

Cones or lines to define the play area.

Activity

1. Specify a locomotor skill to be used in each round.
2. Select two or three students to be taggers.
3. Taggers try to tag as many players as possible within a set time period (e.g., 1 to 2 minutes).
4. When tagged, a player must go to the specified area and demonstrate a movement concept you have chosen. The player could be asked to demonstrate different pathways, different types of force, different levels, and so forth.
5. Once the player has demonstrated the concept correctly, he returns to the game.
6. Most of the locomotor skills can be used with this game.

Extensions

- When a tagger touches a player, the player becomes a tagger and the tagger becomes a player.
- A player is safe if she can tell the tagger a cue word of the locomotor skill being used before being tagged.

ROADWAY SIGNS

Objective

To practice a variety of locomotor skills.

Equipment

Traffic cones and easy-to-read signs that list individual locomotor movements.

Activity

1. Write on heavy paper the names of (or show pictures of) the different locomotor movements to be used. The signs should be large enough to read but small enough to be attached to a traffic cone.
2. Scatter the signs (and cones) throughout the play area.
3. The students move through the area performing the appropriate locomotor movements. When a student comes to a sign, she reads the locomotor movement on the sign and uses that skill until she comes to a new sign.
4. To ensure that all movements are practiced, you may want to put down floor or painter's tape that the students follow. The tape road should lead the students past each cone.

Extensions

- Include movement concepts on the locomotor cards (e.g., running at a slow speed, galloping in a zigzag pathway).
- Use different-colored tape to make a variety of roads. Specify which color of road everyone should follow. Students move to the specified color by following the road until they find an intersection.

PARACHUTE GO-ROUNDS

Objective

To use a variety of locomotor movements while using the parachute.

Equipment

Parachute.

Activity

1. Students hold the parachute at waist level with one hand.
2. Students turn a side to the parachute so all are facing in the same direction (except for sliding, when they will keep both hands on the parachute to prepare for the slide movement).
3. You select a locomotor movement they will use when moving in a circle while holding on to the parachute.
4. When you say *switch,* the students turn and change the direction of travel while performing the locomotor skill.

Extensions

- Divide students into groups. When a group is called, those students go under the uplifted parachute and use the specified locomotor skill to move to the opposite side.
- When a group is called, those students go under the uplifted parachute using a specified skill and say the cues out loud, then return to their original locations.

ON THE MOVE

Objective

To practice a variety of locomotor skills.

Equipment

One percussion instrument.

Activity

1. Students stand in their own self-space.
2. Tell the students to begin walking. While the students are walking, tell them what skill will be practiced next. When you strike the instrument once, the students change to that locomotor skill. Then tell the students which skill will come next.
3. You might choose to have a set pattern (e.g., one hit is walking, two hits is running, three hits is galloping).

Extensions

- Once students have mastered a variety of locomotor skills, allow them to select their own locomotor skills to perform each time you strike the instrument.
- Each student may create his own locomotor routine. The routine should consist of the following:
    1. Start—a statue
    2. Action—three different locomotor movements
    3. Stop—a statue

After the student has had time to practice the individual routines, he may perform the routine for another student or the class. The routines may be done in groups of two to four students. You may select the groups, or the students may form their own.

MOVER'S LICENSES

Objective

To demonstrate the ability to perform the locomotor skills.

Equipment

Mover's licenses for each student. See the following Advance Preparation section.

Activity

1. Students may earn their mover's licenses by correctly demonstrating the skills in any of the previous activities or in combinations of several activities.

2. Or, you may award licenses for demonstrating competencies on a specified number of skills.

Extensions

- Students may be given the licenses to keep.

- Licenses may be posted on the bulletin board and grouped by class. If a student has difficulty maintaining self-space or moving safely, the license may be moved to a section marked "driving school." That student will then practice those skills so that he may graduate from driving school and return to the other activities.

Advance Preparation

Making mover's licenses can be as simple or as complex as you choose.

- *Less complex:* Design your mover's license on the computer (see figure). Once these are duplicated, students may write their names on the licenses. Alternatively, many school administrative assistants are able to use the school's database to print the names of all students on labels. These labels can be placed on the cards so they look more official.

- *More complex:* Every year when individual students' photographs are taken, the photographer returns extra strips or groups of pictures to the school. The school administrative assistant will know if there are extra photographs you can use.

A sample mover's license.

These individual photographs can be attached to the basic license. When the photograph is combined with the student's name (from a label), it looks like a real license. If time and resources allow, laminating the cards will make them more official and a definite keepsake.

Be as creative and realistic with your licenses as resources allow. Include height, weight, a signature, and so on. We have found this project to be a wonderful public relations tool. When students understand the criteria for earning a license, earning one becomes a form of assessment. Many parents are very impressed by this project and often agree to help make the licenses.

SUMMARY

While some locomotor skills (e.g., walking, running) are used daily, others (e.g., sliding, leaping) are used in more specific settings. The challenge for those teaching locomotor skills is to present them in fun and interesting ways in order to keep students motivated and involved in the lesson. Unfortunately, many teachers are not sure how to do this. By using the movement concept approach (Graham et al., 2013) and the specific activities outlined in this chapter, we believe your lessons will be exciting and motivating. These lessons are the first step in helping your students to become skillful movers.

3

Underhand Rolling

The remaining chapters in this book address manipulative skills, which are skills that involve using an object to accomplish a task. A very motivating manipulative skill for kindergarteners and first graders is underhand rolling. The obvious connection between underhand rolling and bowling makes this a fun skill for children to learn.

A key element of underhand rolling is the step. Since stepping in opposition is essential for mastering nearly all manipulative skills, underhand rolling may be a logical way to introduce this concept to young children. *National Standards & Grade-Level Outcomes for K-12 Physical Education* (SHAPE America, 2014) states that a kindergartener should be able to step in opposition while throwing underhand (S1. E13.K), so this action should easily transfer to the underhand roll.

Children do not have to use a bowling ball to bowl. Kindergarteners can be successful with balls that are of the appropriate size and weight (e.g., tennis balls, softballs). For older children, many commercially owned bowling alleys have pins, lanes, and plastic balls that may be used by schools.

Critical Elements

Ready position

Knees bent, facing target, feet shoulder-width apart, eyes on target, object held in preferred hand (palm up) in front of the body.

Arm back

Swing the rolling arm back at least to waist level.

Step and roll

Step forward with the opposite foot, swing the rolling arm forward, and release the ball on the ground (low level) while bending at the knees and waist. The front body surface should be facing the target.

Follow through

The rolling hand continues toward the target in front of the body and finishes above the waist with the palm facing upward.

Cue Words

The cue words you select for each phase of the skill will depend on the age of the students you are teaching and your areas of emphasis. Younger students (kindergarten through grade 2) learn more easily with fewer, but concise, cues. They do not process or retain large quantities of information. In usable sets are some of the cue words that we use to teach underhand rolling. You may use each set individually or mix and match the cue words as needed. We have found that it is beneficial to have the students say the cue words out loud as they practice the skill.

Ready—knees bent, facing target, feet shoulderwidth apart, eyes on target, object held in preferred hand (palm up) in front of the body.

Arm back—swing the rolling arm back at least to waist level.

Step and roll or step and sweep—step forward with the opposite foot, bring the rolling arm forward, and release the ball on the ground (low level) while bending at the knees and waist. The front body surface should be facing the target.

Use your stepping foot—step forward with the opposite foot.

Sneak up on the target—bring the rolling arm forward and release the ball on the ground (low level) so that there is no bounce.

Follow through or Statue of Liberty—rolling hand continues toward the target in front of the body and finishes above the waist with the palm facing upward.

Spider on the shoulder—rolling hand continues toward the target in front of the body and finishes above the waist with the palm facing upward. Follow-through continues until the fingers of the rolling hand touch the top of the shoulder of the rolling hand.

> *Cue set 1:* ready, arm back, step and roll, follow through
> *Cue set 2:* ready, arm back, step and sweep, Statue of Liberty
> *Cue set 3:* ready, arm back, step and roll, spider on the shoulder
> *Cue set 4:* ready, use your stepping foot, sneak up on the target

SUGGESTED ACTIVITIES FOR REINFORCING AND ASSESSING THE CRITICAL ELEMENTS

In the learning process, it is essential that students know how a skill looks, what its critical elements are, and how to perform each element correctly. In the preceding section, we provided pictures and descriptions of underhand rolling, divided it into its critical elements, and provided possible cue words. Chapter 1 has nine generic activities that reinforce these concepts for underhand rolling as well as for all locomotor and manipulative skills. In addition to the material in chapter 1, the following section provides specific activities for reinforcing the critical elements unique to underhand rolling.

PARTNER SKILL CHECK

Objective

To allow partners to assess each other's progress in learning the skill.

Equipment

Partner skill check assessments and one ball for each set of partners. If the students cannot read or do not speak English, the picture version of the partner skill check assessment may be useful.

Activity

1. One partner observes the other student to see if she has the correct form for the ready position.
2. If the ready position is correct, then the partner places a *Y* in the first box. If the ready position is incorrect, he places an *N* in the first box. Nonreaders can put a smiling face if the ready position is correct or a frowning face if the ready position is incorrect.
3. This evaluation continues until each of the critical elements has been assessed five times.
4. A partner skill check sheet is used for each student.

Extensions

- You can use the partner skill check assessment to measure the skill development of each student.
- You can send partner skill check assessments home with report cards or as individual skills develop.

PARTNER SKILL CHECK

Skill: Underhand Roll

Roller's name: _____ Watcher's name: _____

1 Ready
1 2 3 4 5

2 Arm back
1 2 3 4 5

3 Step and roll
1 2 3 4 5

4 Follow through
1 2 3 4

PARTNER SKILL CHECK

Skill: Underhand Roll

Roller's name: _____ Watcher's name: _____

Watch your partner and mark each critical element of the skill. Let your partner do the skill five times. Each time your partner does it right, mark a Y in the box. If your partner doesn't do it right, mark an N in the box.

START	TRIALS

Ready position
1. Eyes on target
2. Knees bent
3. Feet shoulder-width apart
4. Object in front of body

1 2 3 4 5

ACTION

Arm back
1. Belt buckle faces target
2. Rolling arm extends back

1 2 3 4 5

Step and roll
3. Step forward on opposite foot
4. Rolling arm comes forward; ball released on the ground; belt buckle faces the target

1 2 3 4 5

STOP

Follow through
1. Rolling hand continues toward target finishing above the waist

1 2 3 4 5

SUCCESS BUILDERS

The success builder activities allow the teacher to address individual needs. If students need additional help on individual elements, the activities listed will reinforce correct performance.

Objective

To allow partners to improve areas of deficiency as measured by the partner skill check assessment.

Equipment

See the following individual stations. We suggest using an unbreakable mirror and a poster of each critical element of the underhand roll at each station. The mirror is particularly helpful in these activities because it allows the children to see what they are doing. The easiest way to make the posters is to print out the drawings from this book and enlarge them. Laminating the posters will ensure their use for many years.

Activity

1. Set up a station for each critical element in the teaching area. Post a description or a picture of the specific element at the corresponding station.
2. The details for each station follow:

READY

Knees bent, facing target, feet shoulder-width apart, eyes on target, object held in dominant hand (palm up) in front of the body.

Equipment

Poster of the ready position, mirror (if available), and partner evaluations.

Activity

The student assumes the ready position. The partner checks to see if her position matches the poster. The student refers to the mirror for help. The student then walks around and, on a signal from her partner, assumes the ready position again. When she has had several successful trials, the partners may return to working on the entire skill.

ARM BACK

Bring the rolling arm back at least to waist level.

Equipment

Critical element poster, mirror (if available), line at waist level on a wall, and partner evaluations.

Activity

The student demonstrates a swinging motion with his arm (keeping the arm close to the body) and raising his hand at least as high as his waist during the swing. The partner checks to see if his position matches the poster. To help the partner see the height of the swing, the student should perform the task standing near a wall with a line marked approximately waist high. The student refers to the mirror for help. Once the student can demonstrate a good arm swing, the partners may return to practicing the entire skill.

STEP AND ROLL

Step forward with the opposite foot, bring the rolling arm forward, and release the ball on the ground (low level) while bending at the knees and waist. The front body surface should be facing the target.

Equipment

Critical element poster, mirror (if available), whisk broom, jump rope, two chairs, and partner evaluations.

Activity

The student steps forward on her opposite foot and sweeps the floor with the rolling hand. The partner checks to see if her position matches the poster. A whisk broom may be added to this activity to facilitate the idea of sweeping the floor. As the student sweeps the floor, she should have her knees bent, and her body should be facing forward in the direction of the sweep. The student refers to the mirror for help. Once the student can demonstrate to her partner a good floor sweep, the partners may return to practicing the entire skill.

To assist students who are having difficulty with the release point, suspend a jump rope between two chairs and have students practice releasing the ball under the rope. The rope should be low enough that the student must roll the ball on the floor in order for the ball to go under the rope.

FOLLOW THROUGH

The rolling hand continues toward the target in front of the body and finishes above the waist with palm facing upward.

Equipment

Critical element poster, mirror (if available), and partner evaluations.

Activity

The student starts with the floor sweep described previously and finishes by giving the partner an upward high five (see figure). The partner checks to see if her position matches the poster. The rolling hand will have to come up to a high level in order for the student to touch her partner's palm. The student refers to the mirror for help. Once the student can give the partner an upward high five, the partners may return to practicing the entire skill.

Follow-through.

SUGGESTED CULMINATING ACTIVITIES TO REINFORCE THE ENTIRE SKILL

Students should be able to perform the critical elements of the skill correctly before emphasizing accuracy. When the teacher emphasizes accuracy before the skill becomes automatic, the student begins to aim his roll and the elements of the skill are diminished. Your targets should be large enough to allow students to perform the critical elements of the skill and to succeed in hitting the target.

INDIVIDUAL ACTIVITIES

BOWLING GOLF

Objective

To improve accuracy of the underhand rolling skill.

Equipment

At least nine targets of varying sizes placed along the walls of the gymnasium. Three distances from each target should be clearly marked with floor (or painter's) tape. A softball and a score sheet (see figure) will be necessary for each student.

Activity

1. Each student will begin on a "golf hole" and stand on the piece of tape that is the greatest distance from the wall.
2. If a student is able to knock down (or hit) the target from the greatest distance on the first roll, she records a 1 for that hole and moves on to the next.
3. If the student is unable to knock down (or hit) the target, then she moves forward to the next-closest line and tries again. If successful, she records a 2 for the hole and moves to the next station.
4. If unsuccessful, the student moves to the closest line and tries again. Whether she is successful or not, a 3 is recorded and the student moves to the next station.
5. At the end of nine holes, the score cards are tallied and collected. During a future class, the students may be given another opportunity to obtain a lower score.

Bowling Golf Score Card

NAME

Hole number	Score (circle your score on each hole)			Total
1	1	2	3	
2	1	2	3	
3	1	2	3	
4	1	2	3	
5	1	2	3	
6	1	2	3	
7	1	2	3	
8	1	2	3	
9	1	2	3	
Total				

Extensions

- For younger students, you may not want to keep score.
- You may adapt the course for the age and ability level of the students. For example, you may use multiple targets that are close together (like bowling pins) and require that *both* targets must be hit for a score to be recorded.
- You can also adapt the course by including a tunnel (folded mat) that the ball must be rolled under or an obstacle that the ball must be rolled around (by banking the ball off a mat or wall). The adaptations are limited only by the available equipment and your imagination.
- You may want to shorten the distance that each rolling line is from the wall for the younger children and lengthen it for the older students.
- You may require that proper form be used or a penalty will be awarded.
- Integration with mathematics is easy to accomplish in this activity. Here are examples:
  - Students must use addition skills to determine their scores.
  - You may assist the students in using addition and division to determine the average score of the class or to determine the average score for a specific hole.
  - The average score of the class may be graphed so that the students are able to see the improvement.
- Students may work in pairs. One student can roll while the other evaluates form and keeps score. Once the target is hit, the partners change duties and continue. This enables each student to play each hole and to receive the peer evaluation.

MATH BOWLING

Objective
To combine practicing underhand rolling with math skills.

Equipment
One softball for each student and note cards with numbers.

Activity
1. Tape numbered note cards to each rolling station in the teaching area. The numbers you select will depend on the age of the students and the answers to the math questions you intend to ask.
2. Call out a math problem (for example, *What is 2 + 1?*).
3. The students try to roll the ball and hit the appropriate answer.

Extensions
- Students may work in pairs to evaluate the critical elements of the underhand roll and to check answers.
- If points are awarded, it is recommended that one point always be given for performing the skill correctly.
- You may want to lengthen or shorten the distance from the targets depending on the skill level of the children.
- Students can also use subtraction, multiplication, or division for math problems, depending on age and ability.
- This activity may be used with other content areas. For example, the note cards could contain shapes, with the challenge to hit triangles, squares, and other shapes. Or the note cards could contain letters, and challenges could include hitting a vowel or a consonant. You may ask, *What letter does* roll *begin with?* or *What letter does* fun *end with?*

- The students may use flash cards with a partner or a small group. The students draw a card and answer the question by rolling the ball to the correct answer.

COLOR TARGETS

Objective

To provide students opportunities to improve rolling accuracy by hitting specific targets.

Equipment

Construction paper of different colors (about 8 to 12 targets of each color) taped to the baseboard of the gymnasium or activity area and a ball for each student (e.g., softball, tennis ball).

Activity

1. Create a color box in which samples from each color of construction paper have been placed. You will need more samples than you have students.
2. Select a student to draw a sample color from the color box.
3. The sample color chosen is the color target all students must locate and try to hit with an underhand roll.
4. Students continue to roll toward the targets of the selected color until you give a stop signal.
5. The activity continues until all students have been given an opportunity to draw from the color box.

Extensions

- Instead of using different colors, students could select different shapes from the shape box, letters from the alphabet box, or words from the word box.
- Students can work with partners. The partner selects the color, shape, letter, or word that will be used for a target. The roller must then try to hit the selected target. Partners take turns selecting targets and rolling.

CREATE A WORD

Objective

To create words by hitting letters using the underhand roll.

Equipment

One ball (softball or tennis ball) per student and four complete sets of alphabet letters scattered and taped to the baseboard of the gymnasium or activity area. It would be advantageous to have extra copies of vowels and selected consonants (e.g., N, R, S, T). You will also need paper and pencils or a dry-erase board and markers to serve as a word bank.

Activity

1. On your start signal, students begin to spell words by hitting letters of the alphabet using underhand rolling.
2. Once a student has created a word, he goes to the word bank (paper or dry-erase board) and writes the word. It will be helpful to have several word banks so students will not have to wait in line to write their words.
3. A word may be written only once.
4. If a student hits a letter that cannot be used to form the word being created, she must hit the letter again to delete it.

Extensions

- Students can work with partners. One student rolls the ball to hit letters to spell a word while the partner records the word and evaluates the roll. The roller may not use the letter until underhand rolling is performed properly. When the first partner has spelled a word, the other partner is then given an opportunity to roll.

- Students working in pairs are given paper and pencil to record the letters they hit and to write down the words they create. Each partner must roll and hit a vowel and two consonants until the pair has six letters to create words. The partners attempt to create six words using one or more of the letters they have hit. Once the partners have created six words and written them down, they will attempt to spell the words by hitting the letters with the ball. Once a word is spelled, it may be checked off the list. If the students are unable to use a letter they have hit, they must hit that letter again to delete it and select another letter.

PARTNER ACTIVITIES

CHALLENGES

Objective

To practice underhand rolling in a variety of situations.

Equipment

One softball, tennis ball, or playground ball per pair of students and laminated challenge cards. Different types of challenges may require additional equipment.

Activity

1. Each student selects a challenge card.
2. Students perform the tasks described on the cards.
3. Possible challenges may include the following:
   - Roll the ball using strong force (light force).
   - Roll the ball along a line on the floor.
   - Roll the ball into a cup, cone, net, or other object.
   - Roll the ball and hit the target from a specific area on the floor.

Extensions

- Place multicolored targets or pictures on a wall (at floor level). Additional targets may be placed against the wall or scattered throughout the play area. These targets could include cones, bowling pins, buckets, or empty 2-liter plastic bottles. Have the partner tell the roller which target to hit.

- Set up game poles or volleyball standards and tie a rope between them. Suspend different objects from the rope (at floor level) and challenge the students to hit them. Possible targets could include hoops, aluminum pie pans, and empty 2-liter plastic bottles.

LOW BRIDGE

Objective

To use underhand rolling to move the ball under a low object.

Equipment

One softball (or tennis ball) and one folding chair per student pair.

Activity

1. Place a folding chair between two students. The students should be about 10 feet (3 m) apart, and the chair should be facing one of the students.
2. The students take turns underhand rolling the ball so that it goes under the chair.
3. After each partner has rolled the ball under the chair five times, all students may take one step backward.

Extensions

- Turn the chairs so that the sides are toward the partners.
- Partners may back up only when you give that direction.
- If a roll is successful (goes under the chair), the roller takes one step backward.
- If both of the partners roll a ball that goes under the chair, then both may back up. If a subsequent roll does not go under the chair, they must return to the starting point.

GROUP ACTIVITIES

OMNIKIN BALL MADNESS

Objective

To perform underhand rolling using a ball to move an object across the play area.

Equipment

The object may be an Omnikin ball or any ball larger than the balls being rolled. The balls being rolled may be playground balls or softballs when aiming at the Omnikin ball. When the target is smaller, tennis balls may be used.

Activity

1. Divide the class into four groups. Each group stands along one side of a square play area. Students must stay behind their lines.
2. Place the Omnikin ball or large ball in the center of the play area.
3. Each group begins the activity with two or more balls.
4. On the start signal, players roll their balls and try to hit the large ball in the center in an effort to move it toward the other group's line.
5. Players continue to roll their balls until the large ball crosses a group's line. Any ball that stays inside of the area enclosed by the four groups is retrieved by the teacher.
6. Players may touch the large ball only with a rolling ball. They may not touch it with their bodies.
7. Once the large ball crosses the designated line, the activity stops and the large ball is returned to the center of the play area.
8. Resume the activity when each group has the same number of balls to roll. Be sure every player is given a chance to start with a ball.

Extensions

- Create two groups rather than four.
- Students roll a variety of balls at the large ball in an effort to move the ball across another group's line. This may lead to discussions on which types of balls are better for the task (e.g., playground balls versus tennis balls).
- Have groups change positions either before the next round or on a signal during the activity. If the students are to change places during the activity, be sure they understand that they may not roll a ball at the large ball until your signal and that they may not take a ball with them as they change sides.

SWITCHEROO

Objective

To use underhand rolling to tag the feet of opposing players in an effort to get all players on one side of the play area.

Equipment

Six to eight 6- to 8-inch (15-20 cm) balls (foam balls or light rubber balls). The number will vary based on the skill level of the students.

Activity

1. Divide the class into two groups and place them on opposite sides of a divided play area.
2. Give each group an equal number of balls to start the activity.
3. On the start signal, players roll the balls and try to hit the feet of the opposing players.
4. If a player is hit, he moves to the other group's side. That player is now a member of the opposing group. When a player changes sides, he may not carry a ball to the opponent's side.
5. Restart the activity when all players are on the same side.

Extension

While the students are performing the activity, watch to see that underhand rolling is being performed correctly. Ask any student having trouble rolling correctly to go to a practice area and work with a partner or designated teacher assistant.

CONE MADNESS

Objective

To use underhand rolling to hit the opposing group's cones.

Equipment

Cones, bowling pins, or empty 2-liter bottles and eight playground balls.

Activity

1. Divide the class into two groups and place them on opposite sides of a divided play area. Give each group four playground balls.
2. Set up cones or bowling pins on the end lines of the play area; these are used as targets (see figure).

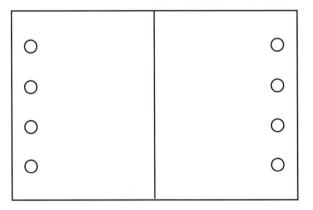

$\bigcirc$ = Cone

Setup for Cone Madness activity.

3. Students may not cross the center line.
4. The balls are rolled to knock down the other group's cones. The defenders may use their hands to stop the balls. If any cones are accidentally knocked down, they may not be put back up.
5. Restart the activity when all of a group's cones are down.
6. Observe for correct form during the activity. If a student demonstrates incorrect form, he must work on the problem area at one of the practice stations.

Extensions

- Use four groups with four sets of cones.
- Use a variety of balls (volleyballs, tennis balls, softballs).

CREATE YOUR OWN ACTIVITY

Objective

To allow students to create their own activities to reinforce underhand rolling skills.

Equipment

One piece of paper and pencil per group and a predetermined list of equipment you will allow the students to use in their activities (e.g., bowling pins, cones, jump ropes, softballs, tennis balls).

Activity

1. Form groups of two to five students. You may select the groups, or the students may form their own.
2. Each group creates an activity using underhand rolling as the basic skill. Students are required to have rules that encourage correct performance of the skill, include all players, and address all safety concerns.
3. The groups write their individual names, the rules of the activity, and the equipment needed on their papers, and then they show their activities to you.
4. After you approve their activities, the groups retrieve the necessary equipment and begin playing.
5. You must approve all changes to the activities.

Extensions

- Groups may teach their activities to other groups.
- Groups may teach their activities to the entire class.

PIN BALL

Objective

To use underhand rolling to hit the opposing group's bowling pins.

Equipment

Balls and three plastic bowling pins (indicated by A and B in the figure) for each group. Bowling pins need to be color coded for each group (e.g., use different-colored tape to mark the pins).

Activity

1. Set up a play area with a center line and two restraining lines that are approximately 12 feet (3.7 m) away from the center line.

2. Divide the class into two equal groups and place the groups behind the restraining lines, facing each other.

3. Set up the six pins along the center dividing line of the play area, alternating colors (see figure).

4. On the start signal, the students roll the balls and try to hit the opposing group's pins. The students may not cross the restraining line.

5. A pin does not stay down if the ball was rolled from in front of the restraining line. If a student knocks down her own pin by mistake, it must stay down.

6. Restart the activity when all of a group's pins have been knocked down.

Adapted, by permission, from K. Thomas, A. Lee, and J. Thomas, 2000, *Physical education for children: Daily lesson plans for elementary school,* 2nd ed. (Champaign, IL: Human Kinetics), 546

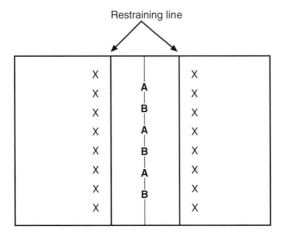

Setup for Pin Ball activity.

Extensions

- Use empty 2-liter bottles, lightweight cones, empty cereal boxes, or other objects as the targets.
- Suspend a rope between two volleyball standards. Hang lightweight targets (e.g., paper, scarves, streamers, crepe paper) on the rope and challenge the students to hit the opposing team's targets.

Adapted, by permission, from K. Thomas, A. Lee, and J. Thomas, 2000, *Physical education for children: daily lesson plans for elementary school,* 2nd ed. (Champaign, IL: Human Kinetics), 546.

CRAZY DOTS

Objective

To combine opportunities to practice underhand rolling and improve accuracy by rolling the ball over the floor dots on the opposing group's side.

Equipment

Six red circles and six blue circles that are approximately 12 inches (30 cm) in diameter and one ball (tennis or softball) per student.

Activity

1. Divide the play area in half with six colored circles randomly placed within each group's area (see figure).
2. Divide the class into two groups.
3. Rolling from his side, each student tries to roll the ball over one of the crazy dots on the opposing group's side.
4. A player may stop a ball from crossing her group's crazy dots by using any part of her body.
5. Each time the student rolls a ball across a crazy dot, he gets a point for the group by placing a tally mark on a designated paper or dry-erase board.
6. At the end of 5 minutes, each group adds up their points.

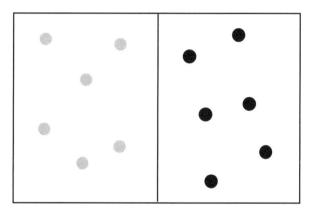

Setup for Crazy Dots activity.

Extensions

- Use more crazy dots.
- Remove a dot after a ball rolls over it. Start a new activity when all of the dots have been removed from one side.

ATHLETE'S FOOT

Objective

To use the underhand rolling motion to slide a beanbag under a rope, trying to hit the feet of the opposing players.

Equipment

Two volleyball standards, one rope, and one beanbag per student. The rope is suspended between the volleyball standards approximately one foot above floor level.

Activity

1. Divide the class into two groups and place one group on each side of the rope.
2. Give each student a beanbag.
3. On the start signal, players slide their beanbags under the rope and try to hit the feet of the opposing players.
4. If a player is hit, she moves to the other group's side, but she may not take the beanbag with her. She is now a member of that group.
5. Restart the activity when all players are on the same side.

Extensions

- Monitor the skill while the students are playing. Direct any student having trouble with the underhand rolling motion to go to the practice area and work with a partner or designated teacher assistant.
- Squash the bug: To work on eye–foot coordination, have the students stop the beanbags by stepping on them.

Adapted from Wessel 1974.

Underhand Rolling Troubleshooting Chart

If you see this	Then try this
1. Eyes not on target	• Have the student roll at a target he has designed. • Use color targets on the floor and roll the ball across them. • Use pie plates for targets and place them on the wall at floor level. • Use targets the student must roll through (e.g., cones, chairs, horseshoes).
2. Arm not swinging back level	• Have the student swing her arm back to touch a target (pie plate) attached to the wall. The target is placed at the student's waist in line with the rolling arm. The student will then roll the ball. • With a partner standing behind the roller, the roller swings his arm back and tries to take an object out of the partner's hand. • Put butcher paper on the wall. The student stands sideways with a marker in her rolling hand. As the student moves the rolling hand back, she draws a curvy line on the paper.
3. Student not stepping in opposition	• Tie a pinny or scarf around the leg opposite of the rolling hand. • Use spots or footprints on the floor to indicate the proper foot placement. • Tape bubble wrap to the floor. Have the student step in opposition on that spot to create a noise.
4. Hand not near the floor on release	• Place a toy truck on the floor where the hand should follow through and have the student push it forward. You could also try this with a tennis ball. • Have the student use a small whisk broom to sweep the ball forward.
5. Knees not bending to allow the hand to get close to the floor or one knee touching the floor	• Slide a beanbag rather than a ball across the floor. • Take a flashlight or projector and shine the light on the student, and have the student watch his shadow as he performs the underhand roll. • Place a 6-inch (15 cm) cone approximately 1 foot (30 cm) in front of the student's nonstepping leg. Have the student practice the skill without a ball and have him touch his knee to the cone.
6. Ball bouncing when released	• Have a partner check the hand position when the ball is released. • Stretch a rope between two chairs so the rope is approximately 1 foot (0.3 m) off the floor. Have the student perform the underhand roll by releasing the ball under the rope.
7. Student not stepping toward a target	• Use a line on the floor or put down tape. Have the student stand behind the line. Challenge the student to step over the line with her stepping foot. • Tape bubble wrap to the floor. Have the student step on the wrap to create a noise. • Place two objects shoe-width apart in front of the student. The objects may be cones, domes, foam bricks, and so on. The student must step so that his foot is placed between the two objects.
8. Body not in proper alignment on the follow-through	• Tell the student to point her belt buckle at the target on the follow-through. • Use a line on the floor or put down tape. Challenge the student to release the ball on the line and bring the rolling arm forward over the line when the ball is released.

SUMMARY

Underhand rolling is a skill that children can learn at an early age as long as the equipment is of the appropriate size. Once your students have mastered the critical elements of the skill, you can add to the challenge by increasing the distance to the target or decreasing the target's size. Later, you could add the four-step approach to complete the transition to the sport of bowling. This will be very motivating for the students!

The skill progression of underhand rolling to underhand throwing to overhand throwing follows a logical sequence: All three skills require the student to step in opposition. As with all physical skills, practice and instruction can greatly enhance the students' mastery of these crucial building-block skills.

UNDERHAND ROLLING LESSON PLAN

(FIRST LESSON)

AGE GROUP: Early primary grades.

FOCUS: Stepping in opposition.

SUBFOCUS: Releasing the ball on the floor.

OBJECTIVES: To step in opposition 80 percent of the time (**cue:** *use your stepping foot*) and release the ball so that there is minimal bouncing four out of five times (**cues:** *let the ball sneak up on your target* and *the ball has to be quiet—shhhh*).

MATERIALS AND EQUIPMENT: One ball and one target (piece of construction paper taped to the baseboard) for each child.

ADVANCE PREPARATION: A learning station for each child may be helpful. Tape pieces of construction paper to the gymnasium baseboard approximately 4 feet (1.2 m) apart. Use as many pieces of construction paper as you have students. In addition, lines that are parallel to the target (construction paper) may be taped (with floor or painter's tape) on the floor at appropriate distances from the wall. This will enable each child to have his own place to practice (see figure).

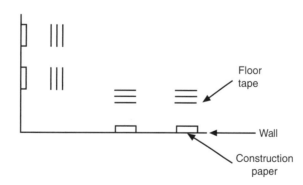

Advance preparation for the underhand rolling activity.

ORGANIZATION AND MANAGEMENT: Students are in self-space for instruction and warm-up. Later, students will find their own learning stations in the gymnasium for practice.

WARM-UP:

Today I would like you to learn the different jobs the arms and legs have. Pretend you are in a parade and you are waving at the crowd. Everyone wave (demonstrate).

Look at your hand that's waving. That is also your rolling hand and it is also your throwing hand.

Today we will call it our rolling hand. Can you remember that? It's called your . . . rolling hand.

INTRODUCTION:

Today we will work on underhand rolling. Everyone stand up. Bring your rolling hand straight back. Excellent.

*Take your foot that's on the same side of your body as your rolling hand and step **back** with it. Can you do that? The foot that's left out in front is your stepping foot. Can you say that? It's your . . . ?*

Let's do this again. Start with your feet together. Place the foot that's on the same side of your body as your rolling hand back. What do we call the foot that's in front? **(Stepping foot.)**

Some children have a different rolling or throwing hand than others. That is okay, as long as everyone has a stepping foot that is on a different side of the body than the hand they use for rolling.

*Let's stand up straight with our feet together. Can you hold up your rolling hand and step **forward** with your stepping foot? Now put your feet back together and hang your arms at your sides. Bring back your rolling hand again and use your stepping foot again.* (This activity is repeated several times.)

Watch for stepping in opposition. Note: Occasionally, a student does not wave with her preferred hand. If there is confusion, place an object on the floor directly in front of the student and ask her to pick it up. Usually she will use her preferred hand. The stepping foot can be taught once hand preference has been determined.

I am going to put on music. I would like you to move around in the general space using any of the locomotor skills we have learned. Who can give me an example of a locomotor skill? (Students provide suggestions.)

Excellent. You will move around, and when the music stops you will freeze, count to three, and then bring your rolling arm back and put your stepping foot forward. Do you understand the directions? (Begin music.)

Repeat this activity for several minutes. Watch to make sure students are stepping in opposition.

Now, when you freeze and put your rolling arm back and your stepping foot forward, I would like you to look at your neighbor and see if he or she is stepping with the proper foot. Again, it doesn't matter if they use a different hand for rolling than you use. What is important is that the stepping foot be on a different side than the rolling hand. (Begin music.)

Repeat this activity for several additional minutes. Watch to make sure students are stepping in opposition.

FORMATION:

Freeze. (Students return to a semicircle formation for instruction.)

Now we will practice using the stepping foot to help roll a ball. This time we will stand up, pull the rolling arm back while stepping with the stepping foot, and roll an imaginary ball. Everyone stand up and find your self-space. Face me. Pull your rolling hand (your waving arm) toward the back wall. Can you step with your stepping foot and bring your rolling hand down until it touches the floor? To do that you may have to bend somewhere.

Watch me. Where do I bend so that I can touch the floor? **(Knees and waist.)** *Let's try it again. Make sure you touch the floor. Ready position, arm back, and step and roll.*

Watch for release point and stepping in opposition.

This time we need to think about a follow-through. This means bringing the arm up after letting go of the ball. Let's practice the roll again. Remember: ready position, arm back, step and roll, and follow through.

Watch for release point, stepping in opposition, and follow-through.

Freeze. We are going to have our own bowling alley today.

Look around the gymnasium. There are pieces of construction paper and balls against the wall. Each of you will have one of these places for your own bowling alley today. Can you find your own bowling alley and sit on the tape closest to the wall? Go.

Pick up the ball and stand on your piece of tape facing the construction paper. Face your target, get in the ready position, pull your arm back, step and roll the ball, and follow through. Go get your ball and return to your piece of tape. (Repeat several times.)

Have the children repeat the cues with you. When you think the children can repeat the cues on their own, allow them to practice independently.

Watch for release point and stepping in opposition.

Freeze. This time our bowling alley will have a secret mission. We need for the balls to sneak up on the target. We don't want the target to hear the balls coming. How could we do that?

Release the balls **on** *the ground.*

Pick up a ball and stand on your piece of tape facing the target. Remember, we are going to be sneaky. Face your target, get in the ready position, pull your arm back, step and roll the ball quietly, and follow through. Go get your ball and return to your piece of tape. Keep practicing.

Freeze. This time I would like you and the person next to you to be partners. One will watch as the other rolls. What do you think you will be looking for? **(Releasing the ball near the ground and using your stepping foot.)** *After each roll, tell your partner how he or she is doing.* (After 5 to 10 rolls, students exchange duties.)

Freeze. Time is up. Please return your ball to its place near the wall and line up.

CLOSURE:

Students are lined up to leave.

How can we sneak up on our bowling pins? How do we know which foot to step with? Next time we will practice bowling from farther back and we will use real bowling pins.

4

Throwing

In this chapter, we discuss the following manipulative skills: underhand throwing, overhand throwing, and two-hand overhead throwing. Since all of these throwing skills, particularly overhand throwing, are used in many lifetime activities, their critical elements should be taught at an early age. *National Standards & Grade-Level Outcomes for K-12 Physical Education* (SHAPE America, 2014) addresses both underhand throwing (S1.E13) and overhand throwing (S1.E14).

UNDERHAND THROWING

While many people believe the only purpose of underhand throwing is pitching a horseshoe, it is in fact an integral part of many sport skills. Underhand throwing is essential to softball pitching, and underhand tossing can also be used to assist a fielder in making an out from a close distance in softball or baseball. In addition, the critical elements of underhand throwing are very similar to those of the underhand volleyball serve. With the addition of a racket, underhand throwing is essential to the game of badminton.

Often, the purpose of underhand throwing will dictate exactly *how* it is performed. Activities requiring height (e.g., slow-pitch softball pitching and horseshoes) will require that the follow-through be very exaggerated. When the distance to the target is short or if the objective is speed, then the follow-through will be much shorter (e.g., in fast-pitch softball pitching). In this section, we emphasize the skills most relevant to young children—that is, those throws requiring an arc.

One factor that greatly affects the initial learning of the underhand throw is the target placement. If a target is placed at a low level, the student may roll rather than throw the ball. If the target is at a high level, the student is more likely to develop incorrect throwing habits. While students are learning and practicing this skill, a medium-level target is best. Once the students understand how to perform the skill, then we encourage the use of large targets that are placed at a variety of heights.

National Standards & Grade-Level Outcomes for K-12 Physical Education (SHAPE America, 2014) (table 4.1) indicates that kindergarteners should be able to throw underhand with the opposite foot forward (S1.E13.K). First graders should be able to throw underhand demonstrating two of the five critical elements (S1.E13.1), and second graders should be able to use a mature pattern (S1.E13.2). In grade 3, students should be able to throw underhand to a partner or target with reasonable accuracy (S1.E13.3). Students will begin using the skill more in grades 4 and 5.

Table 4.1 Grade-Level Outcomes for Underhand Throwing (S1.E13)

	Kindergarten	Grade 1	Grade 2	Grade 3	Grade 4	Grade 5
S1.E13 Underhand throwing	Throws underhand with opposite foot forward. (S1.E13.K)	Throws underhand demonstrating 2 of the 5 critical elements of a mature pattern. (S1.E13.1)	Throws underhand using a mature pattern. (S1.E13.2)	Throws underhand to a partner or target with reasonable accuracy. (S1.E13.3)	Applies skill. (S1.E13.4)	Throws underhand using a mature pattern in nondynamic environments (closed skills) with different sizes and types of objects. (S1.E13.5a) Throws underhand to a large target with accuracy. (S1.E13.5b)

Critical Elements

Ready position	**Arm back**	**Step**	**Release**	**Follow through**
Knees bent, facing target, feet shoulder-width apart, eyes on target, object held in preferred hand (palm up) in front of the body.	Swing the throwing arm back to at least waist level.	Step forward with the opposite foot and bring the throwing arm forward.	Release the ball between the knee and waist level. The arm stays straight throughout the entire movement.	The throwing hand continues toward the target in front of the body with the palm facing upward.

Cue Words

The cue words you select for each phase of the skill will depend on the age of the students you are teaching and your areas of emphasis. Younger students (kindergarten through grade 2) learn more easily with fewer concise cues. They do not process or retain large quantities of information. In usable sets are some of the cue words we use to teach underhand throwing. You may use each set individually or mix and match the cue words as needed. We have found that it is beneficial to have the students say the cue words out loud as they practice the skill.

Ready—knees bent, facing target, feet shoulder-width apart, eyes on target, object held in preferred hand (palm up) in front of the body.

Arm back—bring the throwing arm back at least to waist level.

Step and release—step forward with the opposite foot, bring the throwing arm forward, and release the ball between the knee and waist level. The arm is extended throughout the entire movement.

Use your stepping foot—step forward with the opposite foot.

Let it go—bring the throwing arm forward and release the ball below the waist. The arm is extended throughout the entire movement. The throwing hand continues toward the target in front of the body and finishes with palm facing upward.

Follow through or **Statue of Liberty**—the throwing hand continues toward the target in front of the body and finishes with palm facing upward.

> *Cue set 1:* ready, arm back, step, release, follow through
> *Cue set 2:* arm back, step, release
> *Cue set 3:* ready, arm back, step, release, Statue of Liberty
> *Cue set 4:* ready, arm back, use your stepping foot, let it go

SUGGESTED ACTIVITIES FOR REINFORCING AND ASSESSING THE CRITICAL ELEMENTS

In the learning process, it is essential that students know how a skill looks, what its critical elements are, and how to perform each individual element correctly. In the preceding section, we provided pictures and descriptions of underhand throwing, divided it into its critical elements, and provided possible cue words. Chapter 1 provided generic activities that will reinforce these concepts for underhand throwing as well as for all locomotor and manipulative skills. In addition to the material in chapter 1, the following section provides specific activities for reinforcing the critical elements unique to underhand throwing.

PARTNER SKILL CHECK

Objective
To allow partners to assess each other's progress in learning the underhand throw.

Equipment
Partner skill check assessments and one ball or beanbag for each set of partners. If the students cannot read or do not speak English, the picture version of the partner skill check assessment may be useful.

Activity
1. One partner observes the other to see if he has the correct form for the ready position.
2. If the ready position is correct, then the partner places a *Y* in the first box. If the ready position is incorrect, she places an *N* in the first box. Nonreaders can put a smiling face if the ready position is correct or a frowning face if the ready position is incorrect.
3. This evaluation continues until each of the critical elements has been assessed five times.
4. A partner skill check assessment is used for each student.

Extensions
- You may use the partner skill check assessment to measure the skill development of each student.
- You may send partner skill check assessments home with report cards or as individual skills develop.

PARTNER SKILL CHECK
Skill: Underhand Throwing

Thrower's name: _____

Watcher's name: _____

① Ready

1   2   3   4   5

② Arm back

1   2   3   4   5

③ Step

1   2   3   4   5

④ Release

1   2   3

⑤ Follow through

1   2   3   4

PARTNER SKILL CHECK
Skill: Underhand Throwing

Thrower's name: _____

Watcher's name: _____

Watch your partner and mark each critical element of the skill. Let your partner do the skill five times. Each time your partner does it right, mark a Y in the box. If your partner doesn't do it right, mark an N in the box.

START

TRIALS

Ready position
1. Eyes on target.
2. Knees bent.
3. Feet shoulder-width apart.
4. Object in front of body.

1   2   3   4   5

ACTION

Arm back
1. Belt buckle facing target.
2. Throwing arm swings back.

1   2   3   4   5

Step
3. Step forward on the opposite foot.

1   2   3   4   5

Release
4. Throwing arm comes forward, ball is released between knee and waist level, and arm stays straight.

1   2   3   4   5

STOP

Follow through
1. Arm continues toward target.

1   2   3   4   5

SUCCESS BUILDERS

The success builder activities allow you to address individual needs. If students need additional help on individual critical elements, the activities listed will help reinforce correct performance.

Objective

To allow partners to improve areas of deficiency as measured by the partner skill check assessment.

Equipment

See the following individual stations. We suggest using an unbreakable mirror and a poster of each critical element of underhand throwing at each station. The mirror is particularly helpful in these activities because it allows children to see what they are doing. The easiest way to make the posters is to print out the drawings from this book and enlarge them. Laminating the posters will ensure their use for many years.

Activity

1. Set up a station for each of the five critical elements in the teaching area. Post a description or a picture of the specific element at the corresponding station.
2. The details for each station follow:

READY

Knees bent, facing target, feet shoulder-width apart, eyes on target, object held in preferred hand (palm up) in front of the body.

Equipment

Poster of the ready position, mirror (if available), and partner assessments.

Activity

The student assumes the ready position, and the partner checks to see if her position matches the poster. The student refers to the mirror for help. The student then walks around and, on a signal from her partner, assumes the ready position again. Once the student can demonstrate to the partner a correct ready position, the partners may return to practicing the entire skill.

ARM BACK

Swing the throwing arm back to at least waist level.

Equipment

Mirror, poster, line at waist level on the wall, and partner assessments.

Activity

The student demonstrates a swinging motion with his arm (keeping the arm close to his body) and raises his hand at least as high as his waist during the swing. The partner checks to see if his position matches the poster. To help the partner see the height of the swing, the student should perform the task standing near a wall with a line marked approximately waist high. The student refers to the mirror for help. Once the student can demonstrate to the partner a good arm swing, the partners may return to practicing the entire skill.

STEP AND THROW

Step forward with the opposite foot.

Equipment

Mirror, poster, footprint outlines or tape (floor or painter's tape), jump rope, two chairs, and partner assessments.

Activity

Place footprints (or floor or painter's tape) on the floor. With the partner's help, the student starts from the ready position and steps with the appropriate foot. The partner checks to see if her position matches the poster. The student refers to the mirror for help.

RELEASE

Bring the throwing arm forward and release the ball between the knee and waist level. The arm is extended throughout the entire movement.

Equipment

Mirror, poster, jump rope, two chairs, and partner assessments.

Activity

To assist who are students having difficulty with the release point, suspend a jump rope between two chairs. The students practice releasing the ball under the rope. Once the students can demonstrate to their partners a correct arm swing, the partners may return to practicing the entire skill.

FOLLOW THROUGH

The throwing hand continues toward the target in front of the body and finishes with palm facing upward.

Equipment

Mirror, poster, basketball goal, rope with ball attached, and partner assessments.

Activity

Suspend a ball from a basketball goal at the level of the follow-through. The student practices her step and release (without using a ball or beanbag) and must touch the suspended ball on the follow-through. The partner checks to see if her position matches the poster. The student refers to the mirror for help. Once the student can demonstrate to the partner a correct follow-through, the partners may return to practicing the entire skill.

SUGGESTED CULMINATING ACTIVITIES TO REINFORCE THE ENTIRE SKILL

Students should master the skill's critical elements before you emphasize accuracy. According to *National Standards & Grade-Level Outcomes for K-12 Physical Education* (SHAPE America, 2014), third graders should be able to throw underhand to a partner or a target with reasonable accuracy (S1.E13.3). In fourth grade, students should be able to apply the skill (S1.E13.4). By fifth grade, students should be able to throw underhand using a mature pattern in nondynamic environments (closed skills) with different sizes and types of objects (S1.E13.5a) and throw underhand to a large target with accuracy (S1.E13.5b) (see table 4.2). When accuracy is emphasized, the students begin to aim and the elements of the skill are often compromised. Therefore, your targets must be large enough to allow the students to perform the critical elements of the skill and have success hitting the targets.

Table 4.2   Grade-Level Outcomes for Underhand Throwing Related to Accuracy (S1.E13)

	Kindergarten–grade 2	Grade 3	Grade 4	Grade 5
S1.E13 Underhand throwing	Accuracy not addressed before grade 3.	Throws underhand to a partner or target with reasonable accuracy. (S1.E13.3)	Applies skill. (S1.E13.4)	Throws underhand using a mature pattern in nondynamic environments (closed skills) with different sizes and types of objects. (S1.E13.5a) Throws underhand to a large target with accuracy. (S1.E13.5b)

Reprinted, by permission, from SHAPE America – Society of Health and Physical Educators, 2014, *National standards & grade-level outcomes for K-12 physical education* (Champaign, IL: Human Kinetics).

INDIVIDUAL ACTIVITIES

COLOR TARGETS

Objective

To improve underhand throwing accuracy.

Equipment

Construction paper of different colors (about 8 to 12 targets of each color and as large as possible) taped to the wall of the gymnasium or activity area and a beanbag or ball (yarn ball or tennis ball) for each student.

Activity

1. Create a color box in which samples from each color of construction paper have been placed. You will need more samples than you have students.
2. Select a student to draw a sample color from the color box.
3. The sample color chosen is the color target all students must locate and try to hit with an underhand throw.
4. Students continue to throw toward the targets of the selected color until you give a stop signal.
5. The activity continues until all students have been given an opportunity to draw from the color box.

Extensions

- Instead of using different colors, students could select different shapes from the shape box, letters from the alphabet box, or words from the word box.
- Students can work with partners. The partner chooses the color, shape, letter, or word that will be used for a target. The thrower must then try to hit the selected target. Partners take turns selecting targets and throwing.

CREATE A WORD

Objective

To create words by hitting letters using underhand throwing.

Equipment

One beanbag or ball (yarn ball or tennis ball) per student and four complete sets of alphabet letters (as large as possible) scattered and taped to the wall of the gymnasium or activity area. It would be advantageous to have extra copies of vowels and selected consonants (e.g., N, S, T, R). You will also need paper and markers or a dry-erase board and markers to serve as a word bank.

Activity

1. On your start signal, students begin to spell words by hitting letters of the alphabet using underhand throwing.

2. Once a student has created a word, he goes to the word bank (paper or dry-erase board) and writes the word. It will be helpful to have several word banks so students will not have to wait in line to write their words.

3. A word may be written only once on the paper or dry-erase board.

4. If a student hits a letter that cannot be used to form the word being created, she must hit the letter again to delete it.

Extensions

- Students can work with partners. One student collects letters to spell a word while the partner records the letters and evaluates underhand throwing. The thrower may not use the letter until underhand throwing is performed properly. When the first partner has spelled a word, the other partner is then given an opportunity to throw.

- Partners are given paper and pencil to record the letters they hit and to write down the words they create. Each partner must throw and hit a vowel and two consonants until the team has six letters to use to create words. The partners attempt to create six words using one or more of the letters they have hit. Once the partners have created six words and written them down, they attempt to spell the words by hitting the letters with the ball. Once a word is spelled, it may be checked off the list. If the students are unable to use a letter they have hit, they must hit that letter again to delete it and select another letter.

PARTNER ACTIVITIES

CHALLENGES

Objective

To practice underhand throwing in a variety of situations.

Equipment

One yarn ball, beanbag, or foam ball per pair of students and laminated challenge cards. Different types of challenges may require additional equipment.

Activity

1. Each student selects a challenge card.

2. Students perform the tasks described on the cards.

3. Possible challenges may include the following:
   - Throw the ball using light force.
   - Throw the ball, releasing at a middle or low level.
   - Throw the ball so that it hits the wall, it bounces once, and you are able to catch it.

Extensions

- You can place multicolored targets, pictures, or hoops on the wall. Other targets may be cones or buckets that are scattered in the play area. The partner can tell the thrower where to aim.
- Set up game poles or volleyball standards and tie a rope between them. Suspend different objects from the rope and challenge the students to hit them. Possible targets could include hoops, aluminum pie pans, and empty 2-liter plastic bottles.
- To create more permanent targets, you may paint them on the wall of your gymnasium (see figure). Often tumbling mats are attached to the wall for storage. If you paint these targets on the wall behind where tumbling mats are attached, you can cover them when they are not in use.
- The pairs keep track of their number of correct throws and you keep a total for the class. In a follow-up lesson, you can challenge the class to increase the total number of correct throws.

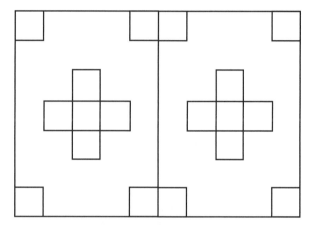

Setup for Challenges activity.

BAG IT

Objective

To underhand throw a ball to a partner who will catch it in a plastic grocery bag.

Equipment

One yarn ball or beanbag and a plastic grocery bag for each set of partners.

Activity

1. Students stand no closer than 10 feet (3 m) from a partner. Students take turns being the thrower and the catcher.
2. The thrower tosses the ball underhand to the catcher, who tries to catch the ball in the plastic grocery bag.
3. The catch counts if the thrower demonstrates all of the elements of underhand throwing and the ball is caught in the bag.
4. Each student has three turns as the thrower and then changes places with his partner to be the catcher.

Extensions

- The partners count the number of catches they are able to make in a set time period or the number they are able to catch consecutively.

- The partners take a step back after each round of successful throws. A round of throws consists of each partner having three throws and three catches.
- Toy stores sell Velcro catching surfaces with tennis balls that are designed to stick to this surface; you can use these items instead of plastic bags. Plastic scoops also make good substitutes for the plastic bags.

GROUP ACTIVITIES

STEW POT

Objective

To demonstrate the proper execution of underhand throwing while throwing a beanbag into a hula hoop.

Equipment

Beanbags and hula hoops.

Activity

1. Divide the class into groups of four.
2. Give each group four beanbags (one per person) and one hula hoop.
3. Directions for making the stew:
   - Have the students make a circle around the pot (a hula hoop placed on the floor); students should stand approximately 2 feet (0.6 m) from the pot.
   - All stew ingredients (beanbags) must get into the pot for the stew to be cooked.
   - Using correct form, everyone in the group must throw her stew ingredient into the pot. If all of the beanbags make it into the pot, the stew is cooked. If any beanbags miss the target, all of the beanbags are retrieved and the group tries again.
   - After each pot of stew is cooked, the students take one step backward from the pot. Students continue to step back after each pot of stew is cooked.

Extensions

- The entire class stands in a large circle. This is the giant stew pot. All of the stew meat and vegetables must get into the pot for the stew to be cooked. The students step back one step after each pot of stew is cooked.
- Since many beanbags come in colors, assign different colors to the different food groups (green for vegetables, red for meats, yellow for pasta, and so on). Then call out specific foods. The children have to decide to which food group their beanbag belongs and then throw it in the pot. For example, when you call out carrots (a vegetable), the children with green beanbags throw their carrots into the stew pot.

CYCLE/RECYCLE

Objective

To improve underhand throwing accuracy while throwing a yarn ball between two volleyball nets.

Equipment

Two volleyball standards, two volleyball nets, and one yarn ball per student. One net should be placed at regular volleyball height and the other at tennis height (on the same standard).

Activity

1. Divide the class in half.
2. Place groups on either side of the nets.
3. On the start signal, everyone throws the ball underhand between the nets.
4. Students count the number of balls they were able to throw between nets.

Extensions

- Have the students total the number of accurate throws made by the entire group. These results can be recorded and later charted or graphed to show class improvement.
- Students who throw the ball between the nets go around the standards and become members of the opposite group.

Reprinted from J.A. Wessel, PhD, 1974, *Project I CAN* (Northbrook, IL: Hubbard).

OMNIKIN BALL MADNESS

Objective

To perform underhand throwing using a playground ball to move an object across the play area.

Equipment

The object to be moved may be an Omnikin ball or any ball larger than the balls being thrown. The balls being thrown may be playground balls or volleyballs when aiming at the Omnikin ball. When the target ball is smaller, tennis balls may be used.

Activity

1. Divide the class into four groups. Each group stands along one side of a square play area. Students must stay behind their lines.
2. Place the Omnikin ball or a large ball in the center of the play area.
3. Each group begins the activity with two or more balls.
4. On the start signal, players throw their balls and try to hit the large ball in the center in an effort to move it toward the other group's line.
5. Players continue to throw their balls until the large ball crosses a group's line. Any ball that stays inside of the area enclosed by the four groups is retrieved by the teacher.
6. Players may touch the large ball only with a thrown ball; they may not touch it with their bodies.
7. Once the large ball crosses the designated line, the activity stops and the large ball is returned to the center of the play area.
8. Resume the activity when each group has the same number of balls to throw. Be sure every player is given a chance to start with a ball.

Extensions

- Create two groups rather than four.
- Try to throw a variety of balls at the large ball in an effort to move the ball across another group's line. This may lead to discussions on which balls are better for the task.
- Have groups change positions either before the next round or on a signal during the activity. If the students are to change places during the activity, be sure they understand that they may not throw a ball at the large ball until your signal and that they may not take a ball with them as they change.

KERPLUNK

Objective

To use underhand throwing to get a ball into the target area behind the opposing group.

Equipment

Two or more Super-Safe balls or balls that are made of soft rubber (8 inches [20 cm] in diameter). The number of balls used will vary based on the skill level and number of students. You will also need tape or cones to mark off a large target area 15 to 20 feet (4.5-6 m) from the center of the playing area. Use a dry-erase board or paper to record the points.

Activity

1. Divide the class into two groups, and place groups on opposite sides of the playing area.
2. Provide each group with an equal number of balls to begin the activity.
3. On the start signal, players use underhand throwing to get the ball into the opposing group's target area.
4. If a player kerplunks the ball into the opposing group's target area, one point is awarded to his group.
5. Players are allowed to catch the ball to prevent it from hitting the target area.
6. Restart the game after one group earns 10 points.

Extensions

- While the students are playing, ensure that underhand throwing is being performed correctly. Instruct any student who is having trouble throwing correctly to go to the practice area and work with a partner or a designated teacher assistant.
- Designate a special ball. If the special ball is kerplunked into the target area, two points are awarded.

CREATE YOUR OWN ACTIVITY

Objective

To allow students to create their own activities to reinforce underhand throwing skills.

Equipment

One piece of paper and pencil per group and a predetermined list of equipment you will allow the students to use in their activities (e.g., bowling pins, cones, ropes, tennis balls, foam balls).

Activity

1. Form groups of two to five students. You may select the groups, or the students may form their own.
2. Each group creates an activity using underhand throwing as the basic skill. Students are required to have rules that encourage correct performance of the skill, include all players, and address all safety concerns.
3. The groups write their individual names, the rules of the activity, and the equipment needed on their papers, and then they show their activities to you.
4. After you approve their activities, the groups retrieve the necessary equipment and begin playing.
5. You must approve all changes to the activities.

Extensions

- Groups may teach their activities to other groups.
- Groups may teach their activities to the entire class.

PIN BALL

Objective

To use underhand throwing to hit the opponents' bowling pins.

Equipment

Balls and three plastic bowling pins (indicated by A and B in the figure) for each group. Bowling pins need to be color coded for each team (e.g., use different-colored tape to mark the pins).

Activity

1. Set up a play area with a center line and two restraining lines that are approximately 12 feet (3.7 m) away from the center line.
2. Divide the class into two equal groups and place the groups behind the restraining lines, facing each other.
3. Set up the six pins along the center dividing line of the play area, alternating colors (see figure).
4. On the start signal, the students throw the balls and try to hit the opposing group's pins. The students may not cross the restraining line.
5. A pin does not stay down if the ball was thrown from in front of the restraining line. If a student knocks down her own pin by mistake, it must stay down.
6. Restart the activity when all of a group's pins have been knocked down.

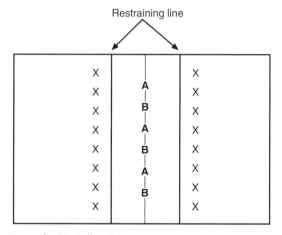

Setup for Pin Ball activity.

Adapted, by permission, from K. Thomas, A. Lee, and J. Thomas, 2000, *Physical education for children: Daily lesson plans for elementary school,* 2nd ed. (Champaign, IL: Human Kinetics), 546.

Underhand Throwing Troubleshooting Chart

If you see this	Then try this
1. Eyes not on target	• Have the student throw at a target he has designed. • Attach a color target to the wall. • Use pie plates for targets and place them on the wall at a medium level. • As an outside activity, have the student throw wet sponges at a target in an effort to soak the target with water.
2. Arm not swinging back	• Have the student swing her arm back to touch a target (pie plate) attached to the wall. The target is placed at the student's waist level in line with the throwing arm. The student then throws the ball. • With a partner standing behind the thrower, the thrower swings his arm back and tries to take an object out of the partner's hand. • Put paper on the wall. Have the student stand sideways with a marker in the throwing hand. As the student moves the throwing hand back, she draws a curvy line on the paper.
3. Student not stepping	• Tie a pinny or scarf around the leg opposite the throwing hand. • Use spots or footprints on the floor to indicate the correct foot placement. • Tape bubble wrap to the floor. Have the student step in opposition on that spot to create noise.
4. Student releases ball too early or too late	• Suspend two ropes between game standards. The student must release the ball between the ropes. As he improves, remove one rope. • Use a partner's hand to indicate where the ball should be released.
5. Student not stepping toward target	• Use a line on the floor or put down tape. Challenge the student to step on the line when the ball is released. • Tape bubble wrap to the floor. Have the student step on the wrap to create noise. • Place two objects shoe-width apart in front of the student. These objects may be cones, domes, or foam bricks. He must step so that his foot is placed between the two objects.
6. Body not in proper alignment on the follow-through	• Tell the student to point her belt buckle at the target on the follow-through. • Use a line on the floor or put down tape. Challenge the student to release the ball on the line and bring the throwing arm over the line as the ball is thrown.
7. Follow-through ends too high	• Suspend two ropes between game standards. The student should touch the top rope on the follow-through. • Use a partner's hand to indicate where the follow-through should end.

SUMMARY

Children begin throwing at an early age. A child may attempt to toss something into the trash can, pitch horseshoes with a grandparent, or throw a ball to a playmate. Regardless of the purpose of the child's first attempts at underhand throwing, this skill will become an integral part of many sports. Therefore, instruction must focus on all of the correct mechanics, especially stepping in opposition and proper release of the object.

By mastering the critical elements of underhand throwing, a foundation is established for the successful performance of lifetime sport skills such as badminton, volleyball, and softball. To ensure success, children need a variety of opportunities for proper practice and instruction, which can greatly enhance their mastery of this crucial building block.

UNDERHAND THROWING LESSON PLAN

(SECOND OR THIRD LESSON)

AGE GROUP: Third grade.

FOCUS: Release point for underhand throwing.

SUBFOCUS: Accuracy.

OBJECTIVES: To release the ball below the waist 80 percent of the time (**cue:** *let it go below your waist*) and to step in opposition, as measured by teacher observation (**cue:** *use your stepping foot*).

MATERIALS AND EQUIPMENT: Targets taped to the walls every 4 feet (1.2 m) and beanbags or yarn balls.

ADVANCE PREPARATION: A learning station for each child is helpful. Each learning station is composed of three targets placed at 4-foot (1.2 m) intervals on the wall (see figure). These targets can be created by making shapes (squares, circles, triangles) with painter's tape (see figure). Targets may also be hula hoops (use duct tape to attach these to the walls), laminated copies of drawings, or construction paper. For the purposes of this lesson, the target is made with five adjacent squares. Ideally, you will have one set of targets for each student. The targets should be at least 2 feet (0.6 m) above floor level. Place a beanbag or a yarn ball at each station and mark three lines for the students to stand behind when practicing. The closest line should be 5 feet (1.5 m) from the wall, the second should be 6 feet (1.8 m) from the wall, and the third should be 7 feet (2 m) from the wall.

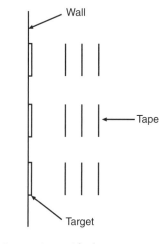

Learning station with three targets.

ORGANIZATION AND MANAGEMENT: Students are in their self-space for instruction and warm-up. Later, students will find their own teaching stations in the gymnasium for practice.

WARM-UP: Music is playing as students enter the gymnasium. They move in general space to teacher-directed locomotor movements (e.g., sliding, galloping, jogging, walking, skipping, hopping, jumping). Later, you may suggest ways to perform the locomotor movements. The students can be challenged to move with varying speeds, levels, and amounts of force or to use a specific pathway. For example, they may begin jogging with light force in a curvy pathway at a high level.

FORMATION: Students find their self-space and sit on the floor facing you.

INTRODUCTION:

Today we are going to work on our underhand throwing again. We need to really think about accuracy today. But let's review first. Who can tell me the parts of under-hand throwing? **(Ready, arm back, step, release, follow through.)**

Who can show me how we step? That's right, we step with the foot on the **other** *side of our body from the hand we throw with.*

Everyone stand up in your self-space. Let's pretend that we have a beanbag in our throwing hand. Let's go through the steps of underhand throwing together: Ready, arm back, step, release, follow through.

Watch for stepping in opposition.

Excellent. Let's talk about accuracy. When we throw a ball, we want it to go to a target. That target might be a person or a place. One thing that really affects whether the ball gets to our target is where we let go of it or release it. Watch as I throw my imaginary beanbag. Where do you think the beanbag will go, high or low? (Release the imaginary beanbag at a high level.)

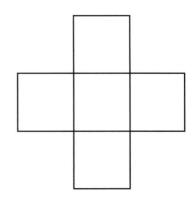

The five squares at each station.

Now where do you think the beanbag will go? (Release the imaginary beanbag at your middle level.) *So if we want the beanbag to go high, we release it high. If we want it to go to a middle level, we release it at that level. Look at the stations that are set up for you. There are five squares at each station* (see figure).

Watch as I demonstrate what you will be asked to do. I would like you to stand on the line closest to the target. Say the cues ready, arm back, step, release, and follow through out loud as you release the beanbag. Your first job will be to use the correct form and perform all of the cues. Later, I will ask you to aim at different targets. When I say go, find a practice space. Go.

Watch for correct form as the students practice the skill and say the cues out loud. After students can perform the skill, provide them with challenges such as the following:

1. Stand on the closest line and do these challenges:
   - Hit the middle target five times in a row.
   - Hit the top target.
   - Hit the target on the left.
   - Hit the target on the right.
   - Hit the lower target.
   - Call out which targets the students should hit before they release the beanbags.
2. Stand on the next line back and repeat the sequence.
3. Stand on the line the greatest distance from the target and repeat the sequence.

Watch for release point and stepping in opposition. Remind the students frequently to release *the beanbag between your knee and waist* and *use your stepping foot.*

Freeze. Everyone please sit down where you are and listen to my directions. When I say go, you will find a partner and sit together at one station. Go. Each of you will underhand throw the beanbag five times in a row. Your target will be the one your partner selects. You may select the distance, but your partner will tell you which one to hit. Remember how many times you are successful. After 5 minutes I'm going to ask you how well you and your partner did.

*Oh, one more condition. The skill must be performed correctly. Remember our cues—ready, arm back, step, release, and follow through. The throw will count only if you say the cues out loud, step with the correct foot, let go of the beanbag below your waist, **and** hit the target. Do you understand these directions? Go.*

Circulate and look for stepping in opposition and proper release point.

CLOSURE:

As students are lined up to leave, play teach the teacher:

1. *Who can tell me how to throw a beanbag underhand correctly?* **(Ready, arm back, step with the opposite foot, release, follow through.)**

Perform an underhand throw. The students tell you how to correct it. Attempt the skill again and step with the wrong foot. Students correct this. Finally, perform the skill correctly. Repeat the cues often.

2. *How can I change where the beanbag goes?* **(Where the ball is released will affect where it goes.)**

3. *Tomorrow we will work on accuracy again. Please walk and get in line.*

OVERHAND THROWING

Perhaps no other manipulative skill is as essential to mastering sports as overhand throwing. Not only is the overhand motion needed in nearly every team sport from the baseball pitch to the overhand volleyball serve, but its mastery is also essential in developing proficiency in badminton and tennis. Overhand throwing usually is mastered later than underhand throwing and is not developmentally appropriate until grade 2. According to *National Standards & Grade-Level Outcomes for K-12 Physical Education* (SHAPE America, 2014), in second grade, students should demonstrate two of the five critical elements of a mature pattern (S1.E14.2). In third grade, students should throw overhand demonstrating three of the five critical elements of a mature pattern in nondynamic environments for distance or force (S1.E14.3). Fourth grade students should be able to demonstrate a mature throwing pattern in a nondynamic environment (S1.E14.4a) and can throw overhand to a partner or a target with accuracy from a reasonable distance (S1.E14.4b). In fifth grade, students should continue to demonstrate a mature throwing pattern, but they now should be able to use balls of different sizes (S1.E14.5a). Accuracy is emphasized (S1.E14/5b). See table 4.3.

Table 4.3 Grade-Level Outcomes for Overhand Throwing (S1.E14)

	Kindergarten	Grade 1	Grade 2	Grade 3	Grade 4	Grade 5
S1.E14 Overhand throwing	Developmentally appropriate and emerging outcomes first appear in grade 2.		Throws overhand demonstrating 2 of the 5 critical elements of a mature pattern. (S1.E14.2)	Throws overhand demonstrating 3 of the 5 critical elements of a mature pattern in nondynamic environments (closed skills) for distance and/or force. (S1.E14.3)	Throws overhand using a mature pattern in nondynamic environments (closed skills). (S1.E14.4a) Throws overhand to a partner or at a target with accuracy at a reasonable distance. (S1.E14.4b)	Throws overhand using a mature pattern in nondynamic environments (closed skills) with different sizes and types of balls. (S1.E14.5a) Throws overhand to a large target with accuracy. (S1.E14.5b)

The outcomes are composed of five critical elements for overhand throwing, beginning with side to the target. We have elected to include a ready position that prepares students to turn their sides to the targets.

Critical Elements

Ready position	Side to target	Arm back	Step	Rotate	Follow through
Facing target, feet shoulder-width apart, knees bent, eyes on target, object held in front of the body in preferred hand.	Body turns as the feet pivot in place and the side opposite the throwing arm is toward the target.	Bring the throwing arm back in a downward circular motion with the throwing hand extended away from the intended line of travel. The elbow is at shoulder height or slightly above, in preparation for action with the elbow leading. The nonthrowing hand points toward the target.	Step with the foot that is opposite the throwing arm.	Hips and shoulders rotate toward the target, the front body surface faces the target, and the arm comes forward past the head.	Throwing hand continues toward the target and continues down diagonally across the body.

Cue Words

The cue words you select for each phase of the skill will depend on the age of the students you are teaching and your areas of emphasis. In usable sets are some of the cue words we use to teach overhand throwing. You may use each set individually or mix and match the cue words as needed. We have found that it is beneficial to have the students say the cue words out loud as they practice.

Ready—facing target, feet shoulder-width apart, knees bent, eyes on target, object held in front of the body.

Side to target (turn)—body turns as the feet pivot in place and the side opposite the throwing arm is toward the target.

Arm back—bring the throwing arm back in a downward circular motion with the throwing hand extended away from the intended line of travel.

Reach back—start with side to the target and reach back with the throwing arm.

Point and look—point and look toward the target.

Step—step with the foot that is opposite the throwing arm.

Step, throw, point or step and throw—step with the foot opposite the throwing arm, hip and shoulder rotate toward the target, arm comes through past the head.

Throw—step and release the ball.

Throw hard—hip and shoulder rotate toward the target as the student throws with strong force.

Squash the bug—the nonstepping foot needs to remain stationary. Students pretend that there is a wasp (or other undesirable insect) under the foot. When they release the ball, they leave that foot still, and their pivot will squash the bug.

Follow through or hug thyself (put your seatbelt on)—the throwing arm continues toward the target and comes down diagonally across the body, almost as if the student is hugging herself (or putting on her seatbelt).

Cue set 1: ready; turn; step, throw, point; follow through
Cue set 2: turn, point and look, step and throw, squash the bug
Cue set 3: turn, step and throw, hug thyself
Cue set 4: reach back, throw
Cue set 5: reach back, step, throw hard

SUGGESTED ACTIVITIES FOR REINFORCING AND ASSESSING THE CRITICAL ELEMENTS

In the learning process, it is essential that students know how a skill looks, what its critical elements are, and how to perform each element correctly. In the preceding section, we provided pictures and descriptions of overhand throwing, divided it into its critical elements, and provided possible cue words. In addition to the material in chapter 1 that reinforces the concepts for all locomotor and manipulative skills, the following section provides specific activities for reinforcing the critical elements unique to overhand throwing.

PARTNER SKILL CHECK

Objective
To allow partners to assess their own skill progress with overhand throwing and to learn to evaluate the skills of others.

Equipment
Partner skill check assessments and one ball for each set of partners. If the students cannot read or do not speak English, the picture version of the partner skill check assessment may be useful.

Activity
1. One partner observes the other to see if he has the correct form for the ready position.
2. If the ready position is correct, then the partner places a *Y* in the first box. If the ready position is incorrect, he places an *N* in the first box. Nonreaders can put a smiling face if the ready position is correct or a frowning face if the ready position is incorrect.
3. This evaluation continues until each of the critical elements has been assessed five times.
4. A partner skill check assessment is used for each student.

Extensions
- You can use the partner skill check assessment to measure the skill development of each student.
- You can send partner skill check assessments home with report cards or as individual skills develop.

SUCCESS BUILDERS

The success builder activities allow you to address individual needs. If students need additional help on a specific critical element, the activities listed here will help reinforce correct performance.

Objective

To allow partners to improve areas of deficiency as measured by the partner skill check assessment.

Equipment

See the following individual stations. We suggest using an unbreakable mirror and a poster of each critical element of overhand throwing at each station. The mirror is particularly helpful in these activities because it allows children to see what they are doing. The easiest way to make the posters is to print out the drawings from this book and enlarge them. Laminating the posters will ensure their use for many years.

Activity

1. Set up a station for each critical element in the teaching area. Post a description or a picture of the specific element at the corresponding station.

2. Following are the details for each station:

READY

Facing target, feet shoulder-width apart, knees bent, eyes on target, object held in front of the body.

Equipment

Poster of the ready position, mirror (if available), and partner assessments

Activity

The student assumes the ready position. The partner checks to see if her position matches the poster. The student refers to the mirror for help. The student then walks around and, on a signal from her partner, assumes the ready position again. When she has had several successful trials, the partners may return to working on the entire skill.

TURN WITH ARM BACK

Body turns as the feet pivot in place and the side opposite the throwing arm is toward the target. Arms are extended with the object held in the throwing hand. The throwing hand is extended away from the intended line of travel with the palm facing upward. The nonthrowing hand points in the direction of travel.

Equipment

Poster of the critical element, mirror (if available), and partner assessments

Activity

The student demonstrates the turn position with the throwing arm back. The partner checks to see if his position matches the poster. The student refers to the mirror for help. The student then assumes the ready position facing a set target. On a signal from his partner, the student demonstrates the turn and arm back position. When he has had several successful trials, the partners may return to working on the entire skill.

STEP, ROTATE, THROW

Step with the foot opposite as the throwing arm moves forward; hip and shoulder rotate as throwing action is executed. The front body surface should be facing the target on release.

STEP

Equipment

Poster showing the step, mirror (if available), footprints or tape (floor or painter's), and partner assessments

Activity

Power stride—Footprints (or tape) are placed on the floor. With the partner's help, the student starts from the ready position, turns with the throwing arm back, and steps with the appropriate foot. The partner checks to see if her position matches the poster. The student refers to the mirror for help. When she has had several successful trials, the partners may return to working on the entire skill.

ROTATE AND THROW

Equipment

Poster of the rotate and throw, mirror (if available), partner assessments, 15- to 20-foot (4.6-6 m) length of cotton or nylon rope, two game standards, 1-inch (2.5 cm) diameter PVC pipe cut to length of four inches. If equipment availability is limited, see extension 1.

Activity

Rocket launcher—Place the game standards 10 to 12 feet 3-3.5 m) apart. Thread the rope through the PVC pipe and then tie the rope between the game standards so it is approximately at students' eye level. Students work in pairs or groups of four, with partners standing at opposite game standards. Students are told to stay clear of the rope while their partners are throwing. One partner starts in the **turn** position with the rocket (PVC pipe) in her throwing hand. The thrower uses step, rotate, throw to propel the rocket down the rope to the opposite standard. The partner at the opposite game standard retrieves the rocket and performs the step, rotate, throw, sending the rocket back toward the partner.

Extensions

- If you have limited space or no game standards, stretch the rope between two chairs. Have the student sit with his nonthrowing side toward his partner and throw the rocket. The student should finish the throw with both hands touching the floor in the direction of the throw.
- Tie a towel, rag, or other object around the rope at the ends, near the game standards, to prevent the rocket from hitting the game standards.

RELEASE POINT

Equipment

Poster of the release point, mirror (if available), jump ropes, two volleyball poles, and partner assessments

Activity

Let 'er rip—Stretch the jump ropes between two volleyball poles, leaving approximately 12 inches (30 cm) between the ropes. The top rope should be at about shoulder height to the thrower. Have the students practice releasing the ball between the ropes. The partner checks to see if the thrower's position matches the poster. The thrower refers to the mirror for help.

FOLLOW THROUGH

Throwing hand continues toward the target and continues down diagonally across the body.

Equipment

Poster of the follow-through, mirror (if available), and partner assessments

Activity

Have the student get into the step and throw position facing a set target. The student practices his step and release (without a ball or beanbag). The partner checks to see if his position matches the poster. The student refers to the mirror for help. When he has had several successful trials, the partners may return to working on the entire skill.

SUGGESTED CULMINATING ACTIVITIES TO REINFORCE THE ENTIRE SKILL

Mastery of critical elements should be accomplished before emphasizing accuracy. According to *National Standards & Grade-Level Outcomes for K-12 Physical Education* (SHAPE America, 2014), children should be able to throw to a partner or at a target with accuracy at a reasonable distance by the fourth grade (S1.E14.4b). By the fifth grade, students should be able to throw overhand to a large target with accuracy (S1. E14.5b). See table 4.4. When accuracy becomes the emphasis before children master the critical elements, children aim at targets and the critical elements of the skill are compromised. Targets should be large enough to allow students to perform the critical elements of the skill and have success hitting the target.

Table 4.4 Grade-Level Outcomes for Overhand Throwing Related to Accuracy (S1.E14)

	Kindergarten–grade 3	Grade 4	Grade 5
S1.E14 Overhand throwing	Accuracy is not addressed until grade 4.	Throws overhand using a mature pattern in nondynamic environments (closed skills). (S1.E14.4a) Throws overhand to a partner or at a target with accuracy at a reasonable distance. (S1. E14.4b)	Throws overhand using a mature pattern in nondynamic environments (closed skills) with different sizes and types of balls. (S1.E14.5a) Throws overhand to a large target with accuracy. (S1.E14.5b)

Reprinted, by permission, from SHAPE America – Society of Health and Physical Educators, 2014, National standards & grade-level outcomes for K-12 physical education (Champaign, IL: Human Kinetics).

INDIVIDUAL ACTIVITIES

COLOR TARGETS

Objective

To improve overhand throwing accuracy by hitting a specified target.

Equipment

Construction paper of different colors (about 8 to 12 targets of each color and as large as possible) taped to the wall of the gymnasium or activity area and a beanbag or ball (yarn ball or tennis ball) for each student.

Activity

1. Create a color box in which samples from each color of construction paper have been placed. You will need more samples than you have students.
2. Select a student to draw a sample color from the color box.
3. The sample color chosen is the color target all students must locate and try to hit with an overhand throw.
4. Students continue throwing toward the targets of the selected color until a stop signal is given.
5. The activity continues until all students have had an opportunity to draw from the color box.

Extensions

- Instead of using different colors, students could select different shapes from the shape box, letters from the alphabet box, or words from the word box.
- Students work with partners. The partner chooses the color, shape, letter, or word that will be used for a target. The thrower must then try to hit the selected target. Partners take turns selecting targets and throwing.

CREATE A WORD

Objective

To create words by using overhand throwing to hit letters.

Equipment

One beanbag or ball (tennis ball or yarn ball) per student and four complete sets of alphabet letters (as large as possible) scattered and taped to the walls of the gym or activity space. It would be advantageous to have extra copies of vowels and selected consonants (e.g., N, R, S, T). You will also need paper and pencils or a dry-erase board and markers to serve as a word bank.

Activity

1. On your start signal, students begin to spell words by hitting letters of the alphabet using an overhand throw.
2. Once a student has created a word, she goes to the word bank (paper or dry-erase board) and writes the word. It will be helpful to have several word banks so students will not have to wait to record their words.
3. A word may be written only once on the paper or dry-erase board.
4. If a student hits a letter that cannot be used to form the word being created, he must hit the letter again to delete it.

Extensions

- Working in pairs, one student hits letters to spell a word while the other records the letters and evaluates the throw. The thrower may not use the letter until overhand throwing is performed properly. When the first partner has spelled a word, the other partner is given an opportunity to throw.
- Partners are given paper and pencil to record the letters they hit and to write down the words they create. Each partner must throw and hit a vowel and two consonants. The pair now has six letters to use to create words. The partners attempt to create six words using one or more of the letters they have hit. Once the partners have created six words and written them down, they will attempt to spell the words by hitting the letters with the ball. Once a word is spelled, it may be checked off the list. If the students are unable to use a letter they have hit, they must hit that letter again to delete it and select another letter.

PARTNER ACTIVITIES

CHALLENGES

Objective

To practice overhand throwing in a variety of situations.

Equipment

One yarn ball, beanbag, or foam ball per pair of students and laminated challenge cards. Different types of challenges may require additional equipment.

Activity

1. Each student selects a challenge card.
2. Students perform the tasks described on the cards.
3. Possible challenges may include the following:
   - Throw the ball using light or strong force.
   - Throw the ball, releasing it at a middle level (high level).
   - Throw the ball so that it hits the wall, it bounces once, and you are able to catch it.

Extensions

- Place multicolored targets, hoops, cones, or buckets on a wall or in the play area and have the partner tell the thrower where to aim.
- Set up game poles or volleyball standards and tie a rope between them. Suspend different objects from the rope and challenge the students to hit them. Possible targets include hoops, aluminum pie pans, and empty 2-liter plastic bottles.
- To create more permanent targets, you may paint them on the wall of your gymnasium. If you paint these targets on the wall behind where tumbling mats are attached for storage, you can cover them when not in use.
- Partners keep track of their number of correct throws and you keep a total for the class. In a follow-up lesson, you can challenge the class to increase the total number of correct throws.

WALL BALL

Objective

To improve overhand throwing and catching while working with a partner.

Equipment

One ball (playground ball or volleyball) per student pair.

Activity

1. Partners stand at least 15 feet (4.5 m) from the wall.
2. One partner throws the ball overhand against the wall. The throw must be at least 10 feet (3 m) high.
3. The other partner has to catch the ball after it comes off the wall but before it hits the ground.
4. When the partner has caught the ball, he overhand throws the ball back to the wall from the place it was caught.
5. Partners count how many successful catches they have in a row.

Extensions

- Allow the ball to bounce once before it is caught.
- Place a target on the wall and challenge the partners to hit it.

GROUP ACTIVITIES

OMNIKIN BALL MADNESS

Objective

To perform overhand throwing using a ball to move an object across the play area.

Equipment

The object may be an Omnikin ball or any ball larger than the balls being thrown. The balls being thrown may be playground balls or volleyballs when aiming at the Omnikin ball. When the target is smaller, tennis balls may be used.

Activity

1. Divide the class into four groups. Each group stands along one side of a square play area. Students must stay behind their lines.
2. Place the Omnikin ball or a large ball in the center of the play area.
3. Each group begins the activity with two or more balls.
4. On the start signal, players throw their balls and try to hit the large ball in the center in an effort to move it toward the other group's line.
5. Players continue to throw their balls until the large ball crosses a group's line. Any ball that stays inside of the area enclosed by the four groups is retrieved by the teacher.
6. Players may touch the large ball only with a thrown ball; they may not touch it with their bodies.
7. Once the large ball crosses the designated line, the activity stops and the large ball is returned to the center of the play area.
8. Resume the activity when each group has the same number of balls to throw. Be sure every player is given a chance to start with a ball.

Extensions

- Create two groups rather than four.
- Try to throw a variety of balls at the large ball in an effort to move the ball across another group's line. This may lead to discussions on which balls are better for the task (e.g., playground balls versus tennis balls).
- Have groups change positions either before the next round or on a signal during the activity. If the students are to change places during the activity, be sure they understand that they may not throw a ball at the large ball until your start signal and that they may not take a ball with them as they change sides.

KERPLUNK

Objective

To use overhand throwing to get a ball into the target area behind the opposing group.

Equipment

Two or more Super-Safe balls or balls that are made of soft rubber (8 inches [20 cm] in diameter). The number of balls used will vary based on the skill level and number of students. You will also need tape or cones to mark off a large target area 15 to 20 feet (4.5-6 m) from the center of the playing area. Use a dry-erase board to record the points.

Activity

1. Divide the class into two groups and place groups on opposite sides of the playing area.

2. Provide each group with an equal number of balls to begin the activity.

3. On the start signal, players use overhand throwing to get the ball into the opposing group's target area.

4. If a player kerplunks the ball into the opposing group's target area, one point is awarded to her group.

5. Players are allowed to catch the ball to prevent it from hitting the target area.

6. Restart the game after one group reaches 10 points.

Extensions

- While the students are playing, ensure that overhand throwing is being performed correctly. Instruct any student who is having trouble throwing correctly to go to the practice area and work with a partner or a designated teacher assistant.

- Designate a special ball. If the special ball is kerplunked into the target area, two points are awarded.

CREATE YOUR OWN ACTIVITY

Objective

To allow students to create their own activities to reinforce overhand throwing skills.

Equipment

One piece of paper and pencil per group and a predetermined list of equipment you will allow the students to use in their activities (e.g., bowling pins, cones, jump rope, softballs, tennis balls).

Activity

1. Form groups of two to five students. You may select the groups, or the students may form their own.

2. Each group creates an activity using overhand throwing as the basic skill. Students are required to have rules that encourage correct performance of the skill, include all players, and address all safety concerns.

3. The groups write their individual names, the rules of the activity, and the equipment needed on their papers, and then they show their activities to you.

4. After you approve their activities, the groups retrieve the necessary equipment and begin playing.

5. You must approve all changes to the activities.

Extensions

- Groups may teach their activities to other groups.
- Groups may teach their activities to the entire class.

PIN BALL

Objective

To use overhand throwing to hit the opposing group's bowling pins.

Equipment

Balls and three plastic bowling pins (indicated by A and B in the figure) for each group. Bowling pins need to be color coded for each group (e.g., use different-colored tape to mark the pins).

Activity

1. Set up a play area with a center line and two restraining lines that are approximately 12 feet (3.7 m) from the center line.

2. Divide the class into two equal groups and place the groups behind the restraining lines, facing each other.

3. Set up the six pins up along the center line of the play area, alternating colors (see figure).

4. On the start signal, the students throw the balls and try to hit the opposing group's pins. The students may not cross the restraining line.

5. A pin does not stay down if the ball was thrown from in front of the restraining line. If a student knocks down his own pin by mistake, it must stay down.

6. Restart the activity when all of a group's pins have been knocked down.

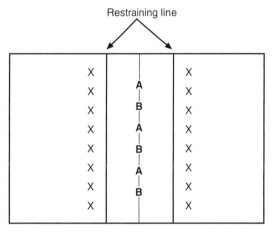

Setup for Pin Ball activity.

Extensions

- Use empty 2-liter bottles, lightweight cones, empty cereal boxes, or other objects as the targets.
- Suspend a rope between two volleyball standards. Hang lightweight targets (e.g., paper, scarves, streamers, crepe paper) from the rope and challenge the students to hit the opposing team's targets.

Adapted, by permission, from K. Thomas, A. Lee, and J. Thomas, 2000, *Physical education for children: Daily lesson plans for elementary school,* 2nd ed. (Champaign, IL: Human Kinetics), 546.

CYCLE/RECYCLE

Objective

To improve overhand throwing accuracy while throwing a yarn ball over a volleyball net.

Equipment

Two game standards, one volleyball net, and one yarn ball per student. The net is placed at regular volleyball height.

Activity

1. Divide the class in half.
2. Place the two groups on either side of the net.
3. On the start signal, everyone throws the ball overhand over the net.
4. Have the students count the number of successful throws they were able to make over the net.

Extensions

- Have the students total the number of accurate throws made by the entire group. These results can be recorded and later charted or graphed to show class improvement.
- Each time a student throws the ball over the net, she goes around the standards and becomes a member of the other group.

Adapted, by permission, from J.A. Wessel, PhD, 1974, *Project I CAN* (Northbrook, IL: Hubbard).

SUMMARY

Although children begin throwing at an early age, a mature throwing pattern will not emerge without proper instruction. Overhand throwing is probably the manipulative skill that is most crucial to later sport skill development. The baseball or softball player who steps with the wrong foot and has trouble throwing the ball in from the outfield probably began as the kindergartner who practiced stepping with the wrong foot or the second grader who never learned to extend the arm back when throwing. The habits that are practiced in the younger grades become permanent motor patterns as students get older.

Since many aspects of overhand throwing transfer to important sport skills (such as the tennis and volleyball serves), this emerging skill should be introduced in the early grades. Proper instruction that begins at this time will provide success and, hopefully, continued participation throughout the student's lifetime. To provide the maximum amount of practice for older children, have them practice throwing to a wall. Throwing to a partner should begin as soon as the students have learned to catch. The next chapter details methods for teaching proper catching skills.

Overhand Throwing Troubleshooting Chart

If you see this	Then try this
1. Eyes not on target	• Have the student throw at a target he has designed. • Attach color targets to the wall. • Place a 2-liter bottle upside down on top of a tall cone and have the student try to knock it off. • As an outside activity, have the student throw wet sponges at a target in an effort to soak the target with water. • Use aluminum plates for targets.
2. Not enough arm extension	• Encourage the student to use stronger force when throwing the object. (Students should be warmed up for all activities, especially this challenge.) • Have the student touch a wall located behind her while extending her arm, and then have her throw the object. • With a partner standing behind him, the thrower swings his arm back and tries to take an object out of his partner's hand.
3. Hand of the throwing arm not going past the ear	• Have the student use the Rocket Launcher activity in the step. rotate, throw station. • Hang a yarn ball from a basketball goal so the ball is at ear height. Put the student in the turn position (side to target) and have her hit the ball with an open palm.
4. Student not stepping in opposition	• Tie a pinny or scarf around the foot opposite the throwing arm. • Use floor spots or footprints on the floor to indicate the proper foot placement. • Tape bubble wrap to the floor. Have the student step in opposition on that spot to create a noise.
5. Limited hip and shoulder rotation	• Have the student check the position of his belt buckle after throwing. The belt buckle should be pointing in the direction of the target. • Have a partner stand behind the thrower. The partner holds rubber tubing or stretch bands to add resistance while the thrower goes through the rotation motion.
6. Student not continuing the follow-through	• Place a tall cone in front of and to the nonthrowing side of the thrower's body. The cone should be far enough away that the student can step and extend the arm on the throw. The student throws the ball and then touches the top of the cone on the follow-through. • Have the student pretend to fasten a seatbelt by crossing the arm across the body while bending forward.

OVERHAND THROWING LESSON PLAN

(SECOND LESSON)

AGE GROUP: Fourth or fifth grade.

FOCUS: Overhand throwing.

SUBFOCUS: Arm extension and force production.

OBJECTIVES: To extend the arm to promote force 80 percent of the time (**cue:** *reach back, throw hard*) and to step in opposition 80 percent of the time, as measured by teacher and peer observation (**cue:** *use your stepping foot*).

MATERIALS AND EQUIPMENT: One yarn ball for each child and music.

ADVANCE PREPARATION: Each child should have her own learning station for this lesson. The learning stations should be spaced around the gymnasium and have three targets taped to the wall. The targets should be at least 2 feet (0.6 m) above the floor, but they may vary in height. Be sure that targets are at the appropriate height for overhand throwing and not underhand throwing or underhand rolling. Targets may be hula hoops (use duct tape to attach these to the wall), laminated copies of drawings, or laminated pieces of construction paper, or you might decide to use tape to make targets (e.g., triangles, squares, rectangles). Place a yarn ball at each station and mark lines for the students to stand behind when practicing. The first line should be at least 5 feet (1.5 m) from the wall, and the remaining lines should be placed at appropriate increments thereafter (see figure).

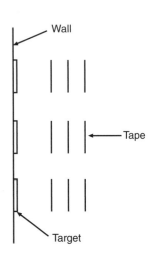

Learning station setup.

ORGANIZATION AND MANAGEMENT: Students are in their self-space for instruction and warm-up. Later, students will find their own learning stations in the gymnasium for practice.

WARM-UP:

Today we are going to use our arms a lot to work on our throwing. When I put on the music, I would like you to begin moving in general space with a locomotor skill of your choice. Who can name a locomotor skill? (Repeat the question several times until skip, slide, gallop, run, and walk are all mentioned.)

When the music stops, I would like you to freeze and perform an arm-stretching exercise. Just in case you can't think of one, who can show me an arm-stretching exercise? (Call on several children. Begin music.)

Watch to make sure students are performing the locomotor skills correctly and using a variety of skills, and ensure that the arm-stretching exercises are sufficient for the day's activity.

FORMATION: Students find their own self-space and sit down.

INTRODUCTION:

Today we will continue working on throwing overhand. Overhand throwing is used in many games. It can be used to throw to people or to targets. Since we will concentrate on throwing hard today, we will practice with targets. Why do you think we will throw at the wall today and not partners? **(We are throwing hard and don't want to hurt anyone.)**

Who can tell me which foot you step with on the overhand throw? **(The stepping foot.)** *Now who can tell me the parts of overhand throwing?* **(Ready; turn; step, rotate, throw; and follow through.)** *Everyone stand up in your self-space and let's practice those steps. Remember to step with the stepping foot.*

Students practice overhand throwing as you repeat the cues out loud. Watch specifically for stepping in opposition.

*Freeze. Please sit down. Let's brainstorm how to throw hard. Watch me as I pretend to throw. Could the ready position help me throw harder? To use stronger force? Could the **turn** make me throw harder? Yes. Because if I stretch my arm out, I can generate more force when I throw. Think about a tiny baseball bat—only a foot long* (use a ruler to demonstrate). *Can I hit a ball farther with a bat this size, or with a longer bat? Yes, the longer bat would be better. So if a longer bat is better for hitting, a longer arm is better for throwing. When we throw, we must reach back, and then when we step, rotate, throw, we will have more force.*

Again, why will we throw at the wall today and not at partners? **(We are throwing hard and don't want to hurt anyone.)** *Should we ever try to throw at a person as hard as we can?* **(No.)**

When I say go, you will find a learning station, pick up the yarn ball, stand on the middle line, and work on extending your arm and throwing hard. Go.

Watch students to ensure that they have full arm extension and are stepping in opposition. Repeat the cues *reach back, rotate, throw hard,* and *use your stepping foot* often.

FORMATION:

After five minutes, tell the students to freeze and sit down at their stations.

You are doing very well extending your arms. We need to work on our accuracy, too. There are three shapes or targets in front of you. You must call out which one you will hit before the ball leaves your hand. Count how many times you are successful. You may stand on any of the three lines. Go.

Watch the students to ensure that they have full arm extension and are stepping in opposition. Repeat the cues *reach back, rotate, throw hard,* and *use your stepping foot* often.

Freeze. How many of you were successful 10 or more times? 20 or more times? Excellent. When I say go, I would like you to find a partner and sit together at one station. Go. Partners, you will challenge your partner to hit a specific target, but he or she may choose the distance. After five throws, you will change jobs. Partners, you must also make sure that the skills are being done correctly, specifically making a turn and stepping with the stepping foot. Go.

Watch the students to ensure that they have full arm extension and are stepping in opposition. Repeat the cues *reach back, rotate, throw hard,* and *use your stepping foot* often.

After 5 minutes, stop the class and have students sit down at their stations.

This time, you and your partner (if you both agree) may change the challenge. You may now tell your partner not only which target to hit but also which line to stand on. If you both don't agree to do this change, that's fine; just keep practicing. Go.

CLOSURE:

As students are lined up to leave, play teach the teacher:

1. *Who can tell me how to perform overhand throwing correctly?* **(Ready; turn; arm back; step, rotate, throw; follow through.)**

2. *How do you add force to the throw?* **(Turn; arm back; step, rotate, throw; follow through.)**

TWO-HAND OVERHEAD THROWING

Two-hand overhead throwing is found primarily in two sports: basketball and soccer. In basketball, two-hand overhead throwing is used to inbound a ball or to throw to a teammate. In soccer, it is used by any player to inbound a ball to a teammate.

National Standards & Grade-Level Outcomes for K-12 Physical Education (SHAPE America, 2014) does not specifically mention two-hand overhead throwing. However, it has been our experience that children should be able to perform this skill by the second grade. Therefore, instruction in two-hand overhead throwing should begin in the primary grades as one of the basic ways to throw a ball.

Critical Elements

Ready position	**Ball behind head**	**Step and throw**	**Follow through**
Facing target, feet shoulder-width apart, knees bent, eyes on target, hands held slightly behind and to the side of the ball. Ball is held at chest level.	Ball is brought above and behind the head. The arms are bent.	Step forward with one foot while extending arms and releasing the ball toward the target. There is a wrist snap with this action.	After the ball is released, hands are turned so that palms are facing away from each other and the thumbs are pointing downward.

Cue Words

The cue words you select for each phase of the skill will depend on the age of the students you are teaching and your areas of emphasis. In the cue sets are some of the cue words we use to teach two-hand overhead throwing. You may use each set individually or mix and match the cue words as needed. We have found that it is beneficial to have the students say the cue words out loud as they practice.

Ready—facing target, feet shoulder-width apart, knees bent, eyes on target, hands held slightly behind and to the side of the ball. Ball held at chest level.

Ball behind head—ball is brought above and behind the head. The arms are bent.

Step and throw—step forward with one foot while extending arms and releasing ball toward target. There is a wrist snap with this action.

Follow through—after the ball is released, hands are turned so that palms are facing away from each other and the thumbs are pointing downward.

Up—bring ball above and behind the head. The arms are bent.

Snap—Wrist snaps as ball is released. Hands are turned so that palms are facing away from each other and the thumbs are pointing downward.

> *Cue set 1:* ready, ball overhead, step and throw, follow through
> *Cue set 2:* ready, up, step and throw, follow through
> *Cue set 3:* ready, up, snap

SUGGESTED ACTIVITIES FOR REINFORCING AND ASSESSING THE CRITICAL ELEMENTS

In the learning process, it is essential that students know how a skill looks, what its critical elements are, and how to perform each individual element correctly. In the preceding section, we provided pictures and descriptions of two-hand overhead throwing, divided it into its critical elements, and provided possible cue words. In addition to the material in chapter 1 that reinforces the concepts for all locomotor and manipulative skills, the following section provides specific activities for reinforcing the critical elements unique to two-hand overhead throwing.

PARTNER SKILL CHECK

Objective

To allow partners to assess their own skill progress with two-hand overhead throwing and to learn to evaluate the skills of others.

Equipment

Partner skill check assessments and one ball for each set of partners. If the students cannot read or do not speak English, the picture version of the partner skill check assessment may be useful.

Activity

1. One partner observes the other to see if he has the correct form for the ready position.
2. If the ready position is correct, then the partner places a *Y* in the first box. If the ready position is incorrect, she places an *N* in the first box. Nonreaders can put a smiling face if the ready position is correct or a frowning face if the ready position is incorrect.
3. This evaluation continues until each of the critical elements has been assessed five times.
4. A partner skill check sheet is used for each student.

Extensions

- You can use the partner skill check assessment to measure the skill development of each student.
- You can send partner skill check assessments home with report cards or as individual skills develop.

SUCCESS BUILDERS

The success builder activities allow you to address individual needs. If students need additional help on specific critical elements, the activities listed here will help reinforce correct performance.

Objective

To allow partners to improve areas of deficiency as measured by the partner skill check assessment.

Equipment

See the individual stations listed below. We suggest using an unbreakable mirror and a poster of each critical element of the two-hand overhead throw at each station. The mirror is particularly helpful in these activities because it allows children to see what they are doing. The easiest way to make the posters is to print out the drawings from this book and enlarge them. Laminating the posters will ensure their use for many years.

Activity

1. Set up a station for each critical element in the teaching area. Post a description or a picture of the specific elements at the corresponding station.
2. Following are the details for each station:

PARTNER SKILL CHECK
Skill: Two-Hand Overhead Throwing

Thrower's name: _____ Watcher's name: _____

1 Ready

1 2 3 4 5

2 Ball behind head

1 2 3 4 5

3 Step and throw

1 2 3 4 5

4 Follow through

1 2 3 4

PARTNER SKILL CHECK
Skill: Two-Hand Overhead Throwing

Thrower's name: _____ Watcher's name: _____

Watch your partner and mark each critical element of the skill. Let your partner do the skill five times. Each time your partner does it right, mark a Y in the box. If your partner doesn't do it right, mark an N in the box.

START

Ready position
1. Facing target.
2. Feet shoulder-width apart.
3. Knees bent.
4. Ball held in front of body with hands on sides of the ball.

TRIALS

1 2 3 4 5

ACTION

Ball behind head
1. Ball is brought above and behind the head with arms bent.

Step and throw
2. Step forward with one foot.
3. Extend arms and release ball toward target.
4. Wrists snap.

1 2 3 4 5

STOP

Follow through
1. Palms are facing away from each other and thumbs are pointed down.

1 2 3 4 5

READY POSITION

Facing target, feet shoulder-width apart, knees bent, eyes on target, hands held slightly behind and to the side of the ball. Ball held at chest level.

Equipment

Poster of the ready position, mirror (if available), and partner assessments.

Activity

The student assumes the ready position. The partner checks to see if her position matches the poster. The student refers to the mirror for help. The student then walks around and, on a signal from her partner, assumes the ready position again. When she has had several successful trials, the partners may return to working on the entire skill.

BALL OVERHEAD

Ball is brought above and behind the head. The arms are bent.

Equipment

Poster of the ball being brought overhead, mirror (if available), and partner assessments.

Activity

The student assumes the ball overhead position. The partner checks to see if his position matches the poster. The student refers to the mirror for help. The student then assumes the ready position facing a set target. On a signal from his partner, the student assumes the ball overhead position. When he has had several successful trials, the partners may return to working on the entire skill.

STEP AND THROW

Step forward with one foot while extending the arms and releasing the ball toward a target. There is a wrist snap with the action.

Equipment

Poster of the step and throw element, mirror (if available), footprints or tape (floor or painter's), and partner assessments.

Activity

Basic stride—Footprints (or tape) are placed on the floor. With the partner's help, the student starts from the ready position, places the ball overhead, and steps forward with one foot. The partner checks to see if her position matches the poster. The student refers to the mirror for help. When she has had several successful trials, the partners may return to working on the entire skill.

Extension

Let it fly—Tie several jump ropes between two volleyball poles, leaving approximately 12 inches (30 cm) between the ropes. The top rope should be at about shoulder height to the thrower. Have the student practice releasing the ball between the ropes. The partner checks to see if the thrower's position matches the poster. The thrower refers to the mirror for help.

FOLLOW THROUGH

After the ball is released, hands are turned so that palms are facing away from each other and the thumbs are pointing downward.

Equipment

Poster of the follow-through, mirror (if available), partner assessments, one playground ball, and target on the wall.

Activity

Imaginary throw—Have the student get into the step and throw position facing a set target. The student practices his step and throw without a ball. The partner checks to see if his position matches the poster. The student refers to the mirror for help. When he has had several successful trials, the partners may return to working on the entire skill.

Extension

Hit the target—Students work in pairs. Students are told to stay away from the target while their partners are throwing. One partner starts with the ball overhead position. The thrower steps and throws the ball toward a target at least 10 feet (3 m) away. The partner watches to see if the partner has completed the follow-through.

SUGGESTED CULMINATING ACTIVITIES TO REINFORCE THE ENTIRE SKILL

Mastery of critical elements should be accomplished before emphasizing accuracy. When accuracy becomes the emphasis before children master the critical elements, children aim at targets and the elements of the skill are compromised. Targets should be large enough to allow students to perform the critical elements of the skill and have success hitting the target.

INDIVIDUAL ACTIVITIES

COLOR TARGETS

Objective

To improve two-hand overhead throwing accuracy by hitting a specified target.

Equipment

Construction paper of different colors (about 8 to 12 targets of each color and as large as possible) taped to the wall of the gymnasium or activity area and a medium-size lightweight ball for each student.

Activity

1. Create a color box in which samples from each color of construction paper have been placed. You will need more samples than you have students.
2. Select a student to draw a sample color from the color box.
3. The sample color chosen is the color target all students must locate and try to hit with a two-hand overhead throw.
4. Students continue to throw toward the targets of the selected color until a stop signal is given.
5. The activity continues until all students have had an opportunity to draw from the color box.

Extensions

- Instead of using different colors, students could select different shapes from the shape box, letters from the alphabet box, or words from the word box.
- Students work with partners. The partner chooses the color, shape, letter, or word that will be used for a target. The thrower must then try to hit the selected target. Partners take turns selecting targets and performing the throw.

CREATE A WORD

Objective

To create words by using two-hand overhead throwing to hit letters.

Equipment

One playground ball per student and four complete sets of alphabet letters (as large as possible) scattered and taped to the walls of the gym or activity space. It would be advantageous to have extra copies of vowels and selected consonants (e.g., N, R, S, T). You will also need paper and pencils or a dry-erase board and markers to serve as a word bank.

Activity

1. On your start signal, students begin to spell words by hitting letters of the alphabet using two-hand overhead throwing.

2. Once a student has created a word, she goes to the word bank (paper or dry-erase board) and writes the word. It will be helpful to have several word banks so students will not have to wait to record their words.

3. A word may be written only once on the paper or dry-erase board.

4. If a student hits a letter that cannot be used to form the word being created, he must hit the letter again to delete it.

Extensions

- Working in pairs, one student hits letters to spell a word while the other records the word and evaluates the two-hand overhead throwing. The thrower may not use the letter until the throw is performed properly. When the first partner has spelled a word, the other partner is given an opportunity to perform the skill.

- Partners are given paper and pencil to record the letters they hit and to write down the words they create. Each partner must throw the ball and hit a vowel and three consonants. The pair now has eight letters to use to create words. The partners attempt to create six words using one or more of the letters they have hit. Once the partners have created six words and written them down, they will attempt to spell the words by hitting the letters with the ball. Once a word is spelled, it may be checked off the list. If the students are unable to use a letter they have hit, they must hit that letter again to delete it and select another letter.

PARTNER ACTIVITIES

BACK IT UP

Objective

To execute two-hand overhead throwing with a partner from varying distances.

Equipment

One playground ball per pair of students.

Activity

1. Students stand approximately 10 feet (3 m) from their partners.

2. The ball is thrown using two-hand overhead throwing. It is caught by the other partner and then thrown back.

3. On completing a successful throw, one partner takes a step backward.

4. The activity is repeated until one student fails to catch the ball or the throw does not reach a partner without hitting the ground.

Based on Bryant and McClean Oliver 1975.

TARGET THROWS

Objective

To execute two-hand overhead throwing to various targets.

Equipment

One piece of construction paper taped to the wall approximately 5 feet (1.5 m) from the floor and one playground ball per student pair.

Activity

1. One partner stands approximately 15 feet (4.6 m) from the target.
2. The other partner calls out where he should throw the ball (e.g., above the target, below the target, to the right, to the left).
3. The partners receive one point if the ball strikes within 1 foot (0.3 m) of the target and in the proper direction.

Extensions

- Partners add their scores together.
- Partners record their scores for several days and chart their improvement.

CHALLENGES

Objective

To practice two-hand overhead throwing in a variety of situations.

Equipment

One playground ball per pair of students and laminated challenge cards. Different types of challenges may require additional equipment.

Activity

1. Each student selects a challenge card.
2. Students perform the tasks described on the cards.
3. Possible challenges may include the following:
   - Throw the ball using light or strong force.
   - Throw the ball, releasing at a high level.
   - Throw the ball so that it hits the wall, it bounces once, and you are able to catch it.

Extensions

- Place multicolored targets, hoops, cones, or buckets on a wall or in the play area and have the partner tell the thrower which target to hit.
- Set up game poles or volleyball standards and tie a rope between them. Suspend various objects from the rope and challenge the students to hit them. Possible targets include hoops, aluminum pie pans, and empty 2-liter plastic bottles.
- To create more permanent targets, you may paint them on the wall of your gymnasium. If you paint these targets on the wall behind where tumbling mats are attached for storage, you can cover them when not in use.
- Partners keep track of their number of correct throws and you keep a total for the class. In a follow-up lesson, you can challenge the class to increase the total number of correct throws.

Based on Bryant and McClean Oliver 1975.

WALL PASS

Objective

To improve two-hand overhead throwing and catching while working with a partner.

Equipment

One ball (playground ball or volleyball) per student pair.

Activity

1. Partners stand at least 15 feet (4.5 m) from the wall.
2. One partner performs a two-hand overhead throw against the wall. The throw must be at least 10 feet (3 m) high.
3. The other partner catches the ball after it bounces off the wall.
4. When the partner has caught the ball, he performs a two-hand overhead throw back to the wall.
5. Partners count how many successful throws they have in a row.

Extension

Allow the ball to bounce several times before catching it.

GROUP ACTIVITIES

OMNIKIN BALL MADNESS

Objective

To perform two-hand overhead throwing to move an object across the play area.

Equipment

The object may be an Omnikin ball or any ball larger than the balls being thrown. The balls being thrown may be lightweight soccer balls aimed at the larger ball.

Activity

1. Divide the class into four groups. Each group stands along one side of a square play area. Students must stay behind their lines.
2. Place the Omnikin ball or a large ball in the center of the play area.
3. Each group begins the activity with two or more balls.
4. On the start signal, players perform two-hand overhead throwing and try to hit the large ball in the center in an effort to move it toward another group's line.
5. Players continue to throw their balls until the large ball crosses a group's line.
6. Players may touch the large ball only with a thrown ball; they may not touch it with their bodies.
7. Once the large ball crosses the designated line, the activity stops and the large ball is returned to the center of the play area.
8. Resume the activity when each group has the same number of balls to throw. Be sure every player is given a chance to begin with a ball.

Extensions

- Have each student start the activity with a ball.
- Create two groups rather than four.
- Try to throw a variety of balls at the large ball in an effort to move the ball across another group's line. This may lead to discussions on which balls are better for the task (e.g., playground balls versus beach balls).
- Have groups change positions either before the next round or on a signal during the activity. If the students are to change places during the activity, be sure they understand that they may not throw a ball at the large ball until your start signal and that they may not take a ball with them as they change sides.

CREATE YOUR OWN ACTIVITY

Objective

To allow students to create their own activities to reinforce two-hand overhead throwing skills.

Equipment

One piece of paper and pencil per group and a predetermined list of equipment you will allow the students to use in their activities (e.g., bowling pins, cones, jump rope, foam soccer balls, playground balls).

Activity

1. Form groups of two to five students. You may select the groups, or the students may form their own.
2. Each group creates an activity using two-hand overhead throwing as the basic skill. Students are required to have rules that encourage correct performance of the skill, include all players, and address all safety concerns.
3. The groups write their individual names, the rules of the activity, and the equipment needed on their papers, and then they show their activities to you.
4. After you approve their activities, the groups retrieve the necessary equipment and begin playing.
5. You must approve all changes to the activities.

Extensions

- Groups may teach their activities to other groups.
- Groups may teach their activities to the entire class.

PIN BALL

Objective

To use two-hand overhead throwing to hit the opposing group's bowling pins.

Equipment

Balls and three plastic bowling pins (indicated by A and B in the figure) for each group. Bowling pins need to be color coded for each group (e.g., use different-colored tape to mark the pins).

Activity

1. Set up a play area with a center line and two restraining lines that are approximately 12 feet (3.7 m) from the center line (see figure).
2. Divide the class into two equal groups and place the groups behind the restraining lines, facing each other.

3. Set the six pins up along the center line of the play area, alternating colors.

4. On the start signal, the students use two-hand overhead throwing and try to hit the opposing group's pins. The students may not cross the restraining line.

5. A pin does not stay down if the ball was thrown from in front of the restraining line.

6. Restart the activity when all of a group's pins have been knocked down.

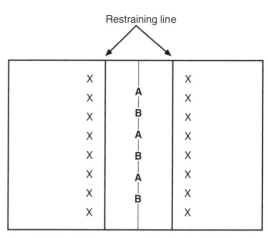

Setup for Pin Ball activity.

Extensions

• Set empty 2-liter bottles, lightweight cones, empty cereal boxes, or other objects on an elevated surface to use as group targets.

• Suspend a rope between two volleyball standards. Hang lightweight targets (e.g., paper, scarves, streamers, crepe paper) from the rope and challenge the students to hit the opposing team's targets.

Adapted, by permission, from K. Thomas, A. Lee, and J. Thomas, 2000, *Physical education for children: Daily lesson plans for elementary school,* 2nd ed. (Champaign, IL: Human Kinetics), 546.

CYCLE/RECYCLE

Objective

To improve accuracy of two-hand overhead throwing while throwing a foam soccer ball over a volleyball net.

Equipment

Two game standards, one volleyball net, and one foam soccer ball for every two students. The net is placed lower than the regular volleyball height.

Activity

1. Divide the class in half and have an equal number of balls on each side.

2. On the start signal, the students perform a two-hand overhead throw over the net.

3. Have the students count the number of successful throws they were able to make over the net.

Extensions

• Have the students total the number of throws the entire group made. These results can be recorded and later charted or graphed to show class improvement.

• Each time a student throws the ball over the net, he goes around the standards and becomes a member of the other group.

• Ask the class to estimate how many correct throws they can perform in 1 minute. Time the students for 1 minute. Evaluate the results.

Reprinted, by permission, from J. Wessel, 1974, *Project I Can* (Northbrook, IL: Hubbard Publishing).

KERPLUNK

Objective

To use two-hand overhead throwing to get a ball into the target area behind the opposing group.

Equipment

Two or more Super-Safe balls or balls that are made of soft rubber (8 inches [20 cm] in diameter). The number of balls used will vary based on the skill level and number of students. You will also need tape or cones to mark off a large target area 15 to 20 feet (4.5-6 m) from the center of the playing area. Use a dry-erase board or paper to record the points.

Activity

1. Divide the class into two groups and place groups on opposite sides of the playing area.
2. Provide each group an equal number of balls to begin the activity.
3. On the start signal, players use two-hand overhead throwing to get the ball into the opposing group's target area.
4. If a player kerplunks the ball into the opposing group's target area, one point is awarded to her group.
5. Players are allowed to catch the ball to prevent it from hitting the target area.
6. Restart the game after one group reaches 10 points.

Extensions

- While the students are playing, ensure that two-hand overhead throwing is being performed correctly. Instruct any student having trouble throwing correctly to go to the practice area and work with a partner or a designated teacher assistant.
- Have a special ball designated. If the special ball is kerplunked into the target area, two points are awarded.

SUMMARY

Throwing a ball to a teammate is crucial in soccer and basketball. Two-hand overhead throwing is required in soccer and is often used in basketball. Learning to properly and accurately throw a ball to a teammate becomes very important to students' overall success in these sports. Students and recreational players can use two-hand overhead throwing effectively once they understand how and when to use it. Maintaining the proper body position, stepping with the throw, and using proper arm movements are elements that students must understand before they have repeated success with this skill.

Two-Hand Overhead Throwing Troubleshooting Chart

If you see this	Then try this
1. Eyes not on target	• Have the student throw to a target he has designed. • Place a 2-liter bottle on top of a cone and have the student try to knock it off. • Use aluminum pie plates for targets.
2. Incorrect hand position	• Draw the hand positions on the ball. • Have the student put her hands in baby powder and then place them on a ball.
3. Student not stepping when throwing the ball	• Have the student step on a mat or a rug as he throws the ball. • Have the student stand near a line (a rope or tape on the floor). She must step over the line while throwing the ball.
4. Arms not fully extended on the throw	• Have the student practice reaching out and grabbing an object placed an arm's length away from the body. • Place a suspended aluminum pie plate in front of the student and have him try to hit the pie plate with his outstretched hands.
5. Body not in proper alignment on the follow-through	• Tell the student to point her belt buckle at the target on the follow-through.
6. Ball hitting the target too high or too low	• Suspend two ropes between two game standards. Place the ropes between waist height and neck height so the ball can be thrown correctly through them and reach the target. • Have the student practice throwing the ball to a target on the wall. • The ball may be too heavy or too light for the student. Either give the student a more appropriately sized ball or move the child closer to (or farther away from) the target.

TWO-HAND OVERHEAD THROWING LESSON PLAN

(FIRST LESSON)

AGE GROUP: Second grade.

FOCUS: Wrist snap on release.

SUBFOCUS: Techniques for generating power through stepping and snapping the wrist.

OBJECTIVES: To execute a two-hand overhead throw by bringing the ball overhead, stepping forward with one foot, and bringing the arms forward and snapping the wrist as the ball is released. This will occur four out of five times and will be assessed by peer observation (**cue:** *snap your wrist*).

MATERIALS AND EQUIPMENT: Construction paper as targets, foam or Gator Skin ball, drawings of the critical elements of two-hand overhead throwing for each student pair, and music.

ADVANCE PREPARATION: Pieces of construction paper are taped to the walls so that the bottom is approximately 5 feet (1.5 m) above the floor. These targets should be approximately 5 feet (1.5 m) apart and will constitute learning stations. Drawings of the critical elements of two-hand overhead throwing are attached beside each target. In front of each station is a line parallel to the wall that is approximately 15 feet (4.5 m) from the wall. A second line, 25 feet (7.6 m) from the wall, is also taped to the floor. A ball that does not rebound quickly from the wall (e.g., foam ball, Gator Skin ball) is placed below each target.

ORGANIZATION AND MANAGEMENT: Students are in self-space for instruction and warm-up. Students work with a partner in individual stations to execute two-hand overhead throwing.

INTRODUCTION AND WARM-UP:

Today we are going to warm up by using a variety of locomotor movements. You will move in general space while maintaining your self-space. When the music starts, you may begin with a jog.

Begin music and call out a variety of locomotor movements (e.g., skip, slide, gallop) as the students move throughout the activity space.

LESSON PROCEDURES:

*Freeze. Please find a personal space (self-space) and sit down. Today we are going to learn how to execute a two-hand overhead throw. It has a great deal in common with overhand throwing and underhand throwing. All three allow us to throw the ball to a teammate, and all three use a **step** to generate power. What can you guess from its name that will make it very different from the other two? **(It uses two hands. It is thrown overhead.)** That's right: It needs two hands and the ball is brought over your head.*

Here are the parts of the skill. (Demonstrate as the cue words are taught.) Ready, ball behind head, step and throw, and follow through. We get our force from the step, but the wrist snap when we release is very important. This time just watch my hands as I throw the ball. (Demonstrate several times again.)

Everyone stand up. Pretend you have a ball in your hand. Let's practice two-hand overhead throwing together as we say the cue words out loud: ready, ball behind head, step and throw, follow through. Practice without a ball several times.

You've got it. This time you may work with a ball, but you will need a partner, too. Please find a partner and stand back to back before I count to three: one, two, three. If you do not have a partner, stand in the middle circle so we can pair you up.

Excellent. When I point to you and your partner, please move and stand in front of a target. Do not touch the equipment. (All student pairs are selected.)

There are two lines in front of you. The thrower stands on the line closer to the wall. The partner stands on the one farther back. Pick up the ball and begin practicing two-hand overhead throwing when I say go. Remember to snap your wrists when you release the ball. Go.

Allow students to practice for several minutes. If possible, stop the practice and point out several students performing the skill correctly. Return to practice.

Watch for students bringing the ball behind the head, stepping with one foot, and snapping the wrist as the ball is released.

Freeze. I am going to give each of you a partner skill check assessment and one pencil. (Teacher distributes assessments and pencils.) *Tell your partner something he or she is doing well and something he or she needs to work on. Your partner should throw five times before you change jobs. Use the partner skill check assessment to help you, but don't write down anything right now. If you understand these directions, clap your hands twice. Excellent. Go.*

Allow students to practice for several minutes. If possible, stop the practice and point out several students performing the skill correctly. Return to practice.

Watch for students bringing the ball behind the head, stepping with one foot, and snapping the wrist as the ball is released.

Freeze. Is there a part of the skill that is giving some of you trouble?

Determine what that is and reteach. Allow additional practice.

Freeze. This time your partner will use the partner skill check and record how well you are doing with each of the elements. Remember, each of you will have five throws before you change jobs.

Allow students to practice and evaluate each other on the skill.

Freeze. Time is up. I know you are just getting used to the skill, but please return your equipment to where it belongs and line up for your teacher.

CLOSURE: Students are lined up to leave.

When I use two-hand overhead throwing, where does the force, or power, come from? **(The step and the wrist snap.)**

Next time we will practice throwing at targets that are moving.

5

Catching

One of the manipulative skills that is most neglected in the elementary grades is catching. Because catching cannot occur without throwing, this skill is dependent on how the ball is thrown or tossed. Unfortunately, well-meaning teachers and coaches often stress how to throw without ever teaching how to catch what is thrown. Because the fear of being hit by a ball can become overpowering, it is essential that the skill of catching be introduced early through self-tosses and controlled tosses with appropriate safety considerations (e.g., using equipment that is soft and easily caught by small hands).

National Standards & Grade-Level Outcomes for K-12 Physical Education (SHAPE America, 2014) (table 5.1) states that kindergarteners should be able to drop a ball and catch it before it bounces twice (S1.E16.Ka). In addition, kindergarteners should be able to catch a large ball tossed by a skilled thrower (S1.E16.Kb). In first grade, children should be able to catch soft objects that are self-tossed (S1.E16.1a) before they bounce and catch objects of various sizes that are self-tossed or tossed by a skilled thrower (S1.E16.1b). Self-tossing and catching well-thrown balls continue in the second grade; children should be able to catch balls with their hands and not trap or cradle the balls against their bodies (S1.E16.2). The proper form for catching is not emphasized until the third grade. The outcomes state that third-grade students should be able to catch a gently tossed hand-sized ball from a partner, demonstrating four of the five critical elements of a mature pattern (S1.E16.3).

Objects may be caught above the waist (with the thumbs together, or thumbs in) or below the waist (with the pinkie fingers together, or thumbs out). The Grade-Level Outcomes suggest that students should be able to differentiate between the types of catches by the fourth grade and demonstrate catches above the waist and below the waist using a mature pattern while stationary (S1.E16.4). Mastery of moving to catch the ball occurs in grade 5 (S1.E16.5).

Regardless of age, appropriate safety precautions should be used. For example, yarn balls, foam balls, or beanbags should be used when children are learning the mechanics of catching. In addition, students should be taught to use the proper amount of force when throwing and to throw *only* when the partner is watching and ready.

Table 5.1   Grade-Level Outcomes for Catching (S1.E16)

	Kindergarten	Grade 1	Grade 2	Grade 3	Grade 4	Grade 5
S1.E16 Catching	Drops a ball and catches it before it bounces twice. (S1.E16.Ka) Catches a large ball tossed by a skilled thrower. (S1.E16.Kb)	Catches a soft object from a self-toss before it bounces. (S1.E16.1a) Catches various sizes of balls self-tossed or tossed by a skilled thrower. (S1.E16.1b)	Catches a self-tossed or well-thrown large ball with hands, not trapping or cradling the ball against the body. (S1.E16.2)	Catches a gently tossed hand-size ball from a partner demonstrating 4 of the 5 critical elements of a mature pattern. (S1.E16.3)	Catches a thrown ball above the head, at chest or waist level, and below the waist using a mature pattern in a nondynamic environment (closed skills). (S1.E16.4)	Catches a batted ball above the head, at chest or waist level, and along the ground using a mature pattern in a nondynamic environment (closed skills). (S1.E16.5a) Catches with accuracy with both partners moving. (S1.E16.5b) Catches with reasonable accuracy in dynamic, small-sided practice tasks. (S1.E16.5c)

Reprinted, by permission, from SHAPE America – Society of Health and Physical Educators, 2014, *National standards & grade-level outcomes for K-12 physical education* (Champaign, IL: Human Kinetics).

Critical Elements

Ready Position	**Step and Reach**	**Fingers Only**	**Give**
Face the target, feet shoulder-width apart, knees bent, eyes on approaching object, elbows bent near sides, hands held in front of body.	As the ball is released, step toward the thrower, extend the arms, and adjust the hands to meet the ball. To catch throws above the waist, hands are held in front of the body (elbows bent near sides) with thumbs together. To catch throws below the waist, hands are held in front of the body (elbows bent near sides) with pinkie fingers together (or thumbs out). The following rhyme may help your students with catching: "If the ball is high, reach to the sky. If the ball is low, reach to your toe."	Use only fingers and thumbs to catch the object. The ball should not be trapped against the body.	Absorb the force of the object by bringing the arms back toward the body.

Cue Words

The cue words you select for each phase of the skill will depend on the age of the students you are teaching and your areas of emphasis. In usable sets are some of the cue words we use to teach catching. You may use each set individually or mix and match the cue words as needed. We have found that it is beneficial to have the students say the cue words out loud as they practice.

Catching Above the Waist

W or ready—feet apart, knees bent, elbows near sides, thumbs up with the hands in front of the chest, and eyes on the approaching object. The tops of the thumbnails are touching. The index finger forms the outside of the W. The rest of the fingers are curved toward each other, leaving an opening large enough to catch the object.

Reach out or reach—step forward with one foot and extend the arms toward the object.

Catch and **use your fingers**—catch the object with the fingers only (do not trap it against the body).

Absorb the force or pull—pull the arms back toward the body.

> *Cue set 1:* W, reach out, catch, absorb the force
> *Cue set 2:* ready, reach, use your fingers, pull

Catching Below the Waist

Ready or form a V—feet apart, knees bent, elbows near sides, pinkies down with the hands below the waist, and eyes on the approaching object. The tops of the pinkies are touching, forming a V (thumbs out). The rest of the fingers are curved toward each other, leaving an opening large enough to catch the object.

Reach down or reach—step forward with one foot and extend the arms downward toward the object.

Catch and **grab**—catch the object with the fingers only (do not trap it against the body).

Absorb the force or **pull**—pull the arms back toward the body.

> *Cue set 1:* V, reach down, catch, absorb the force
> *Cue set 2:* ready, reach, grab, pull

SUGGESTED ACTIVITIES FOR REINFORCING AND ASSESSING THE CRITICAL ELEMENTS

In the learning process, it is essential that students know how a skill is supposed to look, what its critical elements are, and how to perform each individual element correctly. In the preceding section, we provided pictures and descriptions of catching, divided it into its critical elements, and provided possible cue words. Chapter 1 provided generic activities that will reinforce these concepts for catching as well as for all locomotor and manipulative skills. In addition to the material in chapter 1, the following section provides activities for reinforcing the elements unique to catching.

SHOW OFF

Objective

To provide opportunities for students to demonstrate the critical elements of catching.

Equipment

One cone and one ball per student and music. Cones should be of varying heights.

Activity

1. Scatter cones around the gymnasium. Place a ball on top of each cone. Use different sizes of cones and balls.
2. Students move around the gymnasium in self-space while listening to the music.
3. When the music stops, the students move to the closest cone.
4. When you say the cue word *W,* the students freeze in the W position. When you say *reach out,* the students reach to the balls. When you say *catch,* the students remove the balls from the cones. When you say *absorb the force,* the students remove the balls from the cones and pull them toward their bodies. (Cues may be given in any order.)
5. When the music starts, the students replace the balls on the top of the cones and they begin moving again.
6. The next time the music stops, the students must go to a different-sized cone.
7. Continue this activity using each critical element.

TOWEL CATCHERS

Objective

To reinforce the concept of absorbing the force of the object being caught by using a towel.

Equipment

A towel for each set of partners and an object to be caught (e.g., beach ball, balloon, beanbag, playground ball).

Activity

1. Students form groups of four (two sets of partners).
2. Partners hold a towel stretched between them so it can be used to catch an object (ball).
3. On your signal, one set of partners throws the ball to the other set of partners, who try to catch the ball in the towel before it touches the floor.
4. The ball can be thrown either with the hands or with the towel.

Extension

Put up a volleyball net and divide the students into two even groups. Using two or three beach balls, have the students throw and catch the balls over the net using only the towels.

PARTNER SKILL CHECK

Objective

To allow partners to assess each other's progress while learning to catch correctly.

Equipment

Partner skill check assessments and one ball for each set of partners. If the students cannot read or do not speak English, the picture version of the partner skill check assessment may be useful.

Activity

1. One partner observes the other to see if she has the correct form for the W position.

2. If the W position is correct, then the partner places a *Y* in the first box. If the W position is incorrect, he places an *N* in the first box. Nonreaders can put a smiling face if the W position is correct or a frowning face if the W position is incorrect.

3. This evaluation continues until each of the elements has been assessed five times.

4. A partner skill check sheet is used for each student.

Extensions

- You can use the partner skill check assessment to measure the skill development of each student.

- You can send partner skill check assessments home with report cards or as individual skills develop.

SUCCESS BUILDERS

The success builder activities allow the teacher to address individual needs. If students need additional help on particular elements, the activities listed here will help reinforce correct performance.

Objective

To allow partners to improve areas of deficiency as assessed by the partner skill check assessment. It also allows the teacher to address individual needs.

Equipment

See the following individual stations. We suggest using an unbreakable mirror and a poster of each element of catching at each station. The mirror is particularly helpful in these activities because it allows the children to see what they are doing. The easiest way to make the posters is to print out the drawings from this book and enlarge them. Laminating the posters will ensure their use for many years.

Activity

1. Set up a station for each of the critical elements in the teaching area. Post a description or a picture of the specific element at the corresponding station.

2. The details for each station follow:

READY

Facing target, feet shoulder-width apart, knees bent, eyes on approaching object, hands held in front of body (elbows near sides and bent) with thumbs together. To catch throws below the waist, hands are held in front of the body (elbows near sides and bent) with pinkie fingers together.

Equipment

Poster of the ready position, mirror (if available), and partner evaluations

Activity

The student assumes the ready position. The partner checks to see if her position matches the poster. The student refers to the mirror for help. The student then walks around and, on a signal from her partner, assumes the ready position again. Once the student can demonstrate to the partner a good ready position, the partners may return to practicing the entire skill.

STEP AND REACH

As the ball is released, step toward the thrower and extend the arms and hands to meet the ball.

Equipment

Poster of the step and reach, mirror (if available), 28-inch (71 cm) cone or adjustable batting tee, tennis ball, and partner evaluations.

Activity

Place a tennis ball on top of a cone or tee. Have the student stand behind the cone. There should be enough room to allow the student to step and fully extend his arms to pick the ball off the cone or tee. To begin, the student assumes the ready position. On a signal from his partner, the student steps forward toward the cone, extends his arms toward the ball, and removes the ball from the cone or tee. The student refers to the mirror for help. Once the student can demonstrate to the partner a good step and reach, the partners may return to practicing the entire skill.

FINGERS ONLY

Use only fingers and thumbs to catch the object. The ball should not be trapped against the body.

Equipment

Poster of the fingers-only element, mirror (if available), balloon or beach ball, and partner evaluations.

Activity

Have the partner toss the balloon or beach ball up into the air. The catcher must move to the balloon or ball and grasp it with his fingers. Partners should do this several times, making sure that the catcher is using the fingers and not the palm or chest when catching. The catcher refers to the mirror for help. Once the student can demonstrate the ability to catch the balloon or ball using only the fingers, the partners may return to practicing the entire skill.

GIVE

Absorb the force of the object by bringing the arms back toward the body.

Equipment

Poster of the give element, mirror (if available), different-sized balls (tennis ball, foam ball, playground ball), and partner evaluations.

Activity

The student bounces the ball on the floor and catches the ball as it comes back down. Stress the idea of giving with the weight of the ball as if catching an egg. Once the student can give with the ball, have her bounce the ball off the wall and give with catching. To enhance the practice, have the student use different-sized balls along with different amounts of force. The student refers to the mirror for help. Once the student can demonstrate the ability to give while catching the ball, the partners may return to practicing the entire skill.

SUGGESTED CULMINATING ACTIVITIES TO REINFORCE THE ENTIRE SKILL

As stated earlier, catching is a complicated skill. Its proper execution is dependent on the throw (e.g., hard or soft, left or right, near or far) as well as its level (e.g., above the waist or below the waist.) To improve skill development, throws used in the activities should be catchable. If necessary, have the students begin by catching balls they have thrown against a wall. In addition, balls should be soft and easily catchable. As always, reinforce the individual critical elements when performing the entire skill.

INDIVIDUAL ACTIVITIES

PARTY TIME

Objective

To provide all students with the opportunity to practice catching by themselves.

Equipment

Nine-inch (23 cm) balloon or small beach ball for each student.

Activity

1. Create different movement challenges for the students to try with the balloon or ball. All catches should be made using the fingers and thumbs of both hands. Emphasize the critical elements of catching while the students are performing these activities.

2. Challenges can include the following:
   - Catch the balloon at a high (middle, low) level.
   - Throw the balloon forward and run under it to catch it.
   - Toss or hit the balloon to a high level and clap (spin, sit then stand up, hit the bottom of the foot with the hand, twiddle the thumbs, slap the knees) before catching it.
   - Bounce the balloon off a body part and catch it.
   - Student-generated challenges can also be used to practice catching.

Extensions

- Try these challenges using a beach ball, soft rubber ball, rubber chicken, or water balloon (if outside).
- Have students count the number of correct catches they make in a set number of throws or in a specified amount of time.
- Have students use playground balls and bounce them off the floor before catching them.
- Put a 6-inch (15 cm) ball inside a stocking. Have the students bounce the ball on the floor and catch it with two hands as it bounces up. They should try to catch the stocking instead of the ball.

HANGING AROUND

Objective

To practice catching a ball as it swings toward you.

Equipment

Rope, two game standards, old stockings or plastic grocery bags, and one 6-inch (15 cm) playground ball per student. Suspend a rope about 6 to 7 feet (1.8-2.1 m) off of the floor between two game standards. Attach to the rope the old stockings or grocery bags with the balls placed inside (see figure).

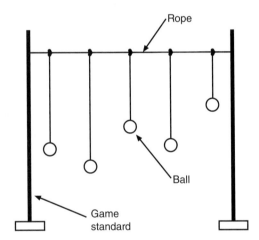

Setup for Hanging Around activity.

Activity

1. This activity can be done with an entire class or as a station with a smaller group of students.
2. Have the student push the ball away from her so it swings away but does not go over the top of the rope.
3. The student catches the ball as it swings back.
4. The ball can be suspended at shoulder or waist height. This can provide practice for both above-the-waist and below-the-waist catching.

Extensions

- Using the 6-inch (15 cm) balls inside the stockings, have the student bounce the suspended ball onto the floor and catch it as it bounces back. For this activity the ball must be suspended at waist level.
- Student pairs stand on opposite sides of the rope, swinging the ball back and forth to each other. See the Swing Catch activity later in the chapter.

PARTNER ACTIVITIES

CHALLENGES

Objective

To practice catching in a variety of situations.

Equipment

One foam ball, soft rubber ball, or playground ball per pair of students and laminated challenge cards.

Activity

1. Each student draws a challenge card.
2. Students perform the tasks described on the cards.
3. Possible challenges could include the following:
   - Bounce the ball to your partner so he can catch it.
   - Throw the ball up in the air for your partner to catch.
   - Toss or bounce the ball to one side of your partner so she must move before catching the ball.
   - Throw the ball to your partner at different levels.

Extensions

- Pairs track the number of correct catches and you keep a total for the class. In a follow-up lesson, challenge the class to increase the total number of correct catches.
- Place multicolored targets on a wall or in the play area. One student throws a ball at the target chosen by her partner. The ball must hit the target and then bounce on the floor to be caught.
- Set up game poles or volleyball standards and tie a rope between them. Suspend hula hoops from the rope and challenge the students to throw balls through the hoops and have their partners catch them on the other side. Every time the ball is caught, the partners earn one point.

SWING CATCH

Objective

To practice catching a ball as it swings toward you.

Equipment

Suspend two ropes between three volleyball standards to create a longer playing area and one stocking with a tennis ball inside per pair of students.

Activity

1. Tie the stocking with the tennis ball inside to a rope.
2. Partners stand on opposite sides of a rope.
3. One partner pushes the ball away so that it swings toward the catcher but does not go over the top of the rope.
4. The other partner catches the ball.
5. The activity continues with partners alternating pushing and catching the ball.

Extensions

- Release the ball using differing amounts of force.
- Use different-sized balls in the stockings.
- Pairs keep track of their number of correct catches and you keep a total for the class. In a follow-up lesson, challenge the class to increase the total number of correct catches.

SURPRISE CATCH

Objective

To practice catching the ball at a variety of levels.

Equipment

Game standards, volleyball net, one soft rubber ball or softball-sized yarn ball for each set of partners.

Activity

1. Set up the volleyball net with the top of the net approximately 6 feet (1.8 m) off the floor.
2. Have one partner throw the ball over or under the net to the other. (Some nets have very large spaces between the net threads. If this is the case, children may be challenged to throw through the nets.)
3. The partner on the other side of the net must try to catch the ball using the correct form (above-the-waist or below-the-waist catch). Then, this partner throws the ball back for the other student to catch.
4. Have the partners keep track of their number of correct catches.

Extensions

- To increase the challenge, students will make a low net with two 28-inch (71 cm) or larger cones and a rope. Tape the rope across the top of the cones (use duct tape) and spread the cones apart. Students toss the ball either over or under the net to their partners. The partners must try to catch the ball using the correct form.
- Place sheets (or a parachute) over a volleyball net so partners cannot see the toss coming over or under the net. Partners must tell each other before they throw the ball. (Yarn balls or foam balls must be used.)
- Stand a folding mat (4 to 6 feet [1.2-1.8 m] wide) on its side to create a wall. Have the partners toss the ball over the mat.
- Partners keep track of their number of correct catches and you keep a total for the class. In a follow-up lesson, challenge the class to increase the total number of correct catches.

PARTNER PASS

Objective

To improve catching skills while working with a partner.

Equipment

Two playground balls per pair of students.

Activity

1. Partners pass a ball back and forth using a chest pass (see chapter 6).
2. After they can perform the chest pass, the students begin using a bounce pass to send the ball back and forth.

3. After the students are able to both bounce pass and chest pass, each student selects the type of pass he will perform. Player A can use *only* the chest pass, while player B can use only the bounce pass.

4. On the start signal (a three-part signal is best, such as ready, set, go), player A chest passes the ball to player B at the same time that player B bounce passes the ball to player A.

5. Repeat this several times, using the start signal each time the passes are attempted.

Extensions

- Have the partners exchange passes so that the bounce passer now practices the chest pass and vice versa.
- Have the students try the activity without using any verbal communication.
- Give the students balls of different sizes to pass to each other.

THREE-BALL JUGGLE

Objective

To control three balls bouncing alternately between partners.

Equipment

Three playground balls per pair of students.

Activity

1. Students work in pairs.

2. Player A starts with two playground balls (ball 1 and ball 3). Player B starts with one playground ball (ball 2).

3. Player A starts the juggle by using one bounce to get ball 1 to player B. Player B must use one bounce to get ball 2 to player A before catching ball 1. Player A must have bounced ball 3 to player B before catching ball 2. Refer to figure.

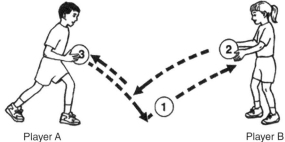

Player A   Player B

4. Once the juggle has started, each partner will have only one ball at a time in her hands (see figure).

Extensions

- Once the partners have mastered the three-ball juggle, have them try the juggle with four or five playground balls.
- Have partners try playing with three or more balls of different sizes.

WALL BALL

Objective

To improve catching and throwing skills while working with a partner.

Equipment

One ball (playground ball or volleyball) per student pair.

Activity

1. Partners stand at least 15 feet (4.5 m) from the wall.

2. One partner throws the ball against the wall at least 10 feet (3 m) high.

3. The other partner has to catch the ball after it comes off the wall but before it hits the ground.

4. When the partner has caught the ball, he must throw the ball back to the wall from the place where it was caught.

5. Partners count how many catches they have in a row.

Extensions

- Allow the ball to bounce once before it is caught.
- Place a target on the wall and challenge the partners to hit it.

GROUP ACTIVITIES

VOLCANO

Objective

To catch balls before they hit the ground.

Equipment

Four folding mats and one yarn or foam ball per student.

Activity

1. Place the folding mats on their sides in the middle of the gymnasium to form the volcano (circle).

2. Place four students inside the volcano.

3. Place the other students outside the volcano (see figure).

4. On the signal, all outside students throw their lava rocks (balls) into the volcano.

5. The students inside the volcano throw the lava rocks out.

6. The students on the outside of the volcano count how many lava rocks they catch with their hands.

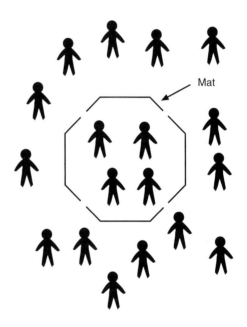

Setup for Volcano activity.

Extensions

- Use balloons or beach balls for the lava rocks.
- Designate a special ball. When a student catches the special ball, she switches places with a player inside the volcano (this is done on a rotating basis).

Based on Nichols 1994.

CYCLE/RECYCLE

Objective

To catch a thrown ball before it hits the floor.

Equipment

Two volleyball standards, one volleyball net, and one yarn ball per student.

Activity

1. Divide the class in half.

2. Place the groups on either side of the net.

3. On the start signal, everyone throws their yarn balls over the net.

4. Students must catch the balls with their hands only.

5. Students count the number of balls they catch.

Extensions

- Students can throw their balls through or under the net instead of over it.
- Every time a student catches a ball with hands only, that student and the student who threw the ball switch sides.
- Every time a student catches a ball with hands only, that student goes around the standards and becomes a member of the other group.

Adapted, by permission, from J.A. Wessel, PhD, 1974, *Project I CAN* (Northbrook, IL: Hubbard).

CATCHBALL

Objective

To catch the ball at a variety of levels.

Equipment

Sixteen 6-inch (15 cm) foam balls (10 are needed for the activity and 6 are required in the practice area) and 6 Frisbees.

Activity

1. Divide the class into two groups and place one group on each side of the play area.

2. Give each group five balls to start the activity.

3. On the signal, players begin to throw or bounce the balls to the other group.

4. Students are expected to catch the balls using only their hands.

5. If a ball is dropped or not caught with the hands, the catcher must go to the practice area.

Practice Area

1. Each group has three balls nearby to create a practice area. Spread the balls apart and place each ball in a Frisbee so it will not roll.

2. To practice, the student picks up a ball, throws it against a wall, and catches it on the rebound.

3. The ball must be caught three consecutive times with the hands only before the student may return to the activity.

Extensions

- While students are playing, observe their skill performance. Instruct any student having trouble catching correctly to go to the practice area and work with you. This practice area is a common area for both groups.
- Any student who has not caught a ball within a 30-second time period must go to the practice area for a predetermined time.

I GOT IT

Objective

To catch a thrown ball in an effort to get all players on the same side of the playing area.

Equipment

Two or more foam balls (8 inches [20 cm] in diameter) (the number of balls used will vary based on the skill level of the students), a net or rope stretched between two game standards 4 to 6 feet (1.2-1.8 m) from the floor, and tape or cones to mark a back line 20 to 30 feet (~6-9 m) from the rope or net.

Activity

1. Divide the class into two groups and place each group on an opposite side of the play area.
2. Give each group an equal number of balls to begin the activity.
3. On the start signal, players with the ball throw them over the net and within the playing area.
4. A player must change sides if he throws a ball out of bounds or if his ball is caught by an opposing player.
5. Restart the activity when all players are on the same side.

Extensions

- While the students are playing, ensure that catching is being performed correctly. Instruct any student having difficulty to go to a practice area and work with a partner or designated teacher assistant.
- Designate a special ball. If the special ball is caught, the thrower and a second student selected by the teacher move to the other side.

STAR PASS

Objective

To improve catching proficiency while working in a group.

Equipment

One fewer ball than the number of students in each group.

Activity

1. Students form a circle of five or more members with one student holding a playground ball.
2. The player with the ball must toss it to another player who is not standing beside her while saying that player's name.
3. The player receiving the ball must toss it to another player who is not standing beside him while saying that player's name.
4. This rotation continues until the ball gets back to the first player who tossed the ball.
5. Once the rotation is completed twice, the first player adds another ball. The passer does not pass ball until he says the receiver's name and the receiver is looking at the passer.
6. After two more completed rotations with two balls, first player adds another ball. This continues until the number of balls equals one fewer than the number of players.

Based on Fluegelman 1981.

TRIANGLE PASS

Objective

To improve catching proficiency while working in a group.

Equipment

Two playground balls per group of three students.

Activity

1. Students form a triangle, and players A and B hold the playground balls.
2. Player A bounce passes to player B as player B bounce passes to player C.
3. Students continue the passing rotation.

Extensions

- Students may use a chest pass instead of a bounce pass.
- It is possible to use two overlapping triangles. Players within each triangle should work only with their group. Group 1 players bounce pass the balls only to other members of group 1. Group 2 players chest pass the balls only to members of group 2 (see figure).

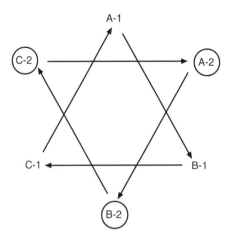

Setup for overlapping triangles extension.

CREATE YOUR OWN ACTIVITY

Objective

To allow students to create their own catching activities.

Equipment

One piece of paper and pencil per group and a predetermined list of equipment you will allow the students to use in their activities (e.g., cones, jump ropes, foam balls, beach balls, yarn balls, softballs, tennis balls).

Activity

1. Form groups of two to five students. You may select the groups, or the students may form their own.
2. Each group creates an activity using catching as the basic skill. Students are required to have rules that promote correct performance of the skill, include all players, and address all safety concerns.
3. The groups write their individual names, the rules of the activity, and the equipment needed on their papers, and then they show their activities to you.
4. After you approve their activities, the groups retrieve the necessary equipment and begin playing.
5. You must approve all changes to the activities.

Extensions

- Groups may teach their activities to other groups.
- Groups may teach their activities to the entire class.

Catching Troubleshooting Chart

If you see this	Then try this
1. Eyes not on the target	• Have the student's partner hold a ball and move it through a variety of levels (depending on the type of catch you are working on) at different speeds. The student tracks the ball with her eyes. • The student hits a balloon up with her hands and tracks the movement of the balloon with her eyes.
2. Hands not in the catching position	• The throwing partner holds a ball and moves it to different levels, depending on the type of catch you are working on. The catching partner must move his hands in response to the ball position. (The ball is not thrown.) • The throwing partner tosses a balloon or beach ball at a variety of levels. Watch for hand positions.
3. Body not in line with the oncoming object	• The partner tosses a balloon, beach ball, or foam ball into the air toward his partner. The receiving partner allows the object to hit his chest. Hands are out to the sides—no catching. • The receiver moves in the direction the partner points.
4. Student not extending arms toward the ball	• Partners stand about arm's-length apart. The throwing partner extends her arms and holds the ball out. The receiving partner steps and extends her arms to take the ball. • Use a balloon or beach ball to provide more time for the receiver to reach out and catch the object.
5. Student not giving with the ball	• Elephant catch—As the receiving partner catches the ball, she pretends the ball is heavy like an elephant and she absorbs the force. • Suspend a ball from the basketball goal. (A tether ball works well for this.) Students work with partners. Partners alternate pushing and catching the ball.
6. Student trapping the ball against the body	• Skunk ball—The student tosses the ball to his partner. If the ball hits the arms or chest as it is caught, the catcher has been sprayed by a skunk and becomes a stinker. Ask the class if there are any stinkers. • Detective—Have the receiving student put baby powder on his hands before catching the ball. The receiving partner tries to catch the ball so he leaves only his fingerprints on the ball.
7. Student turns head as the ball approaches	• To build confidence, begin with a balloon, progress to a beach ball, and then move on to a soft-textured ball. • Have the partner bounce the ball to the student. As he improves his catching, have the partner underhand toss the ball and, finally, throw the ball overhand with light force.

SUMMARY

The skill of catching is essential for most games and sports. Catching cannot occur without a thrown object, which is why catching should be taught simultaneously with throwing. Since these skills are so essential to games and sports, they should be introduced in kindergarten, incorporated into the activities you teach, and reviewed often. With proper instruction and appropriate equipment, children can master throwing and catching by the fourth grade.

The catching skills learned in this chapter will greatly assist your students with the skill addressed in the next chapter, passing. Again, proper instruction, appropriate use of force when passing, and safe equipment will enhance student learning of these important skills.

CATCHING LESSON PLAN

(FIRST LESSON)

AGE GROUP: First grade.

FOCUS: Catching a self-tossed object.

SUBFOCUS: Reaching forward to catch the ball.

OBJECTIVES: To step and reach forward to catch a balloon (and later a playground ball) on four out of five attempts (**cue:** *reach*) and to catch a balloon (and later a playground ball) with fingers and thumbs only on four out of five attempts (**cue:** *use your fingers*).

MATERIALS AND EQUIPMENT: One balloon, one playground ball, and one beanbag for each child and music.

ORGANIZATION AND MANAGEMENT: Students are in self-space for warm-up, instruction, and practice. Review movement concepts during warm-up.

WARM-UP:

Today we're going to warm up with music again. When the music starts, I would like you to move in general space. When the music stops, you will freeze in your self-space. What are some of the safety ideas we need to remember when moving in general space? (**Watch where you're going. Keep space between each person.**) (Begin music.)

Watch for students moving safely.

Stop the music and remind the children about moving safely. Restart the music and add variations to the movement.

Can you walk at a high level? A middle level? A low level? Can you move in a zigzag pathway? A curvy pathway? A straight pathway? Can you move with strong force? Light force? Can you find a way to move sideways? Backward? Can you move at a slow speed? A fast speed? Can you move at a low level and a low speed?

Observe children for problem areas with each of the movement concepts and provide instruction and corrections as needed.

FORMATION: Students find their self-space in the gymnasium and sit and face you.

INTRODUCTION:

Today we are going to work on catching. To catch properly, we need to really reach to catch the ball. Stand up in your self-space. Show me how you reach forward. Now reach high. Reach to one side. Reach to the other side. Pretend you are reaching to catch a butterfly (or a firefly). Notice that you are stepping when you catch and you are reaching your arms out. This is very important if you want to be a good catcher.

I will give each of you a balloon. You will sit in your space with the balloon in your lap and your hands on your knees as I finish passing out the balloons. When I say go, I would like you to stand up in your self-space, hit the balloon into the air, and catch it. Remember to keep your self-space. Go.

Focus on students staying in their own self-space.

Freeze. Please sit down and place your balloon in your lap and your hands on your knees. When you were catching your balloon, did you have to reach to catch it? (**Yes.**) *This time, just before you catch your balloon, I want you to say the word* reach. *Go.*

Watch students reaching (and saying *reach*) as they catch. Be sure to also monitor proper use of self-space.

Freeze. Please sit down and place the balloon in your lap and your hands on your knees. I watched each of you very carefully when you were catching. I saw all of you reaching. That's terrific. What part of your body did you use to catch the balloon? (Students usually respond with **hands.**) *Not just your hands. You really catch with . . .* (**your fingers**). *Excellent. When we use our fingers and thumbs to catch, we have 10 chances to catch or 10 fingers working to help us catch. It is much better to use your* *fingers and thumbs than just your arms. When you use only your arms, you have only two chances to catch; 10 chances are much better.*

This time, when I say go, I'd like you to hit the balloon into the air and say the word reach *as you reach and the word* fingers *when you catch the balloon. Raise your hand if you think you can do that. Great. Go.*
Watch students reaching (and saying *reach*) and using fingers (and saying *fingers*) as they catch. Be sure to also monitor proper use of personal space.

Freeze. Please sit down and place the balloon in your lap and your hands on your knees. You did a wonderful job keeping your self-space, reaching for the balloon, and using just your fingers to catch. Balloons are pretty easy to catch. Why? **(They move slowly.)** *That's right. Raise your hand if you are ready to try something a little harder. I knew you were.*

Students return balloons to the storage bin. Each student selects a playground ball. When this is accomplished, each child finds self-space on the floor.

When we catch balls, we use the same skills we used when catching balloons. What were the two things we concentrated on with the balloons? **(Reaching and using our fingers.)** *That's right. When I say go, I would like you to stand up in your self-space, drop the ball, and catch it.* (Demonstrate several times.) *Make sure you reach and use your fingers. It might help if you say those words out loud. Go.*
Observe students for reaching and using fingers.

Freeze. Stand where you are and place the ball between your feet. This time, when I walk around the gymnasium, I will be looking for good reachers and good finger users. If you are reaching and using your fingers, I will let you go to the wall and bounce your ball against the wall. This will give you a little different way to catch. Be careful to use those 10 fingers to catch and not your arms. Go.

Invite students who are performing the skill correctly to bounce the ball against the wall. Again, monitor students closely to make sure they are not catching the balls in their outstretched arms but are actually using their fingers and thumbs.

After several minutes of successful practice, children exchange playground balls for beanbags. Each student finds his self-space and balances the beanbag on his head.

This time we will combine tossing with catching. When I say go, I would like you to toss the beanbag at a middle level (demonstrate this) *and catch it by reaching and using your fingers. If I see you tossing at a middle level, reaching, and using your fingers, I may ask you to try tossing at a high level. But right now, everyone will toss at a middle level. If you understand, clap once. Go.*

Observe students for proper tossing, reaching, and use of fingers to catch the beanbags. Invite students who are performing well to try tossing the beanbags at a higher level. At the end of practice, children return beanbags to the storage bin and line up for their teacher.

CLOSURE: Students are lined up to leave.

Girls and boys, who can tell me some things I must remember when catching? **(Reach and use your fingers.)** *Good.*

Watch me catch using just my arms (demonstrate). *What's wrong with that? That's right, I have only two chances to catch rather than 10. Excellent! You did very well, and we will continue catching next time.*

6

Passing

A variety of sports require accurate passing for successful play. These sports include football, water polo, and team handball (which use one-hand passing), and basketball and soccer (which use two-hand overhead passing).

In this chapter, we focus on bounce passing and chest passing, which are used in basketball. While these are distinct skills, they are very similar. The unique features of each of these skills are addressed in individual descriptions, critical elements, cues, several specific activities, partner skill check sheets, and success builder activities.

All of the culminating activities, however, are easily adapted for either chest passing or bounce passing. Moreover, all of the activities described in this chapter pertain to passing in general, but specific adaptations are included if needed.

BOUNCE PASSING

Although we often think bounce passing is strictly used in basketball, variations of this skill are found on any playground. Children quickly grasp the concept of bouncing a ball to a partner, but they often push the ball *down* rather than *away*. Connecting the movement concepts of near and far with the bounce pass will help children master it. Although *National Standards & Grade-Level Outcomes for K-12 Physical Education* (SHAPE America, 2014) does not address this skill specifically, it has been our experience that children should be able to perform bounce passing by the second grade. Therefore, instruction in this manipulative skill should begin in the primary grades.

Critical Elements

Ready Position	**Step and Push**	**Follow Through**
Facing target, feet shoulder-width apart, knees bent, eyes on target, ball held with thumbs together on the back of the ball and fingers on the sides of the ball. Hold the ball close to the body at chest level.	Step forward with one foot while extending the arms forward and downward, and release the ball so that it bounces closer to the target than to the passer.	After the ball is released, hands are turned so that palms are facing away from each other with the thumbs pointing downward. The wrist snaps with this action.

Cue Words

The cue words you select for each phase of the skill will depend on the age of the students you are teaching and your areas of emphasis. In usable sets are some of the cue words we use to teach bounce passing. You may use each set individually or mix and match the cue words as needed. We have found that it is beneficial to have the students say the cue words out loud as they practice the skill.

Ready—facing target, feet shoulder-width apart, knees bent, eyes on target, ball held with thumbs together on the back of the ball and fingers on the sides of the ball. Hold the ball close to the body at chest level.

Step and push—step forward with one foot while extending the arms and release the ball toward the target.

Push—hold the ball near the body at chest level with the thumbs together on the back of the ball and fingers on the sides of the ball. Push the ball from the chest.

Follow-through and **thumbs down**—after the ball is released, hands are turned so that palms are facing away from each other with the thumbs pointing downward. The wrist snaps with this action.

Away—step forward with one foot while extending arms and release the ball toward the target. After the ball is released, hands are turned so that palms are facing away from each other with the thumbs pointing downward. The wrist snaps with this action.

> *Cue set 1:* ready, step and push, follow through
> *Cue set 2:* ready, step and push, thumbs down
> *Cue set 3:* push, away

SUGGESTED ACTIVITIES FOR REINFORCING AND ASSESSING THE CRITICAL ELEMENTS OF BOUNCE PASSING

In the learning process, it is essential that students know how a skill looks, what its critical elements are, and how to perform each individual element correctly. The preceding section has pictures and descriptions of bounce passing, divided it into its critical elements, with possible cue words. Chapter 1 contains generic activities that will reinforce these concepts for bounce passing as well as for all locomotor and manipulative skills. In addition to the material in chapter 1, the following section provides specific activities for reinforcing the critical elements unique to bounce passing.

PARTNER SKILL CHECK

Objective
To allow partners to assess each other's progress learning the skill.

Equipment
Partner skill check assessments and one ball for each set of partners. If the students cannot read or do not speak English, the picture version of the partner skill check assessment may be useful.

Activity
1. One partner observes the other to see if she has the correct form for the ready position.
2. If the ready position is correct, then the partner places a *Y* in the first box. If the ready position is incorrect, he places an *N* in the first box. Nonreaders can put a smiling face if the ready position is correct or a frowning face if the ready position is incorrect.
3. This evaluation continues until each of the critical elements has been assessed five times.
4. A partner skill check assessment is used for each student.

Extensions
- Use the partner skill check assessment to measure the skill development of each student.
- Send partner skill check assessments home with report cards or as individual skills develop.

Skill: Bounce Passing

Passer's name: _____ Watcher's name: _____

❶ Ready

1 2 3 4 5

❷ Step and push

1 2 3 4 5

❸ Thumbs down

1 2 3

PARTNER SKILL CHECK

Skill: Bounce Passing

Passer's name: _____ Watcher's name: _____

Watch your partner and mark each critical element of the skill. Let your partner do the skill five times. Each time your partner does it right, mark a Y in the box. If your partner doesn't do it right, mark an N in the box.

START	TRIALS

Ready Position
1. Eyes facing target.
2. Knees bent.
3. Feet shoulder-width apart.
4. Object held in front of body.

□ □ □ □ □
1 2 3 4 5

ACTION

Step and Push
1. Step forward with one foot.
2. Belt buckle faces target.
3. Arms extended.
4. Push the ball out and downward.

□ □ □ □ □
1 2 3 4 5

STOP

Follow Through
1. Thumbs point down.

□ □ □ □ □
1 2 3 4 5

SUCCESS BUILDERS

The success builder activities allow you to address individual needs. If students need additional help on specific critical elements, the activities listed here will help reinforce correct performance.

Objective

To improve areas of deficiency as measured by the partner skill assessment.

Equipment

See the following individual stations. We suggest using an unbreakable mirror and a poster of each critical element of bounce passing at each station. The mirror is particularly helpful with these activities because it allows children to see what they are doing. The easiest way to make the posters is to print out the drawings from this book and enlarge them. Laminating the posters will ensure their use for many years.

Activity

1. Set up a station for each of the three critical elements in the teaching area. Post a description or a picture of the specific element at the corresponding station.

2. The details for each station follow:

READY

Facing target, feet shoulder-width apart, knees bent, eyes on target, ball held with thumbs together on the back of the ball and fingers on the sides of the ball. Hold the ball at chest level.

Equipment

Poster of the ready position, mirror (if available), and partner evaluations.

Activity

The student assumes the ready position. The partner checks to see if her position matches the poster. The student refers to the mirror for help. The student then walks around and, on a signal from her partner, assumes the ready position again. Once the student can demonstrate proper position for holding the ball (with thumbs behind the ball and at chest level), the partners may return to practicing the entire skill.

STEP AND PUSH

Step forward with one foot while extending arms forward and downward and release the ball so that it bounces closer to the target than to the passer.

Equipment

Mirror, poster, tape (floor or painter's) or circle target on the floor, partner evaluations, and rope suspended between two chairs.

Activity 1

The student demonstrates a step forward and pushes toward a target on the floor. The student should push his arms and hands toward the marked target. The partner checks to see if his position matches the poster. The student refers to the mirror for help. Once the student can demonstrate to the partner a good step and push, the partners may return to practicing the entire skill.

Activity 2

The student attempts to bounce pass the ball to her partner by passing it under the rope.

Activity 3

The student attempts to see how far apart he can stand from his partner and still bounce pass the ball under the rope and have his partner catch it before it bounces more than once.

FOLLOW THROUGH

After ball is released, hands are turned so that palms are facing away from each other with the thumbs pointing downward. The wrist snaps with this action.

Equipment

Mirror, poster of the follow-through, projector (or some means of shining light onto the student), and partner evaluations.

Activity

The student demonstrates the follow-through in front of the mirror or light. The partner looks for the wrist snap as the student demonstrates this critical element. The partner checks to see if her position matches the poster. The student refers to the mirror for help. Once the student can demonstrate to the partner a good follow-through, the partners may return to practicing the entire skill.

SUGGESTED CULMINATING ACTIVITIES TO REINFORCE THE ENTIRE BOUNCE PASSING SKILL

Students should master the skill's critical elements before you emphasize accuracy. When accuracy becomes the emphasis too early, the critical elements of the skill disappear as the children begin to aim at their targets. Targets should be large enough to allow students to perform the critical elements of the skill and have success hitting the target.

PARTNER ACTIVITIES

NOT ON MY SIDE

Objective

To develop the bounce passing skill while trying to push an object across a partner's line.

Equipment

One ball (playground ball or lightweight rubber ball), one dome cone or other object that will slide when hit with a ball, and two restraining lines (court markings or painter's tape spaced approximately 3 feet [1 m] apart) between the two partners.

Activity

1. Partners stand behind the restraining lines and face each other, with the dome cone placed between the two lines.
2. Each partner performs a bounce pass and tries to hit the dome cone and push it across the line onto the partner's side. The object may be moved only with a bounce pass.
3. If one of the partners uses any other pass to move the dome cone, the cone is returned to the starting position and the activity is restarted.
4. The activity continues until the dome cone has been pushed completely across the restraining line. Then, restart the game.

Extensions

- Use empty cereal boxes, paper plates, flat playground balls, hula hoops, or other objects instead of dome cones.
- Increase the challenge by using a hula hoop and requiring that the student specify where on the hoop the ball should hit (e.g., outside edge of the hoop, inside edge of the hoop).

THREE-BALL JUGGLE

Objective

To control three balls bouncing alternately between partners.

Equipment

Three playground balls per pair of students.

Activity

1. Students work in pairs.

2. Player A starts with two playground balls (ball 1 and ball 3). Player B starts with one playground ball (ball 2).

3. Player A starts the juggle by using one bounce to get ball 1 to player B. Player B must use one bounce to get ball 2 to player A before catching ball 1. Player A must have bounced ball 3 to player B before catching ball 2 (see figure).

4. Once the juggle has been started, each partner will have only one ball at a time in his hands (see figure).

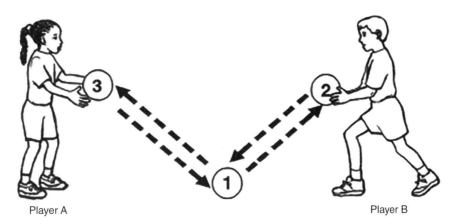

Player A   Player B

Setup for Three-Ball Juggle activity.

Extensions

- Once the partners have mastered the three-ball juggle, have them try the juggle with four or five playground balls.

- Have partners try playing with three or more balls of different sizes.

GROUP ACTIVITIES

IT'S YOURS, NOT MINE!

Objective

To use bounce passing to push all objects onto the opponent's side.

Equipment

Eight to 10 playground balls or light rubber balls and 12 to 15 objects (e.g., hoops, dome cones, empty boxes) that can slide on the floor when hit by a ball.

Activity

1. Set up a play area with a center line and two restraining lines that are approximately 8 feet (2.4 m) away from the center line.

2. Divide the class into two equal groups and place the groups behind the restraining lines, facing each other.

3. Set up the target objects along the center dividing line (see figure).

4. Give each group four or five balls.

5. On the start signal, the students bounce pass the balls and try to hit the targets in the middle of the play area. The students may not cross the restraining line when they bounce pass the ball.

6. Players try to hit the targets and slide them past the opposing group's restraining line.

7. Restart the activity when all of the targets have been pushed into one group's play area.

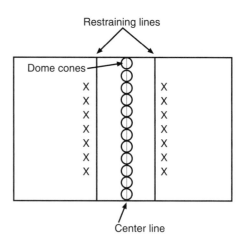

Setup for the It's Yours, Not Mine! activity.

Extension

Set a time limit for the activity and count the number of targets that are hit and moved during the specified time.

KERPLUNK

Objective

To use bounce passing to get a ball into the target area behind the opposing group.

Equipment

Two or more soft rubber balls (8 inches [20 cm] in diameter). The number of balls used will vary based on the skill level and number of students. You will also need tape or cones to mark off a large target area 15 to 20 feet (4.5-6 m) from the center of the playing area. Use a dry-erase board or paper to record the points.

Activity

1. Divide the class into two groups, and place groups on opposite sides of the playing area.

2. Provide each group with an equal number of balls to start the activity.

3. On the start signal, players use bounce passing to get the ball into the opposing group's target area.

4. If a player kerplunks the ball into the opposing group's target area, one point is awarded to her group.

5. Players are allowed to catch the ball to prevent it from hitting the target area.

6. Restart the game after one group reaches 10 points.

Extensions

- While the students are playing, ensure that bounce passing is being performed correctly. Instruct any student having trouble passing correctly to go to the practice area and work with a partner or a designated teacher assistant.

- Designate one ball to be worth more points. If that special ball is kerplunked into the target area, two points are awarded.

OMNIKIN BALL MADNESS

Objective

To perform bounce passing using a ball to move an object across the play area.

Equipment

The object may be an Omnikin ball or any ball larger than the balls being passed. The balls being passed may be playground balls, basketballs, or volleyballs when aiming at the Omnikin ball.

Activity

1. Divide the class into four groups. Each group stands along one side of a square play area. Students must stay behind their lines.
2. Place the Omnikin ball or a large ball in the center of the play area (see figure).
3. Each group begins the activity with two or more balls.
4. On the start signal, players pass their balls and try to hit the large ball in the center in an effort to move it toward the other group's line.
5. Players continue to pass their balls until the large ball crosses a group's line. Any ball (used for passing) that stays inside of the area enclosed by the four groups' lines is retrieved by the teacher.
6. Players may touch the large ball only with a passed ball; they may not touch it with their bodies.
7. Once the large ball crosses the designated line, the activity stops and the large ball is returned to the center of the play area.
8. Resume the activity when each group has the same number of balls to pass. Be sure every player is given a chance to start with a ball.

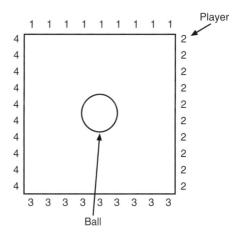

Setup for Omnikin Ball Madness activity.

Extensions

- Create two groups rather than four.
- Try to pass a variety of balls at the large ball in an effort to move the ball across another group's line. This may lead to discussions on which balls are better for the task (e.g., basketballs versus foam balls).
- Have groups change positions either before the next round or on a signal during the activity. If the students are to change places during the activity, be sure they understand that they may not pass a ball at the large ball until your signal and that they may not take a ball with them as they change.

PIN BALL

Objective
To use bounce passing to hit the opposing group's bowling pins.

Equipment
Three balls and three plastic bowling pins (indicated by A and B in the figure) for each group. Bowling pins need to be color coded for each group (e.g., use different-colored tape to mark the pins).

Activity

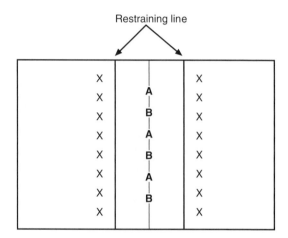

Restraining line

Setup for Pin Ball activity.

1. Set up the play area with a center line and two restraining lines that are approximately 8 feet (2.4 m) away from the center line.

2. Divide the class into two equal groups and place the groups behind the restraining lines, facing each other.

3. Set up the six pins along the center dividing line of the play area, alternating colors (see figure).

4. Give each group three balls.

5. On the start signal, the students bounce pass the balls and try to hit the opposing group's pins. The students may not cross the restraining line.

6. A pin does not stay down if the ball was passed from in front of the restraining line.

7. Restart the activity when all of a group's pins have been knocked down.

Extensions

- Use empty 2-liter bottles, lightweight cones, empty cereal boxes, or other objects as the targets.
- Suspend a rope between two volleyball standards. Hang lightweight targets (e.g., paper, scarves, streamers, crepe paper) from the rope and challenge the students to hit the opposing team's targets.

Adapted, by permission, from K. Thomas, A. Lee, and J. Thomas, 2000, *Physical education for children: Daily lesson plans for elementary school,* 2nd ed. (Champaign, IL: Human Kinetics), 546.

Additional activities to work on bounce passing can be found in the Suggested Culminating Activities to Reinforce Bounce Passing and Chest Passing Skills section later in the chapter.

Bounce Passing Troubleshooting Chart

If you see this	Then try this
1. Eyes not on the target	• Have the student pass to a target he has designed.
	• Have students pass to different-colored targets on the wall.
	• Place an empty 2-liter bottle on top of a tall cone and have the student try to knock it off.
	• Place aluminum pie plates on the wall for targets.
2. Incorrect hand position on the ball	• Draw the hand positions on the ball.
	• Have the student put her hands in baby powder and then place them on a ball.
	• Use commercially available balls that already have handprints on them.
3. Student not stepping when passing the ball	• Have the student step on a mat or a rug as she passes the ball.
	• Have the student stand near a line (a rope or tape on the floor can be used). She must step over the line while passing the ball.
	• Tape bubble wrap to the floor. Have a student step on that spot while passing to create a noise.
4. Arms not fully extended on the pass	• Have the student practice reaching out and grabbing an object placed an arm's length away from the body.
	• Place a suspended aluminum pie plate in front of the student and have him try to hit the pie plate as he pushes his hands out for the bounce pass.
5. Body not in proper alignment on the follow-through	• Tell the student to point her belt buckle at the target on the follow-through.
	• Have a partner watch to make sure the chest is even with (or past) the stepping foot on the follow-through.
6. Ball not bouncing in the proper spot (hitting the ground too close or too far away from the target)	• Place two targets (pieces of tape or hula hoops) on the floor between the partners for them to hit. They should aim for the target that is closer to their partner.
	• Have the partners pass the ball under a rope (or volleyball net).
	• Place a dome cone between two partners. Have each partner try to hit the dome and push it past his partner.

CHEST PASSING

Chest passing is usually considered to be specific to the game of basketball, but it appears in other sports as well, such as team handball and speedball. We suggest teaching chest passing after teaching bounce passing. The additional strength required for chest passing makes it more challenging for young children (since the ball must be pushed out, not down). In addition, because a bounce pass is easier to catch than a chest pass, it will be easier to practice.

Children should use balls that they can hold properly. A playground ball is the appropriate size for young children. If the ball is too large or too heavy, the children will get under the ball and throw it in an arc rather than throwing it straight.

Although *National Standards & Grade-Level Outcomes for K-12 Physical Education* (SHAPE America, 2014) does not address chest passing, we have found that students can usually master this skill in the third grade. It should be introduced when children have achieved a competent level in catching, and it should be introduced early in the primary curriculum if possible.

Critical Elements

Ready Position

Facing target, feet shoulder-width apart, knees bent, eyes on target, ball held with thumbs together on the back of the ball and fingers on the sides of the ball. Hold the ball close to the body at chest level.

Step and Push

Step forward with one foot while extending arms and release the ball toward the target.

Follow Through

After the ball is released, hands are turned so that palms are facing away from each other with the thumbs pointing downward. The wrist snaps with this action.

Cue Words

The cue words you select for each phase of the skill will depend on the age of the students you are teaching and your areas of emphasis. In usable sets are some of the cue words we use to teach chest passing. You may use each set individually or mix and match the cue words as needed. We have found that it is beneficial to have the students say the words out loud as they practice the skill.

Ready—facing target, feet shoulder-width apart, knees bent, eyes on target, ball held with thumbs together on the back of the ball and fingers on the sides of the ball. Hold the ball close to the body at chest level.

Push—hold the ball near the body at chest level with the thumbs together on the back of the ball and fingers on the sides of the ball. Push the ball from the chest.

Step and push—step forward with one foot while extending the arms and release the ball toward the target.

Follow through and **thumbs down or away**—after the ball is released, hands are turned so that palms are facing away from each other with the thumbs pointing downward. The wrist snaps with this action.

> *Cue set 1:* ready, step and push, follow through
> *Cue set 2:* ready, step and push, thumbs down
> *Cue set 3:* ready, away
> *Cue set 4:* push, away

SUGGESTED ACTIVITIES FOR REINFORCING AND ASSESSING THE CRITICAL ELEMENTS OF CHEST PASSING

In the learning process, it is essential that students know how a skill looks, what its critical elements are, and how to perform each element correctly. In the preceding section, we provided pictures and descriptions of chest passing, divided it into its critical elements, and provided possible cue words. Chapter 1 provided generic activities that will reinforce these concepts for chest passing as well as for all locomotor and manipulative skills. In addition to the material in chapter 1, the following section provides specific activities for reinforcing the critical elements unique to chest passing.

PARTNER SKILL CHECK

Objective
To allow partners to assess each other's progress in learning the skill.

Equipment
Partner skill check assessments and one ball for each set of partners. If the students cannot read or do not speak English, the picture version of the partner skill check assessment may be useful.

Activity
1. One partner observes the other to see if he has the correct form for the ready position.
2. If the ready position is correct, then the partner places a *Y* in the first box. If the ready position is incorrect, she places an *N* in the first box. Nonreaders can put a smiling face if the ready position is correct or a frowning face if the ready position is incorrect.
3. This evaluation continues until each of the critical elements has been assessed five times.
4. A partner skill check sheet is used for each student.

Extensions
- You can use the partner skill check assessment to measure the skill development of each student.
- You can send partner skill check assessments home with report cards or as individual skills develop.

First sheet

Skill: Chest Passing

Passer's name: _____

Watcher's name: _____

❶ Ready

1   2   3   4   5

❷ Step and push

1   2   3   4   5

❸ Thumbs down

1   2   3

Second sheet

PARTNER SKILL CHECK
Skill: Chest Passing

Passer's name: _____   Watcher's name: _____

Watch your partner and mark each critical element of the skill. Let your partner do the skill five times. Each time your partner does it right, mark a Y in the box. If your partner doesn't do it right, mark an N in the box.

START	TRIALS

Ready Position
1. Eyes facing target.
2. Knees bent.
3. Feet shoulder-width apart.
4. Object held in front of body.

1   2   3   4   5

ACTION

Step and Push
1. Step forward with one foot.
2. Belt buckle faces target.
3. Arms extended.
4. Push the ball out.

1   2   3   4   5

STOP

Follow Through
1. Thumbs point down.

1   2   3   4   5

SUCCESS BUILDERS

The success builder activities allow you to monitor student progress and address individual needs. If students need additional help on individual critical elements, the activities listed here will help reinforce correct performance.

Objective

To improve areas of deficiency as assessed by the partner skill check assessment.

Equipment

See the following individual stations. We suggest using an unbreakable mirror and a poster of each critical element of chest passing at each station. The mirror is particularly helpful in these activities because it allows the children to see what they are doing. The easiest way to make the posters is to print out the drawings from this book and enlarge them. Laminating the posters will ensure their use for many years.

Activity

1. Set up a station for each of the three critical elements in the teaching area. Post a description or a picture of the specific element at the corresponding station.
2. The details for each station follow:

READY

Knees bent, facing target, feet shoulder-width apart, eyes on target, ball held with thumbs together on the back of the ball and fingers on the sides of the ball. Hold the ball at chest level.

Equipment

Poster of the ready position, mirror (if available), and partner evaluations.

Activity

The student assumes the ready position. The partner checks to see if his position matches the poster. The student refers to the mirror for help. The student then walks around and, on a signal from his partner, assumes the ready position again. Once the student can demonstrate to the partner a good ready position, the partners may return to practicing the entire skill.

STEP AND PUSH

Step forward with one foot while extending the arms and release the ball toward the target.

Equipment

Mirror, poster of the step and push, tape (floor or painter's) or circle target on the floor, and partner evaluations

Activity 1

The student demonstrates a step forward and push toward a target on the wall. The student should push her arms and hands toward the marked target. The partner checks to see if her position matches the poster. The student refers to the mirror for help. Once the student can demonstrate to the partner a good step and push, the partners may return to practicing the entire skill.

Activity 2

Place several targets on the wall. The partner selects the target to be hit. The student steps and pushes the ball toward the appropriate target. Once the student can demonstrate to the partner a good step and push, the partners may return to practicing the entire skill.

FOLLOW THROUGH

After the ball is released, hands are turned so that palms are facing away from each other with the thumbs pointing downward. The wrist snaps with this action.

Equipment

Mirror, poster of the follow-through, projector (or some means of shining light onto the student to project his shadow or image onto a wall), and partner evaluations

Activity

The student demonstrates the follow-through in front of the mirror or light. The partner looks for the wrist snap as the student demonstrates this component. The partner checks to see if the student's position matches the poster. The student refers to the mirror for help. Once the student can demonstrate to the partner a good follow-through, the partners may return to practicing the entire skill.

SUGGESTED CULMINATING ACTIVITIES TO REINFORCE BOUNCE PASSING AND CHEST PASSING SKILLS

Students should master the skill's critical elements before you emphasize accuracy. When accuracy becomes the emphasis too early, the critical elements of the skill disappear as the children begin to aim at their targets. Targets should be large enough to allow students to perform the critical elements of the skill and have success hitting the target.

INDIVIDUAL ACTIVITIES

COLOR TARGETS

Objective

To improve passing accuracy by hitting a specific target.

Equipment

Construction paper of different colors (about 8 to 12 targets of each color) taped to the floor of the gymnasium or activity area and a ball (playground ball or foam ball) for each student.

Activity

1. Create a color box in which samples from each color of construction paper have been placed. You will need more samples than you have students.
2. Select a student to draw a sample color from the color box.
3. The sample color chosen is the color target all students must locate on the floor and try to hit with a bounce pass.
4. Students continue to pass toward the targets of the selected color until you give a stop signal.
5. The activity continues until all students have had an opportunity to draw from the color box.

Adaptation for chest passing: Targets should be placed on the wall instead of the floor. Proper distance from the wall will be dictated by student ability and safety.

Extensions

- Instead of using different colors, students could select different shapes from the shape box, letters from the alphabet box, or words from the word box.
- Students work with partners. The partner chooses the color, shape, letter, or word that will be used for a target. The passer must then try to hit the selected target. Partners take turns selecting targets and passing. Targets may be spread throughout the activity area, and the partner may catch the pass.

- Targets may be placed on the floor and wall so that the student has to stand at an appropriate distance and bounce pass the ball to the floor target and then to the wall target.

CREATE A WORD

Objective
To create words by hitting letters using bounce or chest passes.

Equipment
One ball (foam ball or playground ball) per student and four complete sets of letters scattered and taped to the wall of the gymnasium or activity area. It would be advantageous to have extra copies of vowels and selected consonants (e.g., N, R, S, T). You will also need paper and markers or a dry-erase board and markers to serve as a word bank.

Activity
1. On your start signal, students begin to spell words by hitting letters using a bounce or chest pass.
2. Once a student has created a word, she goes to the word bank (paper or dry-erase board) and writes the word. It will be helpful to have several word banks so students will not have to wait in line to write their words.
3. A word may be written only once on the paper or dry-erase board.
4. If a student hits a letter that cannot be used to form the word being created, she must hit the letter again to delete it.

Extensions
- Students work with partners. One student hits letters to spell a word while the other partner records the word and evaluates the student's passing. The passer may not use the letter unless the passing skill is properly performed. When the first partner has spelled a word, the other partner is then given a turn.
- Students work with partners. Partners are given paper and pencil to record the letters they hit and to write down the words they create. Each partner must pass and hit a vowel and two consonants until the pair has six letters to use to create words. The partners attempt to create six words using one or more of the letters they have hit. Once the partners have created six words and written them down, they attempt to spell the words by hitting the letters with the ball. Once a word is spelled, it may be checked off the list. If the students are unable to use a letter they have hit, they must hit that letter again to delete it and select another letter.

PARTNER ACTIVITIES

HOT POTATO

Objective
To improve chest passing accuracy while passing the ball through a hoop.

Equipment
One hula hoop suspended from either a basketball rim or a rope between two game standards and one ball for each set of partners.

Activity
1. Partners stand on opposite sides of the suspended hoop.
2. On your signal, the partners use chest passing to get the ball through the hoop.

3. Partners count the number of times the ball goes through the hoop during the time limit.

4. Students may only count the passes that go through the hoop and are performed correctly.

Extensions

- Try the activity without a time limit. This will remove the speed component and allow you to place extra emphasis on correct skill performance.
- Use two nets instead of suspended hoops. Place one at tennis height and the other at volleyball height and have students chest pass between the nets.

BACK IT UP

Objective

To develop passing skills while trying to increase the distance between partners.

Equipment

One ball (playground ball or lightweight rubber ball) for each set of partners.

Activity

1. Students face each other and pass the ball back and forth once.

2. If the ball is passed and caught without difficulty, the students take one step backward and chest pass the ball back and forth again.

3. After each successful pass and catch, the partners each take another step backward.

4. This continues until either the distance between the two cannot be covered or the skill is no longer being performed correctly. When this occurs, the partners return to the starting point and begin again.

Extensions

- Introduce the idea of measurement and have the partners place a cone (or other object) to show the farthest distance they were able to attain. They may use a tape measure to determine the exact distance. This measurement can be recorded and compared to class totals or later results, or it can be graphed and displayed on the bulletin board.
- If the ball is passed and caught without difficulty, the student who threw the ball takes one step backward. After each successful pass and catch, the partner who threw the ball takes a step backward. This continues until the distance between the two cannot be covered by one pass or until the pass is not caught. When this occurs, the two return to the starting point and begin again.

Based on Bryant and McLean Oliver 1975.

CHALLENGES

Objective

To practice passing in a variety of situations.

Equipment

One playground ball, light rubber ball, or basketball per pair of students and laminated challenge cards. Different types of challenges may require additional equipment.

Activity

1. Each student selects a challenge card.

2. Students perform the tasks described on the cards.

3. Possible challenges may include the following:

- Pass the ball using strong force (light force).
- Pass the ball toward your partner's chest.
- Pass the ball so that it hits the wall, it bounces once, and you or your partner is able to catch it.
- Pass the ball and hit a target (chest high) on the wall.
- Pass the ball through a hoop held chest high by your partner or through a suspended hoop.

Extensions

- Place multicolored targets, hoops, cones, or buckets in the play area or on the wall (chest high) and have the partner tell the passer which target to hit.
- Set up game poles or volleyball standards and tie a rope between them. Suspend different objects from the rope and challenge the students to hit them. Possible targets include hoops, aluminum pie pans, and empty 2-liter plastic bottles.
- To create more permanent targets, you may paint them on the wall of your gymnasium. Often, tumbling mats are attached to the walls for storage. If you paint these targets on the wall behind where tumbling mats are attached, you can cover them when they are not in use.
- Pairs keep track of their number of correct passes and you keep a total for the class. In a follow-up lesson, challenge the class to increase the total number of correct passes.

SLIDE AND PASS

Objective

To improve passing accuracy while moving.

Equipment

One ball (playground ball, volleyball, or basketball) per pair of students.

Activity

1. Student partners face each other and pass the ball back and forth.
2. After the second pass, each partner slides once (in the same direction), stops, and passes again.
3. This activity is repeated across the entire length of the gymnasium.

Extensions

- Students pass and slide without stopping.
- Students face each other, dribble the ball twice, and then pass to their partners. After the second pass, each partner slides once (in the same direction), stops, dribbles, and passes again. This activity is repeated for the entire length of the gymnasium.

NET PASS

Objective

To improve passing accuracy by passing a ball through a target.

Equipment

Three volleyball standards, two volleyball nets, one hula hoop per pair, rope and string, and one playground ball for each pair. The nets should be placed at the regular volleyball height. Tie the hoops to the bottom of the nets.

Activity

1. Partners stand on opposite sides of the hoop.
2. Partners must pass the ball to each other so it goes through the hoop.
3. Partners must let the ball bounce before catching it.
4. Students count the number of balls they were able to pass through the hoops.

Extensions

- Students total the number of passes the entire group made. These results can be recorded and later charted or graphed.
- Each time a student passes the ball through the hoop, she takes one step back. This continues until the student can no longer pass the ball through the hoop. The student then starts over.

GROUP ACTIVITIES

CYCLE/RECYCLE

Objective

To practice passing accuracy in a movement setting.

Equipment

Two volleyball standards, one volleyball net, and one playground ball per student. The net should be placed at regular volleyball height.

Activity

1. Divide the class in half.
2. Place the groups on either side of the net.
3. On the start signal, everyone uses a bounce pass to pass the ball under the net.
4. Students count the number of balls they were able to pass under the net.

Adaptation for chest passing: Place a second net between the standards at tennis height. Students chest pass the ball between the two nets.

Extensions

- Students total the number of passes the entire group made. These results can be recorded and later charted or graphed to show class improvement.
- Each time a student passes the ball under (or between) the net(s), he goes around the standards and becomes a member of the other group.

Adapted, by permission, from J.A. Wessel, PhD, 1974, *Project I CAN* (Northbrook, IL: Hubbard).

CREATE YOUR OWN ACTIVITY

Objective

To allow students to create their own activities to reinforce passing skills.

Equipment

One piece of paper and pencil per group and a predetermined list of equipment you will allow the students to use in their activities (e.g., bowling pins, cones, ropes, playground balls, light rubber balls).

Activity

1. Form groups of two to five students. You may select the groups, or the students may form their own.

2. Each group creates an activity using passing (either bounce or chest) as the basic skill. Students are required to have rules that encourage correct performance of the skill, include all players, and address all safety concerns.

3. The groups write their individual names, the rules of the activity, and the equipment needed on their papers, and then they show their activities to you.

4. After you approve their activities, the groups retrieve the necessary equipment and begin playing.

5. You must approve all changes to the activities.

Extensions

- Groups may teach their activities to other groups.
- Groups may teach their activities to the entire class.

TRIANGLE PASS

Objective

To improve passing proficiency while working with a group.

Equipment

Two playground balls per group of three students.

Activity

1. Students form a triangle. Players A and B each have a playground ball.

2. Player A bounce passes her ball to player B as he bounce passes his ball to player C.

3. When this is accomplished, player B bounce passes the ball to player C as soon as player C has passed her ball to player A.

Extensions

- Chest passing may be used.
- It is possible to employ two overlapping triangles. Players within each triangle should work only with their group. Group 1 players bounce pass the balls only to other members of their group. Group 2 players chest pass the balls only to members of that group (see figure).

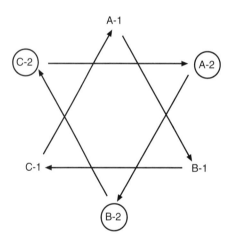

Setup for the second extension.

STAR PASS

Objective

To improve passing proficiency while working with a group.

Equipment

One fewer ball than the number of students in each group.

Activity

1. Students form a circle with one player holding a playground ball.
2. The player with the ball bounce passes it to another player who is not standing beside her while saying that player's name.
3. The player receiving the ball passes it to another player who is not standing beside him while saying that player's name.
4. This rotation continues until the ball gets back to the first player who passed the ball.
5. Once the rotation is completed twice, the first player adds another ball.
6. After two more completed rotations, the first player adds another ball. This continues until the number of balls equals one fewer than the number of players.

Extensions

- Chest passing may be used.
- A combination of bounce passing and chest passing may be used.

Based on Fluegelman 1981.

Chest Passing Troubleshooting Chart

If you see this	Then try this
1. Eyes not on the target	• Have the student pass to a target she has designed. • Have students pass to different-colored targets on the wall. • Use aluminum pie plates for targets.
2. Incorrect hand position on the ball	• Draw the hand positions on the ball. • Have the student put his hands in baby powder and then place them on a ball. • Use commercially available balls that already have handprints on them.
3. Student not stepping when passing the ball	• Have the student step on a mat or rug as she passes the ball. • Have the student stand near a line (rope or tape on the floor can be used). She must step over the line while passing the ball. • Tape bubble wrap to the floor. Have the student step on that spot while passing the ball to create a noise.
4. Arms not fully extended on the pass	• Have the student practice reaching out and grabbing an object placed an arm's length away from the body. • Place a suspended aluminum pie plate in front of the student and have him try to hit the pie plate as he pushes his hands out for the chest pass.
5. Body not in proper alignment on the follow-through	• Tell the student to point her belt buckle at the target on the follow-through. • Have a partner watch to make sure the chest is even with or past the stepping foot on the follow-through.
6. Ball hitting the target at a level that is too high or too low	• Suspend two ropes between two game standards. Place the ropes between waist and neck height so that the ball can be passed correctly through them and reach the target. • Have the student practice passing the ball to a target on the wall. • The ball may be too heavy or too light for the student. Either give the student a more appropriately sized ball or move the child closer to (or farther away from) the target.

SUMMARY

Basketball has become one of the most popular sports in the United States. There are professional teams for both women and men that provide *all* students—girls and boys—with potential role models. When students play basketball during recess, at home, in youth leagues, or at camps, they often try to move the ball like one of the professional players. Without proper instruction, students do not learn to perform the skills correctly. Correcting these skills later can be challenging.

One of the most efficient ways to move the ball down the court is to pass it. Learning to properly and accurately pass a ball to a partner or teammate becomes very important to the student's overall success in basketball. Students and recreational players can use bounce passing and chest passing effectively once they understand how and when to execute a pass. Maintaining the proper body position, stepping with the pass, and pushing the ball out are critical elements that students must understand before they will experience repeated success with passing skills.

Teachers are usually the first people students will come in contact with who are able to provide instruction by using the critical elements and cues for a skill. This is an opportunity we should take seriously. As you help students become skillful movers, they may, in turn, become more interested in participating in physical activities outside of the physical education classroom setting.

BOUNCE PASSING LESSON PLAN

(FIRST LESSON)

AGE GROUP: First grade.

FOCUS: Pushing the ball away from the passer.

SUBFOCUS: Movement concepts of force and direction (down and away).

OBJECTIVES: To push the ball away in the bounce pass so that the ball bounces closer to the receiver than to the passer four out of five times, as measured by peer observation (**cue:** *push away*).

MATERIALS AND EQUIPMENT: One playground ball, one hula hoop, and one target for each child. One dome cone (or other object that can be pushed across the floor) is needed for each pair of children.

ADVANCE PREPARATION: Place targets around the gymnasium. These targets may be hoops, construction paper, or other objects. Each student will need one target. The targets should be no higher than 3 feet (1 m) above the floor. Place floor tape (or painter's tape) on the floor about 8 to 10 feet (2.4-3 m) in front of the target.

ORGANIZATION AND MANAGEMENT: Students are in self-space for instruction and warm-up. Later, students will find their own learning stations in the gymnasium for practice.

INTRODUCTION AND WARM-UP:

*Today we are going to learn some directions and practice using them. The direction words are **up** and **down** and **away** and **near**. When I start the music, we will move around the gymnasium in general space using a locomotor skill that I call out. When the music stops, I will ask you to march in place and make your arms go **up** or **down** or to have your arms **near** or **away** from your body. Do you understand these directions?*

Begin music and call out jog, skip, gallop, walk, or slide. Add directions of *up* or *down* or *near* or *far* when music stops. Watch for correct performance of locomotor skills and correct use of directions.

*Freeze. Now I want you to pretend that you have a ball in your hand. Show me how you would make it go **down**. Go **up**. Go **away**. Stay **near**. Excellent. Now, we are going to use our locomotor movements again, and when the music stops, you will freeze and make your imaginary ball go in the direction I call out. Do you understand these directions?* (Begin music.)

Watch for correct performance of locomotor skills and correct use of directions.

*Freeze. Please find your self-space and sit down. This time we will practice using these directions with a real ball. We are going to learn the bounce pass. To do this skill, we stand up, hold the ball at our chest, and **step** and **push** it down and away from us. It is important that the ball go **away** from us. Watch as I bounce pass the ball near the wall.* (Demonstrate passing the ball to the floor area near a wall.)

*Notice that I can bounce the ball off the floor and have it hit the target. To do that, I have to **push** the ball **away** from me. To keep my balance, it helps to put one foot in front when I pass the ball. It really doesn't matter which foot is in front. And this is for what? **(Balance.)** Great.*

Look around the gymnasium. There are pieces of construction paper and balls against the wall. Each of you will have your own place to work on bounce passing. Can you find your own target and sit on the tape in front of it? Go.

Pick up the ball and stand on your piece of tape facing the construction paper. Face your target, get in the ready position, step and push the ball away from you, and try to hit the target. Go get your ball and return to your piece of tape. (Repeat several times.)

The children repeat the cues with you. When they can repeat the cues (*push away*) on their own, they are allowed to practice independently.

Watch for students pushing the ball away.

Freeze. If you are able to hit your target three times in a row, you may take one giant step backward. Whenever you are able to bounce pass the ball and hit the target three times in a row, you may take another step back. Do you understand these directions? Go.

Watch for students pushing the ball away. Repeat the cue *push away* frequently.

Freeze. Everyone sit down where you are. If you are able to perform bounce passing easily, you may try this next challenge. (Demonstrate as you explain.) *You will place a hula hoop one step away from the wall. You will have to bounce the ball so that it hits the floor inside the hula hoop and then it bounces up to hit your target on the wall. Do you understand these directions? If you think you are ready to try this, raise your hand.* (Dismiss children in small groups to obtain hula hoops.) *Everyone return to your targets. Go.*

Watch for students pushing the ball away. Repeat the cue *push away* frequently.

Freeze. Everyone find a partner and sit down. You are doing very well pushing the ball away. Are you ready for something really challenging? You and your partner will need only one ball for the two of you and one dome cone. One of you can bring the hoop and put it on the pile and then pick up a dome cone. The other one can return one of the balls you have. (Dismiss children by groups to obtain and return equipment.) *Excellent.*

*Now watch (student) and me perform this skill. We have a dome cone between us. We will take two steps back from the dome cone. I want to **push** the ball **away** so that it hits the dome cone and pushes the cone closer to (student). (Student) will try to bounce pass the dome cone back toward me. When I say go, you and your partner will find a space in the gymnasium, place your dome cone on the floor, and take two steps back from the dome cone. You may then try to push the dome cone away from each other using bounce passes. Do you understand these directions? Go.*

Watch for the students pushing the ball away. (Contact with the dome cone is of secondary concern.) Repeat the cue *push away* frequently.

Freeze. Time is up. Please return your equipment to where it belongs and line up for your teacher.

CLOSURE: Students are lined up to leave.

*Do you think it is more important to pass the ball down or away for the bounce pass? **(Away.)** We spent a lot of time pushing the ball away. If (student) is my partner and I bounce pass to (student), does the ball hit the ground closer to her or to me on a good pass? **(Student.)***

Next time we will practice passing the ball to a moving target.

7

Striking

Striking is an integral part of many sport activities. The strike can take the form of an underhand strike, as in a volleyball serve; a sidearm strike, as in a tennis forehand; or a two-hand sidearm strike, as in batting.

Children's first attempts at striking tend to be uncontrollable swats or hits *at* an object. As children develop their skills, the swat becomes more recognizable as a strike. Unfortunately, when first learning striking, children tend to hit an object as hard as they can. The challenge for teachers is to provide adequate cues and activities to help children control the striking movement. This allows them to control the force of the strike and the direction of the object being struck.

In this chapter, we examine three of the primary striking patterns: underhand striking (volleyball serve), sidearm striking (tennis forehand), and two-hand sidearm striking (batting). Because of the complexity of each skill and the use or nonuse of equipment, the age for mastering each skill varies. *National Standards & Grade-Level Outcomes for K-12 Physical Education* (SHAPE America, 2014) addresses underhand striking (S1.E22) as an underhand volley. In addition, the outcomes address striking with short-handled implements (S1.E24) and long-handled implements (S1.E25). However, in this text, we address sidearm striking and two-hand sidearm striking without being specific about the length of the implement. The outcomes for each are addressed in their corresponding sections.

UNDERHAND STRIKING

The critical elements of underhand throwing are very similar to those of underhand striking or underhand serving in volleyball. Once a child becomes proficient with underhand throwing, it is easier for him to develop the underhand striking skill. When this movement pattern is set, the addition of implements can transform the skill into a serve in badminton.

National Standards & Grade-Level Outcomes for K-12 Physical Education (SHAPE America, 2014) does not directly address underhand striking. However, the underhand volley described in the outcomes will be referred to as an underhand strike in this text (table 7.1). The outcomes indicate that kindergarteners should be able to strike a lightweight object (balloon), sending it upward (S1.E22.K), and that first graders should be able to strike an object with an open palm, sending it upward (S1.E22.1). In the second grade, students should be able to volley an object upward with consecutive hits (S1.E22.2). By grade 3, students should be able to strike an object with an underhand striking pattern, sending it forward over a net, to the wall, or over a line to a partner while demonstrating four of the five critical elements of a mature pattern (S1.E22.3). Application of the skill in a dynamic environment should occur in grades 4 and 5 (S1.E22.4 and S1.E22.5).

We have found that mastery of underhand striking may not occur until the third or fourth grade. It should, however, be introduced in kindergarten.

Table 7.1   Grade-Level Outcomes for Underhand Volleying (S1.E22)

	Kindergarten	Grade 1	Grade 2	Grade 3	Grade 4	Grade 5
S1.E22 Underhand volleying	Volleys a lightweight object (balloon), sending it upward. (S1.E22.K)	Volleys an object with an open palm, sending it upward. (S1.E22.1)	Volleys an object upward with consecutive hits. (S1.E22.2)	Volleys an object with an underhand or sidearm striking pattern, sending it forward over a net, to the wall, or over a line to a partner while demonstrating 4 of the 5 critical elements of a mature pattern. (S1.E22.3)	Volleys underhand using a mature pattern in a dynamic environment (e.g., 2 square, 4 square, handball). (S1.E22.4)	Applies skill. (S1.E22.5)

Critical Elements

Ready Position

Face the direction of the strike, feet shoulder-width apart, eyes looking at the ball, ball held in nonpreferred hand in front of the body at waist level.

Arm Back

Pull striking arm back to at least waist level.

Step and Swing

Lean forward and step forward with opposite foot while the preferred hand strikes the ball in front of the body at waist level or below.

Hit

Strike the underside of the ball with the heel of the hand while continuing the step with the foot opposite the striking hand.

Follow Through

Hand continues in the direction of the ball but does not go beyond shoulder height.

Cue Words

The cue words you select for each phase of the skill will depend on the age of the students you are teaching and your areas of emphasis. We list, in usable sets, some of the cue words we use to teach underhand striking. You may use each set individually or mix and match the cue words as needed. We have found that it is beneficial to have the students say the words out loud as they practice the skill.

Ready—face the target, feet shoulder-width apart, eyes on the ball, ball held in nonstriking hand in front of the body at waist level.

Start—face the direction of the strike, feet shoulder-width apart, eyes looking forward.

Hold it low and **extend**—ball is held in nonstriking hand and arm is extended and in front of the body at waist level.

Step—step forward with foot opposite the striking hand.

Hit/strike—strike the ball on the underside.

Arm back—pull the striking arm back in a straight pathway behind the body at about waist level.

Step and swing and **step and hit**—step forward with foot opposite the striking hand. The striking hand contacts the ball in front of the body at waist level or below. Hit the underside of the ball with the heel of the hand.

Follow through—the hand continues in the direction of the ball but does not go beyond shoulder height.

> *Cue set 1:* ready, step, strike
> *Cue set 2:* hold it low, step, hit
> *Cue set 3:* start, extend, step and swing, follow through
> *Cue set 4:* ready, arm back, step and hit, follow through

SUGGESTED ACTIVITIES FOR REINFORCING AND ASSESSING THE CRITICAL ELEMENTS

In the learning process, it is essential that students know how a skill is supposed to look, what its critical elements are, and how to perform each individual element correctly. In the preceding section, we provided pictures and descriptions of underhand striking, divided it into its critical elements, and provided possible cue words. In addition to the material in chapter 1 that reinforces the concepts for all locomotor and manipulative skills, the following section provides specific activities for reinforcing the critical elements unique to underhand striking.

PARTNER SKILL CHECK

Objective

To allow partners to assess each other's progress learning the skill.

Equipment

Partner skill check assessments, pencils, and one ball for each set of partners. If the students cannot read or do not speak English, the picture version of the partner skill check sheet may be useful.

Activity

1. One partner observes the other to see if she has the correct form for the ready position.

2. If the ready position is correct, then the partner places a *Y* in the first box. If the ready position is incorrect, he places an *N* in the first box. Nonreaders can put a smiling face if the ready position is correct or a frowning face if the ready position is incorrect.

3. This evaluation continues until each of the critical elements has been assessed five times.

4. A partner skill check assessment is used for each student.

Extensions

- You may use the partner skill check assessment to measure the skill development of each student.

- You may send the partner skill check assessment home with report cards or as individual skills develop.

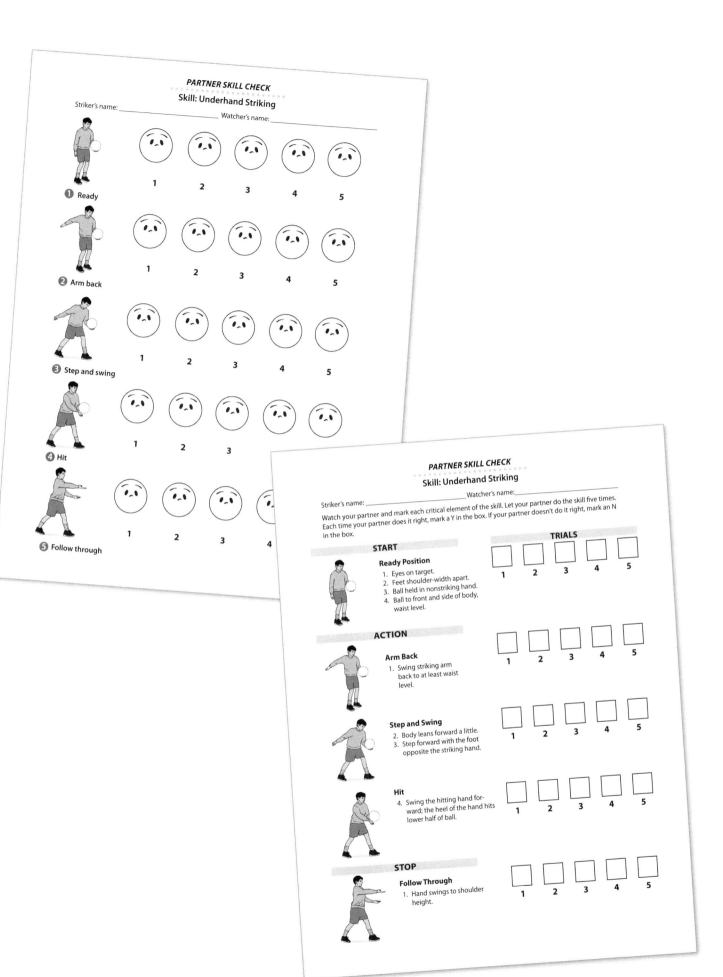

PARTNER SKILL CHECK
Skill: Underhand Striking

Striker's name: _____

Watcher's name: _____

1 Ready

1 2 3 4 5

2 Arm back

1 2 3 4 5

3 Step and swing

1 2 3 4 5

4 Hit

1 2 3

5 Follow through

1 2 3 4

PARTNER SKILL CHECK
Skill: Underhand Striking

Striker's name: _____

Watcher's name: _____

Watch your partner and mark each critical element of the skill. Let your partner do the skill five times. Each time your partner does it right, mark a Y in the box. If your partner doesn't do it right, mark an N in the box.

TRIALS

START

Ready Position
1. Eyes on target.
2. Feet shoulder-width apart.
3. Ball held in nonstriking hand.
4. Ball to front and side of body, waist level.

1 2 3 4 5

ACTION

Arm Back
1. Swing striking arm back to at least waist level.

1 2 3 4 5

Step and Swing
2. Body leans forward a little.
3. Step forward with the foot opposite the striking hand.

1 2 3 4 5

Hit
4. Swing the hitting hand forward; the heel of the hand hits lower half of ball.

1 2 3 4 5

STOP

Follow Through
1. Hand swings to shoulder height.

1 2 3 4 5

SUCCESS BUILDERS

The success builder activities allow you to address individual needs. If students need additional help on individual critical elements, the activities listed here will reinforce correct performance.

Objective

To allow partners to improve areas of deficiency as assessed by the partner skill check assessment.

Equipment

See the following individual stations. We suggest using an unbreakable mirror and a poster of each critical element of underhand striking at each station. The mirror is particularly helpful in these activities because it allows the children to see what they are doing. The easiest way to make the posters is to print out the drawings from this book and enlarge them. Laminating the posters will ensure their use for many years.

Activity

1. Set up a station for each of the five critical elements in the teaching area. Post a description or a picture of the specific element at the corresponding station.
2. The details for each station follow:

READY

Face target, feet shoulder-width apart, eyes looking forward, object held in nonpreferred hand at waist level in front of the body.

Equipment

Poster of the ready position, mirror (if available), and partner evaluations.

Activity 1

The student assumes the ready position. The partner checks to see if her position matches the poster. The student refers to the mirror for help. The student pretends to strike a ball and, on a signal from her partner, assumes the ready position again. Once the student can demonstrate the ready position to the partner, both may return to practicing the entire skill.

Activity 2

Sometimes children bend the arm that is holding the ball, which causes an improper hit. An elbow pad can help the student feel the elbow bend during practice and cue him to keep that arm straight. As soon as possible, remove the elbow pad and encourage the student to practice without it.

ARM BACK

Pull the striking arm back past the midline of the body to waist level.

Equipment

Poster of the arm-back part of the skill.

Activity

Have a student stand with his back to the wall and reach back with the preferred hand and touch the wall. When working with a partner, the student can reach back and try to touch his partner's hand. Once this is mastered, the students may return to practicing the entire skill.

STEP AND SWING

Step forward with opposite foot while the preferred hand strikes the ball in front of the body at waist level or below.

Equipment

Poster of the step and swing, tape (floor or painter's), and partner evaluations.

Activity

The student assumes a stride position with the leg opposite the striking hand forward. (If necessary, use floor or painter's tape on the floor or other visual cues that will assist the student in stepping in opposition.) The student should begin practicing from this position, then progress to starting with feet together and then stepping with the opposite foot. Once the student can demonstrate a good step and swing to the partner, both may return to practicing the entire skill.

HIT

Strike the ball on the underside with the heel of the hand while continuing to step with the foot opposite the striking hand.

Equipment

Poster of the hit, playground balls or volleyballs, and partner evaluations.

Activity

Use a magic marker to draw a 3-inch (7.6 cm) diameter circle on the ball. The student holds the ball so that she can easily hit the circle with the striking hand. Have the student practice striking the ball so that she can see the heel of the striking hand hitting the circle drawn on the ball.

FOLLOW THROUGH

The hand continues in the direction of the ball but does not go beyond shoulder height.

Equipment

Poster of the follow-through, projector, unbreakable mirror, and partner evaluations.

Activity 1

The student stands so that he is between the projector and a wall. It should be possible for the partner to cast a shadow on the wall while the other student practices. The student practices underhand striking, and his partner places a piece of tape on the wall showing how far his hand went after the strike. The partners continue the drill until the student consistently stops the follow-through before reaching the shoulder level.

Activity 2

The student faces the mirror and practices underhand striking without a ball. The student watches the mirror to determine where she ends the follow-through. The partner may also evaluate the student.

SUGGESTED CULMINATING ACTIVITIES TO REINFORCE THE ENTIRE SKILL

Mastery of critical elements should be accomplished before emphasizing accuracy. When accuracy is emphasized too early, the students begin to aim and the elements of the skill disappear. Your targets should be large enough to allow the students to perform the critical elements of the skill and have success hitting the target.

INDIVIDUAL ACTIVITIES

COLOR TARGETS

Objective

To improve underhand striking by hitting a specific target.

Equipment

Construction paper of different colors and sizes (about 8 to 12 targets of each color) taped to the wall of the gymnasium or activity area and a ball (volleyball, playground ball, foam ball) for each student.

Activity

1. Create a color box in which samples from each color of construction paper have been placed. You will need more samples than you have students.
2. Select a student to draw a sample color from the color box.
3. The sample color chosen is the color target all students must try to hit using underhand striking.
4. Students continue striking the targets of the selected color until you give a stop signal.
5. The activity continues until all students have been given an opportunity to draw from the color box.

Extensions

- Instead of using different colors, students could select different shapes from the shape box, letters from the alphabet box, or words from the word box.
- Students work with partners. The partner chooses the color, shape, letter, or word that will be used for a target. The student must hit the selected target using underhand striking. Partners take turns selecting targets and striking.

CREATE A WORD

Objective

To create words by hitting letters using underhand striking.

Equipment

One ball (volleyball, playground ball, foam ball) per student and four complete sets of alphabet letters scattered and taped to the wall of the gymnasium or activity area. It would be advantageous to have extra copies of vowels and selected consonants (e.g., N, R, S, T). You will also need paper and pencils or a dry-erase board and markers to serve as a word bank.

Activity

1. On your start signal, students begin to spell words by striking different letters of the alphabet.
2. Once a student has created a word, he goes to the word bank (paper or dry-erase board) and writes the word. It will be helpful to have several word banks so students will not have to wait in line to write their words.

3. A word may be written only once on the paper or dry-erase board.

4. If a student strikes a letter that cannot be used to form the word being created, she must strike the letter again to delete it.

Extensions

- Students work with partners. One student hits letters to spell a word while his partner records the word and evaluates the underhand striking. The striker may not use the letter until underhand striking is performed properly. When the striker has spelled a word, the partner is then given an opportunity to collect letters using underhand striking.
- Students work with partners. Partners are given paper and pencil to record the letters they hit and to write down the words they create. Each partner must strike a vowel and two consonants until the pair has six letters to use to create words. The partners attempt to create six words using one or more of the letters they have hit. Once the partners have created six words and written them down, they attempt to spell the words by using underhand striking to hit the letters with the ball. Once a word is spelled, it may be checked off the list. If the students are unable to use a letter they have hit, they must strike that letter to delete it and select another letter.

PARTNER ACTIVITIES

CHALLENGES

Objective

To practice underhand striking in a variety of settings.

Equipment

One playground ball or volleyball per pair of students and laminated challenge cards.

Activity

1. Each student selects a challenge card.

2. Students perform the tasks described on the cards.

3. Possible challenges may include the following:

   - Strike the ball using strong force (light force).
   - Strike the ball to hit targets at different levels (high, middle).
   - Strike the ball at the same time your partner does.

Extensions

- Place multicolored targets on the wall and have the partner tell the striker which target to hit.
- Set up game standards with a volleyball net or rope between them. The striker must strike the ball over the net or rope. Use different heights for the net or rope.
- Suspend a rope between two game standards. Attach various objects (e.g., empty 2-liter plastic bottles, hoops, aluminum pie pans) to the rope. Students must call out which object they will hit before they strike the ball.

WALL BALL

Objective

To improve the underhand striking skill by hitting a ball to a wall.

Equipment

One ball (playground ball or volleyball) per student pair.

Activity

1. Partners stand at least 15 feet (4.5 m) from the wall.

2. One partner uses underhand striking to hit the ball against the wall.

3. Her partner has to catch the ball after it comes off the wall but before it hits the ground.

4. When the partner has caught the ball, she must underhand strike the ball back to the wall from the place it was caught.

5. Partners count how many successful strikes and catches they have in a row.

Extensions

- Allow the ball to bounce once before it is caught.

- Place a target on the wall and challenge the partners to strike it.

BACK IT UP

Objective

To improve the underhand striking skill by hitting a ball to a partner from varying distances.

Equipment

One ball (e.g., volleyball, 8-inch [20 cm] foam ball) per student pair.

Activity

1. Students stand approximately 10 feet (3 m) apart and face each other.

2. The student with the ball underhand strikes the ball to his partner, who must catch it.

3. After the partner catches it, she underhand strikes it back to her partner, who must catch it.

4. Once the ball has been hit and caught twice, one of the partners takes a step backward and the process is repeated.

5. If the ball is not hit correctly or caught, the partners must return to their original locations.

Extensions

- After a correct strike, you may allow the ball to bounce once before it is caught without returning to the original location.

- A volleyball net (or rope) may be used so that the students have to strike the ball over it to a partner.

Based on Fluegelman 1981.

THROUGH THE HOOP

Objective

To improve underhand striking accuracy by hitting a ball through a suspended hoop.

Equipment

A large hula hoop suspended from an overhead structure (e.g., game standards, basketball backboard) and one playground ball or volleyball per student pair.

Activity

1. Partners stand on each side of the hoop.

2. Partners take turns trying to underhand strike the ball so that it goes through the hoop.

Extensions

- Partners may count how many successful strikes they have in a specified time period (e.g., 1 minute).

- Partners may be required to have a correct underhand strike and a successful catch before the strike is counted.

GROUP ACTIVITIES

CREATE YOUR OWN ACTIVITY

Objective

To allow students to create their own activities to reinforce underhand striking skills.

Equipment

One piece of paper and pencil per group and a predetermined list of equipment you will allow the students to use in their activities (e.g., bowling pins, cones, ropes, hula hoops, volleyballs, suspended volleyball net, foam balls).

Activity

1. Form groups of two to five students. You may select the groups or the students may form their own.
2. Each group creates an activity using underhand striking as the basic skill. Students are required to have rules that encourage correct performance of the skill, include all players, and address all safety concerns.
3. The groups write their individual names, the rules of the activity, and the equipment needed on their papers, and then show their activities to you.
4. After you approve their activities, the groups retrieve the necessary equipment and begin playing.
5. You must approve all changes to the activities.

Extensions

- One group may teach their activity to another group.
- Groups may teach their activities to the entire class.

CYCLE/RECYCLE

Objective

To improve underhand striking skills by striking balls over a net.

Equipment

Two game standards, a net at volleyball height, and one soft ball (e.g., Super-Safe ball, Gator Skin ball, beach ball, foam ball) per student.

Activity

1. Divide the class in half.
2. Place the two groups on either side of the net.
3. On the start signal, everyone strikes the balls over the net.
4. Students count the number of balls they strike over the net.

Extensions

- Have the students total the number of correct strikes (strikes over the net) the entire group made. These results can be recorded and later charted or graphed to show class improvement.
- Each time a student strikes the ball over the net, she goes around the standards and becomes a member of the other group.

Adapted, by permission, from J.A. Wessel, PhD, 1974, *Project I CAN* (Northbrook, IL: Hubbard).

Underhand Striking Troubleshooting Chart

If you see this	Then try this
1. Ball not held in front of body	• Place a mirror in front of the student so he can see his arm and hand placement. • The student works with a partner. The student gets into the correct position, and the partner places the ball into her hand.
2. Arm not going back far enough	• Hang a balloon from a net or rope suspended between two game standards. Have the student stand in front of the balloon and swing his arm back until it hits the balloon. This can also be done with the student standing with his back to the wall and swinging his arm back to touch the wall. • Place a large piece of paper on the wall. Have the student stand sideways to the paper while you mark her waist height. Swing the student's arm back and draw the arc of the backswing on the paper for her to see.
3. Student not stepping or stepping forward on the wrong foot	• Tie a pinny or scarf on the opposite leg. • Place a spot or footprint in front of the student. He must step onto the spot or footprint before hitting the ball. • Tape bubble wrap to the floor. Have the student step in opposition on that spot to create a noise.
4. Student throwing the ball up in the air before striking	• Have a partner touch the arm holding the ball. The partner needs to apply enough resistance so the student can feel the arm remaining stationary. • Hang a balloon from a net or rope suspended between two game standards. Have the student hold the balloon and strike it. If the student tosses the balloon, she will see a bend in the balloon rope.
5. Student not using the heel of the hand to strike the ball	• Hang a damp sponge from a volleyball net or rope suspended between two game standards. Have the student hit the sponge with the heel of his hand. Check to see where the water is on the hand. • Partners face each other; one has her hand outstretched with the palm down. Using light force and an underhand motion, the other partner swings his arm and strikes the first partner's outstretched hand with the heel of his hand.
6. Swing arm not following through	• Suspend a net or rope between two game standards so the bottom of the rope is at the student's shoulder height. Have the student perform the skill without a ball, continuing the arm swing until the heel of the hand touches the net. • Partners face each other; one has her hand outstretched with the palm down at shoulder height. Using light force and an underhand motion, the other partner swings his arm and strikes the first partner's outstretched hand with the heel of his hand.

SUMMARY

Playing a game of volleyball can be a very frustrating experience for older students who are poorly skilled in underhand striking. Many are unable to execute even a basic underhand serve. We have observed that these students do not hold the ball low before contact, and the resulting hit goes up toward the ceiling. Another major problem is when a child bends her holding arm and a mis-hit occurs. While both of these mechanical problems are easy to correct in elementary school, the motor pattern may be difficult to alter in later years. During initial instruction, elementary school–aged children do not need the challenge of hitting a ball over a net. Proper instruction and plenty of practice opportunities while working with a wall or a partner will ensure improved mechanics and better participation in later grades.

UNDERHAND STRIKING LESSON PLAN

(SECOND LESSON)

AGE GROUP: Third grade.

FOCUS: Extension of the nonstriking arm.

SUBFOCUS: Bending and extending body parts and stepping in opposition.

OBJECTIVE: To fully extend the nonpreferred arm before the ball is contacted during underhand striking four out of five times, as measured by teacher observation (**cues:** *extend your arm, arm straight, keep it low*).

MATERIALS AND EQUIPMENT: One Super-Safe ball or beach ball (or similar ball) per student.

ORGANIZATION AND MANAGEMENT: Students are in self-space for warm-up, instruction, and practice. Set up teaching stations with one ball beside the wall and a line parallel to and at least 15 feet (4.6 m) from the wall.

WARM-UP:

Today we're going to warm up with music. When the music starts, I would like you to jog in general space. When the music stops, you will freeze in your own self-space.

Watch for students moving safely.

(Stop music.) *Everyone stand where you are and look toward me. I would like to make your warm-ups more challenging by teaching you the words* bend *and* extend. *Watch as I bend my arm; now I extend the arm to make it straight. Can you bend one leg? Can you extend that leg to make it straight? Can you bend your wrist? Can you extend your wrist? Excellent.*

This time, I'm going to use the words we just learned to make our warm-ups more challenging. Use the locomotor movement that I call out and, when the music stops, freeze in a position where you will either bend or extend the body part I name. (Select two students to demonstrate skipping and, on freeze, tell the students to fully extend their arms.) *Do you understand what you are to do? Go.*

Watch for students correctly performing the locomotor skills and following the bend and extend commands correctly. Stop the children several times to change the locomotor movement and the limb to bend or extend.

FORMATION: Students find self-space and sit and face you.

INTRODUCTION:

Today, we will put the extend *and* bend *words to use with underhand striking. Who can tell me how to do this underhand striking skill?* (Using the teach the teacher technique, review the key elements of ready, arm back, step and swing, hit, and follow through, placing particular emphasis on stepping in opposition.) *Excellent. Everyone stand up. Let's pretend that we have an imaginary ball in our hand. Get ready, swing your arm back, step with your opposite foot, hit, and follow through.* (Children practice several times.)

Watch for stepping in opposition and following through.

Excellent. When we did our warm-ups today, I had you practice bending and extending different parts of your body. To do the underhand strike correctly, we have to really extend one arm, and that's what we are going to stress today. Everyone stand up in your self-space. Face me. Bring your striking arm backward. Take your other arm and extend it downward in front of you so that your hand makes an L (see figure).

It is very important that the arm be almost straight. Excellent.

Watch for straight arms extended in front of the body.

Pretend you have a ball in that hand. Really extend that arm; keep it straight. Can you step, hit the ball, and follow through? Let's try that a few times with our imaginary balls.

Watch for straight arms extending in front of the body, stepping in opposition, and following through.

Freeze. You are doing very well. Help me remember, how do I hold the ball? **(Straight arm.)** *Excellent. Now you are ready to work with a ball. Watch as I strike the ball.* (Demonstrate several times.) *Who can tell me where I strike the ball?* **(Bottom half.)** *Excellent! What can you tell me about my feet?* **(They're stepping in opposition** or **you're using the stepping foot.)** *What about the arm that holds the ball?* **(Extend it.)**

Note that the hand makes an L.

It's time to practice. There are balls placed against the walls and there are lines marked off in front of them. When I tell you to go, you will find a station, pick up the ball, and stand on your line, but still face me. (Dismiss students by groups.)

Terrific. When I say go, you may begin striking the ball toward the wall. Remember to extend your arm and hold the ball low. Go.

Watch for arm extension and stepping in opposition. Children practice for 3 to 5 minutes.

Freeze. Everyone find a partner and sit down together on one of your lines. Go. Now, we will need only one ball for the two of you. One of you return a ball and then come back to your line. Go.

This time you are going to help each other with the skill. Your partner will underhand strike the ball against the wall and you will really watch to make sure he or she is holding the ball low to begin with and is stepping with the correct foot. You have to make sure your partner can do those things. I will tell you when to change jobs. Do you understand these directions? Go.

Watch for arm extension and stepping in opposition. Children practice for 2 to 3 minutes, then switch.

Freeze. All of you are doing very well. This time you and your partner are going to play a cooperative activity. It is called Wall Ball. Watch as (student) and I demonstrate. I will underhand strike the ball to the wall and, when it comes off the wall, (student) will catch it. It's okay to let it bounce once. But I have to strike it so (student) can be there to catch it. Then, (student) will strike the ball and I'll catch it. We want to count how many times we can do this in a row. You must really work together. Do you understand the directions? Go.

Watch for arm extension, stepping in opposition, and good catching techniques. If any skill problems occur, stop the class and reteach the skills. Children practice for 5 to 7 minutes.

CLOSURE: Line up the students to leave.

Girls and boys, who can tell me how to hold the ball in my hand? **(Make an L and really extend the arm.)** *Where do I strike the ball?* **(On the bottom half.)** *Which foot do I step with when I strike the ball?* **(Opposite foot** or **stepping foot.)** *Next time we are going to practice striking the ball to a target.*

SIDEARM STRIKING

Sidearm striking can be performed by striking the ball out of the hand, as in the sidearm volleyball serve, or off of a bounce, as in handball. When first learning a skill, children perform better without any equipment. As they progress, short-handled implements (e.g., paddles) may be added. Once striking with short-handled implements is mastered, long-handled implements (e.g., tennis rackets) may be introduced. It is essential that students make these progressions and that equipment of the appropriate size and weight be used.

When equipment is added, the sidearm strike can become the forehand stroke for pickleball (short-handled implement) or tennis (long-handled implement). For young children, however, the addition of an implement to strike an object may be challenging. They can, however, become proficient in using the sidearm striking technique to hit a bounced playground ball. The following section focuses on the mechanics of sidearm striking without using an implement. Later, as the child's eye–hand coordination improves, you can add smaller balls, paddles, and rackets. *National Standards & Grade-Level Outcomes for K-12 Physical Education* (SHAPE America, 2014) addresses striking with short- and long-handled implements, but not as they apply specifically to sidearm striking.

Critical Elements

Ready Position	T	Step and Hit	Follow Through
Front of the body toward the target, eyes on the target, feet shoulder-width apart, knees bent, hands parallel with palms facing each other and fingers pointing forward.	Body turns as the feet pivot in place, side to target, arms extended in the shape of a T. Extend the striking hand away from the intended line of travel with the palm facing outward. Hold the ball toward the target in the nonstriking hand. Drop the ball. Eyes are on the ball throughout the movement.	Step toward the target with the foot opposite the striking arm. The arm swings through as the hips and shoulders rotate toward the target, allowing the front body surface to face the target.	The hand continues in the direction of the strike.

Cue Words

The cue words you select for each phase of the skill will depend on the age of the students you are teaching and your areas of emphasis. In usable sets we list some of the cue words we use to teach sidearm striking. You may use each set individually or mix and match the cue words as needed. We have found that it is beneficial to have the students say the words out loud as they practice the skill.

Ready—face the target, feet shoulder-width apart, weight evenly distributed on both feet, ball is held in nonstriking hand.

Start and drop—nonstriking side toward the target, feet shoulder-width apart, and weight evenly distributed on both feet. Bring the striking hand back parallel to the ground. Drop the ball from the nonstriking hand. Eyes are on the ball throughout the movement.

T—body turns as the feet pivot in place, side to target, arms extended in the shape of a T. Extend the striking hand away from the intended line of travel with the palm facing outward. Hold the ball in the nonstriking hand toward the target. Drop the ball from the nonstriking hand. Eyes are on the ball throughout the movement.

Step—step toward the target with the foot opposite the striking arm. The arm swings through as the hip and shoulder rotate toward the target, allowing the front body surface to face the target (use the cue "belt buckle" to help reinforce correct body position).

Go—step forward with opposite foot while bringing the striking hand forward.

Step and hit—step toward the target with the foot opposite the striking hand. Hips and spine rotate as the arm is brought forward. Strike object with hand.

Hit and **whack it**—strike ball with preferred hand.

Follow through—striking hand continues in the direction of the hit.

Reach high—hand continues in the direction of the strike.

> *Cue set 1:* ready, T, step, follow through
>
> *Cue set 2:* start, go, hit
>
> *Cue set 3:* drop, go, whack it
>
> *Cue set 4:* start, step and hit, reach high

SUGGESTED ACTIVITIES FOR REINFORCING AND ASSESSING THE CRITICAL ELEMENTS

In the learning process, it is essential that students know how a skill is supposed to look, what its critical elements are, and how to perform each individual element correctly. In the preceding section, we provided pictures and descriptions of sidearm striking, divided it into its critical elements, and provided possible cue words. In addition to the material in chapter 1 that reinforces the concepts for all locomotor and manipulative skills, the following section provides specific activities for reinforcing the critical elements unique to sidearm striking.

PARTNER SKILL CHECK

Objective

To allow partners to assess each other's progress in learning the skill.

Equipment

Partner skill check assessments, pencils, and one ball for each set of partners. If the students cannot read or do not speak English, the picture version of the partner skill check assessments may be useful.

Activity

1. One partner observes the other to see if he has the correct form for the ready position.
2. If the ready position is correct, then the partner places a *Y* in the first box. If the ready position is incorrect, he places an *N* in the first box. Nonreaders can put a smiling face if the ready position is correct or a frowning face if the ready position is incorrect.
3. This evaluation continues until each of the critical elements has been assessed five times.
4. A partner skill check assessment is used for each student.

Extensions

- You may use the partner skill check assessment to measure the skill development of each student.
- You may send partner skill check assessments home with report cards or as individual skills develop.

PARTNER SKILL CHECK
Skill: Sidearm Striking

Striker's name: _____   Watcher's name: _____

❶ Ready 1 2 3 4 5

❷ T 1 2 3 4

❸ Step and hit 1 2 3 4

❹ Follow through 1 2 3 4 5

PARTNER SKILL CHECK
Skill: Sidearm Striking

Striker's name: _____   Watcher's name: _____

Watch your partner and mark each critical element of the skill. Let your partner do the skill five times. Each time your partner does it right, mark a Y in the box. If your partner doesn't do it right, mark an N in the box.

START | **TRIALS**

Ready Position
1. Eyes on the target.
2. Knees bent.
3. Feet shoulder-width apart.
4. Hands apart in front of the body.

1 2 3 4 5

ACTION

T
1. Side to target.
2. T—hitting hand back and other hand pointing at target.

1 2 3 4 5

Step and Hit
3. Step forward on opposite foot.
4. Hip and shoulder turn to target; palm of hand points in direction of hit.

1 2 3 4 5

STOP

Follow Through
1. Arm continues across body after the release and belt buckle points toward target.

1 2 3 4 5

SUCCESS BUILDERS

The success builder activities allow you to address individual needs. If students need additional help on individual critical elements, the activities listed here will help reinforce correct performance.

Objective

To allow partners to improve areas of deficiency as assessed by the partner skill check.

Equipment

See the following individual stations. We suggest using an unbreakable mirror and a poster of each element of sidearm striking at each station. The mirror is particularly helpful in these activities because it allows the children to see what they are doing. The easiest way to make the posters is to print out the drawings from this book and enlarge them. Laminating the posters will ensure their use for many years.

Activity

1. Set up a station for each of the four critical elements in the teaching area. Post a description or a picture of the specific component at the corresponding station.

2. The details for each station follow:

READY

Front of the body toward the target, eyes on the target, feet shoulder-width apart, knees bent, ball is held in nonpreferred hand.

Equipment

Poster of the ready position, mirror (if available), and partner evaluations.

Activity

The student assumes the ready position. The partner checks to see if his position matches the poster. The student refers to the mirror for help. The student pretends to strike a ball and, on a signal from his partner, assumes the ready position again. Once the student can demonstrate the ready position to the partner, partners may return to practicing the entire skill.

T

Body turns as the feet pivot in place, side to target, arms extended in the shape of a T. Extend the striking hand away from the intended line of travel with the palm facing outward. Hold the ball in the nonstriking hand toward the target. Drop the ball from that hand. Eyes are on the ball throughout the movement.

Equipment

Poster of the T position, tape (floor or painter's), and partner evaluations.

Activity 1

The student turns his nonstriking side toward the target and assumes a stride position with the leg opposite the striking hand stepping forward. (If necessary, use floor or painter's tape on the floor or other visual cues that will assist the student in stepping in opposition.) The arms extend to make a T. The student should begin practicing from this position, then progress to starting with feet together (ready) and then pivoting to the T (ready, T). Once the student can demonstrate a good turn to the T position to the partner, the partners may return to practicing the entire skill.

Activity 2

Sometimes children will bend the arm that is to strike the ball, which will cause an improper hit. An elbow pad can help the student feel the elbow bend during practice, cueing her to keep that arm straight when striking the ball. As soon as possible, remove the elbow pad and encourage the student to practice without it.

STEP AND HIT

Step toward the target with the foot opposite the striking hand. The arm swings through as the hip and shoulder rotate toward the target, allowing the front body surface to face the target (use the cue "belt buckle" to help reinforce correct body position).

Equipment

Poster of the step and hit, pie plate with duct tape on the bottom (allows plate to be attached to the student's shirt), PVC pipe or wooden dowel 3 to 4 feet (~1 m) in length, and partner evaluations.

Activity 1

The student begins this activity from the T position, with her nonstriking side to the mirror or partner. The student holds the PVC pipe (or dowel) behind her neck with both hands at the end of the PVC pipe that faces the target. The student rotates the hips and shoulders, turning so the length of pipe is parallel to the mirror or partner. The student practices this several times before returning to practicing the entire skill.

Activity 2

The student attaches the pie plate to his shirt and works with a partner. He begins this activity from the T position, with his nonstriking side to the partner. On a signal from the partner, the student swings the striking arm while rotating his hips and shoulders. The student should finish the movement with the pie plate facing the partner. If a mirror is used, it should be placed in the same position as the partner. The student practices this several times before returning to practicing the entire skill.

FOLLOW THROUGH

Hand continues in the direction of the strike.

Equipment

Poster of the follow-through, unbreakable mirror, and partner evaluations.

Activity

The student faces the mirror and practices sidearm striking without a ball. The student watches the mirror to determine when she ends the follow-through. A partner may also evaluate the student.

SUGGESTED CULMINATING ACTIVITIES TO REINFORCE THE ENTIRE SKILL

Mastery of critical elements should be accomplished before emphasizing accuracy. Although *National Standards & Grade-Level Outcomes for K-12 Physical Education* (SHAPE America, 2014) does not specifically address sidearm striking, they do address the skill briefly within the underhand volley outcome. The outcome states that third graders should be able to use a sidearm striking pattern to send an object over a net, to the wall, or over a line to a partner (S1.E22.3).

As with all manipulative skills, the critical elements should be mastered before accuracy is emphasized. When accuracy becomes the primary goal, the students will often compromise technique for accuracy. Therefore, wait until third grade to begin emphasizing accuracy. Use targets that are large enough to allow the students to perform the critical elements of the skill and have success hitting the target.

INDIVIDUAL ACTIVITIES

COLOR TARGETS

Objective

To provide students with opportunities to practice sidearm striking while hitting a specific target.

Equipment

Construction paper of different colors and sizes (about 8 to 12 targets of each color) taped to the wall of the gymnasium or activity area and a ball for each student (volleyball, beach ball, foam ball).

Activity

1. Create a color box in which samples from each color of construction paper have been placed. You will need more samples than you have students.
2. Select a student to draw a sample color from the color box.
3. The sample color chosen is the color target all students must locate and strike using sidearm striking.
4. Students continue striking the target until you give a stop signal.
5. The activity continues until all students have been given an opportunity to draw from the color box.

Extensions

- Instead of using different colors, students could select different shapes from the shape box, letters from the alphabet box, or words from the word box.
- Students work with partners. The partner chooses the color, shape, letter, or word that will be used for a target. The student must strike the selected target. Partners take turns selecting targets and striking.

CREATE A WORD

Objective

To create words by hitting letters using sidearm striking.

Equipment

One ball (volleyball, beach ball, foam ball) per student and four complete sets of alphabet letters scattered and taped to the wall of the gymnasium or activity area. It would be advantageous to have extra copies of vowels and selected consonants (e.g., N, R, S, T). You will also need paper and pencils or a dry-erase board and markers to serve as a word bank.

Activity

1. On your start signal, students begin to spell words by striking different letters of the alphabet.
2. Once a student has created a word, he goes to the word bank (paper or dry-erase board) and writes the word. It will be helpful to have several word banks so students will not have to wait in line to write their words.
3. A word may be written only once on the paper or dry-erase board.
4. If a student strikes a letter that cannot be used to form the word being created, he must strike the letter again to delete it.

Extensions

- Students work with partners. One student hits letters to spell a word while the partner records the word and evaluates the sidearm strike. The striker may not use the letter until sidearm striking is performed properly. When the first partner has spelled a word, the other partner is given an opportunity to strike letters.

- Students work with partners. Partners are given paper and pencil to record the letters they hit and to write down the words they create. Each partner must perform a sidearm strike and hit a vowel and two consonants until the pair has six letters to use to create words. The partners attempt to create six words using one or more of the letters they have hit. Once the partners have created six words and written them down, they attempt to spell the words by using the sidearm strike to hit each letter. Once a word is spelled, it may be checked off the list. If the students are unable to use a letter they have hit, they must strike that letter to delete it and select another letter.

PARTNER ACTIVITIES

CHALLENGES

Objective

To practice sidearm striking in a variety of settings.

Equipment

One ball (playground ball, foam ball, or volleyball) per pair of students and laminated challenge cards.

Activity

1. Each student selects a challenge card.
2. Students perform the tasks described on the cards.
3. Possible challenges may include the following:
   - Strike the ball using strong force (light force).
   - Strike the ball at targets at different levels (middle, low).
   - Strike the ball at the same time your partner does.

Extensions

- Place multicolored targets on the wall (no higher than 5 feet [1.5 m] above the floor) and have the partner tell the striker which target to hit.
- Suspend a rope between two game standards. Attach various objects (e.g., empty 2-liter plastic bottles, hoops, aluminum pie pans) to the rope. Students must call out which object they will hit before they strike the ball.

BACK IT UP

Objective

To sidearm strike the ball to a partner from different distances.

Equipment

One ball (volleyball, playground ball, or foam ball) per student pair.

Activity

1. Partners stand approximately 10 feet [3 m] apart and face each other.
2. The student with the ball sidearm strikes it to his partner, who must catch it after one bounce.

3. After the partner catches it, she sidearm strikes it back to the first student, who must catch it after only one bounce.

4. Once the ball has been hit and caught twice, one of the partners takes a step backward and the process is repeated.

5. If the ball is not struck correctly or caught, the partners must return to their original locations.

Extensions

- After the ball is struck correctly, the ball may bounce more than once before it is caught without students returning to their original locations.
- A volleyball net (or rope) may be used so that the students have to strike the ball over the net or rope and to their partners.

Based on Bryant and McLean Oliver 1975.

THROUGH THE HOOP

Objective

To improve the accuracy of sidearm striking by hitting a ball through a suspended hoop.

Equipment

One large hula hoop and one ball (beach ball, foam ball, or volleyball) per student pair. Suspend the hula hoop from an overhead structure (e.g., volleyball standards or basketball goals) approximately 2 feet (0.6 m) above the floor.

Activity

1. Partners stand on each side of the hoop.

2. Partners take turns trying to hit the ball using the sidearm strike so that the ball goes through the hoop.

Extensions

- Partners may count how many successful strikes they have in a specified time period (e.g., 1 minute).
- Partners may be required to have a successful catch before the strike is counted.

GROUP ACTIVITIES

CREATE YOUR OWN ACTIVITY

Objective

To allow students to create their own activities to reinforce sidearm striking skills.

Equipment

One piece of paper and pencil per group and a predetermined list of equipment you will allow the students to use in their activities (e.g., bowling pins, cones, ropes, hula hoops, beach balls, playground balls, volleyballs, foam balls, tennis balls).

Activity

1. Form groups of two to five students. You may select the groups or the students may form their own.

2. Each group creates an activity using sidearm striking as the basic skill. Students are required to have rules that encourage correct performance of the skill, include all players, and address all safety concerns.

3. The groups write their individual names, the rules of the activity, and the equipment needed on their paper, and then they show their activities to you.

4. After you approve their activities, the groups retrieve the necessary equipment and begin playing.

5. You must approve all changes to the activities.

Extensions

- One group may teach the activity to another group.
- Groups may teach their activities to the entire class.

CYCLE/RECYCLE

Objective

To practice sidearm striking by hitting all of the balls over a net.

Equipment

Two volleyball standards, a net placed at tennis height, and one foam ball per student.

Activity

1. Divide the class in half.
2. Place groups on either side of the net.
3. On the start signal, everyone sidearm strikes the balls over the net.
4. Students count the number of balls they strike over the net.

Extensions

- Students total the number of correctly performed sidearm strikes the entire group made over the net. These results can be recorded and later charted or graphed to show class improvement.
- Each time a student strikes the ball over the net, he goes around the standards and becomes a member of the other group.
- Place an additional net at volleyball height and challenge the students to strike the balls between the two nets.

Adapted, by permission, from J.A. Wessel, PhD, 1974, *Project I CAN* (Northbrook, IL: Hubbard).

KEEP IT GOING

Objective

To practice sidearm striking while hitting the ball over a net.

Equipment

Two volleyball standards, a net placed at tennis height, and one foam ball per group of four students.

Activity

1. Divide the students into groups of four.
2. Gather the students in a shuttle formation: Make one line with two students standing front to back on one side of the net and a line of two students standing front to back on the other side of the net.
3. The first student in line starts with a ball.

4. As soon as the first student in line strikes the ball over the net, she moves and stands behind the second student on the same side of the net.

5. After the ball goes over the net it must bounce. The first student in line on the opposite side of the net must strike it back.

6. That student then moves behind the second student on the same side of the net.

7. The striking continues until the ball cannot be struck after one bounce.

Extensions

- Students total the number of properly performed sidearm strikes the entire group made. These results can be recorded and later charted or graphed to show class improvement.

- Students are placed in groups of six to eight. Each time a student strikes the ball over the net, he goes around the standards and becomes a member of the other group. If the ball does not go over the net, the student tries the strike again.

SUMMARY

Perhaps the area of biggest concern with sidearm striking is the inability of the student to pivot or turn his side to the target. When that first action is omitted, the rest of the skill deteriorates. Unfortunately, this poor movement may be a result of the way he was taught. During initial instruction, it helps to have the students already assume a side orientation while they practice the other elements. As soon as the students begin to grasp the skills, however, be sure to include the pivot. Once the students are successful with this addition, increase the distance they have to move in order to strike the ball. This sequence will ensure a logical skill progression and make the practice more gamelike, and it will provide a better transition into future sport participation.

Sidearm Striking Troubleshooting Chart

If you see this	Then try this
1. Student not keeping eyes on the ball	• Place an empty 2-liter bottle upside down on top of a cone and have the student try to knock it off. • Draw a picture on the ball and have the student focus on this as he watches the ball. If the ball has words on it, just use the words. • The student's partner bounces a ball to her using light force. She must move so the ball will touch her belt buckle.
2. Student not turning side to the target	• Draw two arrows on the floor perpendicular to each other in front of both of the student's feet as he is standing in the ready position. Have the student practice rotating on the balls of his feet to turn his side to the target. • Have the student's partner give a verbal cue to turn as the ball comes toward the student. • Have the student's partner bounce a ball to her. The student must rotate so the ball will touch the side of her body.
3. Student not pulling the striking arm back	• Have the student turn and touch a wall behind him with the striking arm. • The student's partner stands behind her with one hand held in the stop position. The student turns and pulls her arm back until it touches the palm of the partner's hand.
4. Student not taking a step forward	• Use spots or footprints on the floor to indicate to the student where the opposite foot should be placed during the strike. • Have the student step over a line or flat object with the opposite foot before striking. • Use a small, nonskid "bug" (floor spot) in front of the stepping foot and ask the student to step on the bug as he strikes the ball. • Tie a pinny or scarf around the opposite leg. • Tape bubble wrap to the floor. Have the student step in opposition on that spot to create a noise.
5. Limited hip and shoulder rotation	• Have the student check her belt buckle position after the strike. It should be facing in the direction of the target. • Have a partner hold rubber tubing or stretch bands to add resistance while the student goes through the rotation motion.
6. Striking arm not coming through in an extended position	• Hang an object (small wind chimes, sheet, pie plates) from a net or rope suspended between two game standards. Have the student touch the object as the striking arm moves forward. • Have the student's partner hold an object (hula hoop, beanbag, plastic bottle). The student takes the object out of the partner's hand as the student moves his arm forward.
7. Student not continuing the follow-through	• Suspend a balloon from a basketball goal. Have the student perform the striking skill and touch the balloon with her hand as she finishes.

SIDEARM STRIKING LESSON PLAN

(FIRST LESSON)

AGE GROUP: First grade.

FOCUS: Dropping the ball and then contacting it.

SUBFOCUS: Stepping with appropriate foot, force, and catching.

OBJECTIVES: To drop a ball and contact it with the preferred hand four out of five times, as measured by teacher observation (**cues:** *drop, step, and hit*) and to step in opposition, as measured by teacher evaluation (**cue:** *use your stepping foot*).

MATERIALS AND EQUIPMENT: One beach ball or foam ball per student.

ADVANCE PREPARATION: A learning station for each child may be helpful. Place two pieces of floor tape or painter's tape on the floor. Use as many pairs of tape as you have students. These pieces of tape should be approximately 1 foot (0.3 m) apart and placed parallel to and approximately 15 feet (4.6 m) from the wall. This will enable each child to have her own place to practice. To facilitate distribution of equipment, place a playground ball or volleyball at each station (see figure).

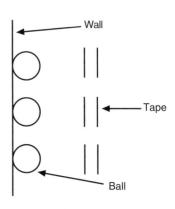

Setup for lesson.

ORGANIZATION AND MANAGEMENT: Students are in self-space for warm-up, instruction, and practice.

WARM-UP: Students enter gymnasium and find self-space.

Today we're going to review two of our locomotor skills, galloping and slow running, which is also called jogging. Let's start with galloping. Who can show me a good gallop? (Choose two students to demonstrate galloping. Stress the key elements of keeping one lead foot and the irregular step-together pattern.)

When I put the music on, I would like you to gallop in general space. When the music stops, you will wait for further directions. Do you understand? (Begin music.)

Watch for lead foot and step-together pattern. Stop music.

Freeze. Now, who can show me how to run slowly? (Choose two students to demonstrate jogging. Stress the key elements of *eyes forward* and *pump your arms.*)

When I put on the music, I would like you to jog in general space. When the music stops, you will freeze where you are and wait for more directions. Do you understand? (Begin music.)

Watch for eyes forward and the proper use of arms. Stop music.

Freeze. Your galloping and jogging are wonderful. Now, I'm going to try to trick you. When I put the music on, you will gallop. When the music stops, you will keep moving, but this time you will jog as I restart the music. When the music stops again, you will gallop. You will change locomotor skills each time the music stops. Now, which skill will we start with? **(Gallop.)** *Excellent. Do you have any questions?* (Begin music.)

Watch for proper skill performance and stop the music several times to allow the students to change skills.

INTRODUCTION:

Freeze. Everyone find their self-space and sit down. Excellent. Today we are going to learn how to strike a ball with our hands. Now, pretend you are in a parade. Wave with one hand. Excellent. Before, when we learned to roll and throw, we called this our throwing arm or strong arm. This same arm is our striking arm.

Hitting or striking a ball is a little different from the underhand roll. This time we have to turn our side to the target so that our striking arm is away from the wall. (Demonstrate.)

To do this, we turn our side to the wall and hold the ball in one hand and strike the ball with the other hand. Which arm would be the best for striking? **(The strong arm.)**

Notice that we have stations around the gymnasium. At each station there is a ball and there are two pieces of tape on the floor. Right now I do not need the ball, but watch as I practice. (Stand on the tape and then extend your preferred hand back.) *Girls and boys, notice that my striking arm is toward the middle of the gymnasium and away from the wall. I have one foot on each piece of tape. I bring back my striking arm and step toward the wall with the foot that is closest to the wall. As I step, I bring my striking arm forward.* (Repeat actions and the cues of *step* and *hit* several times.)

I need some helpers. (Select about five students, one of whom should be left-handed.) *Each of you find a station and stand on the tape with your striking arm toward the middle of the gymnasium.* (Watch for extension of the proper hand.) *Excellent. Now, girls and boys, notice that (student) has a striking arm that is different from the other students'. That's fine. What's important is that you use your striking arm. You do not have to be exactly like everyone else. It's y**our** striking arm.*

Let's see how well these students step and strike the ball. (Children repeat the action three or more times.)

Excellent. It's time for everyone to practice. When I call out a color you are wearing, I would like you to find a station and stand on the tape so that your striking arm is toward the middle of the gymnasium. (Call out colors until all children are at a station.) *Make sure you have your striking arm toward the middle of the gymnasium.*

Look for extension of the correct arm and make sure children are standing on the pieces of tape.

Very well done. Now, let's all practice stepping and striking the ball. Just like in underhand rolling and throwing, we have to step with our stepping foot. As I say the words step *and* hit, *you will step toward the wall with your foot that is closest to the wall—that's your stepping foot—and bring your striking arm forward.* (Repeat the cues *step* and *hit* at least five times.)

Look for extension of the correct arm and make sure children are stepping toward the wall.

Excellent. Now I think you're ready to try something a little harder. I want you to pretend that there is a ball in your other hand. You are going to pretend to drop it, then step and hit. Watch as I do this. (Demonstrate and say the cues *drop* and *step and hit.*) *Remember that we have to step and strike the ball at the same time. Everyone stand up and try this as I say the words.*

Repeat the cues *drop* and *step and hit* several times as you look for dropping the ball, extension of the correct arm, and children stepping toward the wall.

Freeze. Now I think you're ready to put everything together. Watch as I take the ball, hold it in one hand, and bring my striking arm back. I still have my feet on the tape, and now I'm going to **drop** *(not throw or bounce) the ball and then* **step** *and* **hit** *the ball with my striking arm.*

Demonstrate several times and repeat the cues *drop* and *step and hit.*

Let's see if some of you are ready. (Select about five children to practice the skill of dropping, stepping, and hitting as the cues are repeated. Correct actions are noted and problem areas addressed.)

Notice that some of the balls are bouncing off the wall too hard. How can we fix that problem? **(Use less force.)** *That's right. In fact, let's make it a rule that the ball must bounce* **once** *before it gets back to you. That way you will use light force.*

When I say go, I would like each of you to pick up the ball next to the wall, stand on your pieces of tape, bring your striking arm back, and hold the ball in your other hand. Do not drop the ball yet. Do you understand these directions? Go.

Watch for striking arm extended and side to the wall.

Now, when I say go, I would like you to drop the ball you are holding, step, and hit it. Make sure it bounces once before you catch it. Go.

Watch for striking arm extended, side to the wall, dropping (not throwing or bouncing) the ball, and contacting the ball with the extended arm.

Freeze. That was very well done. Now, I would like you to say the words drop, step, *and* hit *out loud as you practice. You may keep striking the ball, catching it, and striking it again as long as you keep repeating the words* drop, step, *and* hit *out loud each time. Remember to use* **light force,** *and remember that the ball must bounce once before it returns to you and the tape. Do you understand these directions? Go.*

Freeze. This time I would like you to count how many times you can strike the ball against the wall **and** *catch it. Remember, the ball has to bounce once. Go.*

Watch for striking arm extended, side to the wall, dropping (not throwing or bouncing) the ball, and contacting the ball with the extended arm.

Freeze. How many of you were able to catch it five times? Eight times? Ten times? Terrific. If you were able to catch it 10 times, you may play wall ball. Find a partner. Watch as (student) and I play. (Demonstrate as you give directions.) I strike the ball to the wall, it bounces, and then (student) catches it. Then he strikes the ball and I catch it. We still have to have our side to the wall, we use our stepping foot, and we drop the ball. We want our partner to be able to catch it, so we still use light force.

If you weren't able to catch it 10 times, you should keep practicing by yourself for the next few minutes. Does everyone understand these directions? Go.

Watch for cooperative play as well as striking arm extended, side to the wall, dropping (not throwing or bouncing) the ball, and contacting the ball with the extended arm.

Freeze. If you have been working alone, I would like you to find a partner and play wall ball. Go.

The activity continues for 3 to 5 minutes.

Freeze. Time is up. Please return the balls to their place near the wall and line up for your teacher.

CLOSURE: Children are lined up to leave.

(Student), tell me one thing I should do to get ready to strike the ball. (Do what the child instructs. Call on another student and do exactly *what the child explains. Keep modifying the movement and asking questions until sidearm striking is performed correctly.)*

Now, help me remember some of the cues we have used. **(Drop, step and hit.)** *Excellent. Next time, we will work on hitting a target with our two-hand sidearm strike.*

TWO-HAND SIDEARM STRIKING

Two-hand sidearm striking is used when batting a ball. Equipment should be of an appropriate weight and size for children in every activity, especially when using long-handled implements. When children use bats that are too heavy, they often use an open grip (hands apart), and they will become fatigued after only a few swings. Because children should practice striking with bats they can control, we recommend using plastic bats initially and then using heavier bats when students are ready for them.

Safety concerns must be addressed with all skills, but especially with batting. Besides using plastic bats, we suggest using yarn, foam, cloth, or *soft* rubber balls. Real softballs and baseballs are inappropriate for physical education classes.

Safety must be taught and practiced. Often young children become so excited about retrieving balls that have been hit that they do not look where they are moving. You must continuously remind children to hold the bat securely, look before they swing, and look where they are moving. We recommend setting up clearly marked areas around the batter so that children are prevented from walking in front of or behind the batter. By properly planning lessons, you can substantially reduce the risk of injuries.

National Standards & Grade-Level Outcomes for K-12 Physical Education (SHAPE America, 2014) addresses two-hand sidearm striking in the section on striking with long-handled implements (S1.E25). This section includes bats, golf clubs, and hockey sticks. However, only the outcomes related to two-hand sidearm striking are addressed in this text. According to the outcomes, sidearm striking is not developmentally appropriate until the second grade; it is recommended that second graders be able to strike a ball off of a tee or cone with a bat using correct grip and proper side and body orientation (S1.E25.2). In the third grade, students can strike a ball with a bat, sending the ball forward, while using the proper grip. In fourth grade, students can strike an object with a bat demonstrating three of the five critical elements of a mature pattern (grip, stance, body orientation, swing, plane, and follow-through) (S1.E25.4) In fifth grade, students can strike a pitched ball with a bat using a mature pattern (S1.E25.5a) and can combine striking with receiving and traveling skills in a small-sided game (S1.E25.5b). Since this skill requires many repetitions, all of our suggested drills and activities assume the use of a batting tee.

Critical Elements

Foot Placement	Ready Position	Step and Swing	Hit	Follow Through
To find proper foot placement, the student's front foot is in line with the tee. The student then extends her arms so that the thickest part of the bat touches the tee. The student takes one small step away from the intended direction of the strike. The side is now toward the area to which the ball will be hit.	When gripping the bat, the preferred hand is above the other hand and is level with the armpit. The chin is placed on the shoulder, looking toward the direction the ball will be hit. The bat is behind the shoulder away from the target, and the back elbow is parallel to the ground.	Step forward with opposite foot while back foot remains stationary. Weight transfers from the back foot to the front foot as the hip and shoulder begin to rotate.	Arms extend and ball is contacted in front of the body and in line with the front foot. Use the upper half of the bat when striking the ball.	The bat continues past the point of the strike, the back shoulder moves to a position under the chin, and both hands remain on the bat.

Cue Words

The cue words you select for each phase of the skill will depend on the age of the students you are teaching and your areas of emphasis. In usable sets we list some of the cue words we use to teach two-hand sidearm striking. You may use each set individually or mix and match the cue words as needed. It is beneficial to have the students say the words out loud as they practice the skill.

Ready and **bat back**—stand with the nonpreferred side toward the intended target. When gripping the bat, the preferred hand is above the other hand and level with the armpit, and the chin is placed on the shoulder looking toward the direction the ball will be hit. The bat is behind the shoulder away from the target, and the back elbow is parallel to the ground.

Step and swing—step forward with the front foot while the back foot pivots but remains stationary. Weight transfers from the back foot to the front foot as the hips and shoulders begin to rotate.

Step—step forward with the foot closest to the target.

Swing—as hips and shoulders rotate, the bat is brought forward and strikes ball. Arms are fully extended.

Step and hit—step with foot closest to target, hips and shoulders rotate, and bat contacts the ball.

Hit—arms extend and ball is contacted in front of the body and in line with the front foot using the upper half of the bat.

Follow through—the bat continues past the point of the strike, the back shoulder moves to a position under the chin, and both hands remain on the bat.

Shoulder—the bat continues past the point of the strike, and the back shoulder moves to a position under the chin. Both hands remain on the bat.

Swing through the ball—step with foot closest to target, hips and shoulders rotate, and the bat contacts the middle of the ball. The bat continues past the point of the strike, the back shoulder moves to a position under the chin, and both hands remain on the bat.

Cue set 1: ready, step and swing, hit, follow through
Cue set 2: ready, step, swing
Cue set 3: bat back, step and hit, shoulder
Cue set 4: ready, swing through the ball

SUGGESTED ACTIVITIES FOR REINFORCING AND ASSESSING THE CRITICAL ELEMENTS

In the learning process, it is essential that students know how a skill is supposed to look, what its critical elements are, and how to perform each individual element correctly. In the preceding section, we provided pictures and descriptions of two-hand sidearm striking, divided it into its critical elements, and provided possible cue words. In addition to the material in chapter 1 that reinforces the concepts for all locomotor and manipulative skills, the following section provides specific activities for reinforcing the critical elements unique to two-hand sidearm striking.

PARTNER SKILL CHECK

Objective
To allow partners to assess each other's progress in learning the skill.

Equipment
Partner skill check assessments, pencils, and one bat and ball for each set of partners. If the students cannot read or do not speak English, the picture version of the partner skill check sheet may be useful.

Activity
1. One partner observes the other to see if she has the correct form for the ready position.
2. If the ready position is correct, then the partner places a *Y* in the first box. If the ready position is incorrect, he places an *N* in the first box. Nonreaders can put a smiling face if the ready position is correct or a frowning face if the ready position is incorrect.

3. This evaluation continues until each of the elements has been assessed five times.

4. A partner skill check assessment is used for each student.

Extensions

- You may use the partner skill check assessment to evaluate the skill development of each student.

- You may send partner skill check assessments home with report cards or as individual skills develop.

SUCCESS BUILDERS

The success builder activities allow you to address individual needs. If students need additional help on specific critical elements, the activities listed here will help reinforce correct performance.

Objective

To improve areas of deficiency as assessed by the partner skill check.

Equipment

See the following individual stations. We suggest using an unbreakable mirror and a poster of each critical element of two-hand sidearm striking at each station. The mirror is particularly helpful in these activities because it allows the children to see what they are doing. The easiest way to make the posters is to print out the drawings from this book and enlarge them. Laminating the posters will ensure their use for many years.

Activity

1. Set up a station for each of the critical elements in the teaching area. Post a description or a picture of the specific element at the corresponding station.
2. Find proper foot placement. The student's front foot should be in line with the tee. The student then extends her arms so that the thickest part of the bat touches the tee. The student then takes one small step away from the intended direction of the strike. The side is now toward the area to which the ball will be hit.
3. The details for each station follow:

READY

Stand with the side toward the intended target. When gripping the bat, the preferred hand is above the other hand and is level with the armpit. The chin is placed on the shoulder, looking toward the direction the ball will be hit. The bat is behind the shoulder away from the target, and the back elbow is parallel to the ground.

Equipment

Poster of the ready position, bat, mirror, and partner evaluations.

Activity

The student assumes the ready position. The partner checks to see if her position matches the poster. The student refers to the mirror for help. The partner then tells the student to put the bat down and get ready, and the activity is repeated until the student can perform the ready position five times in a row. When the student is successful, she may return to the rest of the group.

STEP AND SWING

Step forward with the front foot while the back foot remains stationary. Weight transfers from the back foot to the front foot as the hip and shoulder rotate.

Equipment

Poster of the step and swing, bat, tape on the floor, and partner evaluations.

Activity

The student stands on tape that is shoulder-width apart with the nonpreferred side toward the target. On his partner's command, he steps toward the target with the front foot, placing it on a piece of tape placed in the appropriate spot (refer to drawing of step and swing). After this can be accomplished without problems, the swing is added. The student assumes the ready position while holding a bat. On his partner's command, he steps toward the target and swings the bat.

HIT

Arms extend and ball is contacted in front of the body and in line with the front foot. Use the thickest part of the bat when striking the ball.

Equipment

Poster of the hit, batting tee (target is the wall), bats, cloth balls, and partner evaluations.

Activity

The student approaches the tee and extends the bat to determine where she must stand in order for the bat to strike the tip of the tee. The partner evaluates the student as she practices the ready and step and swing, and then she strikes the very tip of the tee. The partner provides feedback so that the student strikes the tee in the proper location. When this can be completed at least five times in a row, a cloth ball is added and the partner continues to evaluate. The student may return to the rest of the class after this activity can be accomplished five times in a row.

FOLLOW THROUGH

The bat continues past the point of the hit and both hands remain on the bat.

Equipment

Poster of the follow-through, bat, and partner evaluations.

Activity

Using the mirror, the student attempts to swing at an imaginary ball. She concentrates on having the bat go through the ball and on finishing with the back shoulder under the chin. After the partner indicates that this has been accomplished five times in a row, the pair may return to the rest of the class.

SUGGESTED CULMINATING ACTIVITIES TO REINFORCE THE ENTIRE SKILL

As in all manipulative skills, the critical elements of two-hand sidearm striking should be mastered before accuracy is emphasized. With two-hand sidearm striking, however, adjusting the step to direct the travel of the ball is a necessary skill. It should not supersede the correct execution of the other aspects of two-hand sidearm striking. As in all target activities, use targets that are large enough to allow the students to perform the critical elements of the skill and have success hitting the target.

INDIVIDUAL ACTIVITIES

BATTING TEE CHALLENGES

Objective

To improve two-hand sidearm striking by hitting balls from a batting tee.

Equipment

Each student pair will need a batting tee (or traffic cone), a bat, one Wiffle ball (or yarn ball), and three targets attached to the wall.

Activity

Tees are placed approximately 15 feet (4.6 m) from the wall, and students attempt to strike the ball toward the wall. Using the batting tee (or traffic cone), students use correct form to do the following:

- Strike the ball to the wall without touching the tee.

- Hit the ball to a target on the wall that is directly in front of the tee.
- Adjust their stance in order to strike the ball to one of three targets that are placed on the wall.

Extensions

- Suspend a net between two game standards. Have the students try to strike the ball into the net.
- Suspend two ropes between two game standards with approximately 2 feet (0.6 m) between them. Have the students attempt to strike the ball so that it travels between the two ropes.

WHACK IT

Objective

To improve two-hand sidearm striking by hitting a suspended ball.

Equipment

One bat and one Wiffle ball suspended by a heavy string from an overhead structure (e.g., basketball goal). The ball should hang within the student's strike zone.

Activity

1. The ball is stationary.
2. The student goes through the ready, step and swing, hit, and follow-through elements while striking the Wiffle ball.

Extensions

- A partner may evaluate the student's technique.
- The student attempts to strike the ball as it gently swings toward her.

PARTNER ACTIVITIES

CHALLENGES

Objective

To practice two-hand striking in a variety of settings.

Equipment

One ball, one bat, and one batting tee (or traffic cone) per pair of students and laminated challenge cards.

Activity

1. Each student selects a challenge card.
2. Students perform the tasks described on the cards.
3. Possible challenges may include the following:
   - Strike the ball using strong force (light force).
   - Strike the ball to hit targets at different levels (high, middle, low).
   - Strike the ball to hit targets in different locations (in front of the batter, to the left, to the right).

Extensions

- Place three targets on the wall side by side (different colors of construction paper work well). Partners challenge each other to strike specific targets.
- Increase the distance between the targets so that students are challenged to hit in a variety of directions.

MOVING TARGET

Objective

To strike a moving ball that a partner is swinging.

Equipment

A bat and one tennis ball inside of one leg of a pair of pantyhose.

Activity

1. This activity should be used with well-skilled fourth or fifth graders only. They should be reminded to hold on to the swinging ball and bat at all times.
2. One partner swings the pantyhose and ball over her head (like a lasso) so that it is in the strike zone of her partner.
3. The student attempts to strike the ball.
4. Students change positions after five hits.

Extensions

- Use the pantyhose with a soft rag ball.
- Count how many times the batter can strike the ball in a row. Have the partners total the strikes and add these to the rest of the class's scores.

GROUP ACTIVITIES

CREATE YOUR OWN ACTIVITY

Objective

To allow students to create their own activities to reinforce two-hand sidearm striking skills.

Equipment

One piece of paper and pencil per group and a predetermined list of equipment you will allow the students to use in their activities (e.g., cloth balls or rag balls, bats, cones, ropes, hula hoops, foam balls).

Activity

1. Form groups of two to five students. You may select the groups, or the students can form their own.
2. Each group creates an activity using two-hand striking as the basic skill. Students are required to have rules that encourage correct performance of the skill, include all players, and address all safety concerns.
3. The groups write their individual names, the rules of the activity, and the equipment needed on their papers, and then they show the activities to you.
4. After you approve their activities, the groups retrieve the necessary equipment and begin playing.
5. You must approve all changes to the activities.

Extensions

- Groups may teach their activities to other groups.
- Groups may teach their activities to the entire class.

SUMMARY

The increasing number of teeball and peewee baseball and softball teams has made learning the skill of batting (two-hand sidearm striking) very important to young children. As teachers, we will inevitably compete with the advice of coaches, parents, and grandparents when we teach this skill. We will also encounter children who want to use heavier bats (as they use in practice) or who possibly practice prebatting rituals like the big-league players do. While these outside influences can be challenging to work with, our focus should remain on proper mechanics and form.

With proper organization of your lesson plans, children will receive many more opportunities to practice two-hand sidearm striking in physical education than they will on recreational teams. The gymnasium can function as the batting clinic that will provide the foundation for later success on the athletic field.

Two-Hand Sidearm Striking (Batting) Troubleshooting Chart

If you see this	Then try this
1. Back elbow not parallel to the ground	• Have the student demonstrate the ready position (without a bat) with the teacher or partner lifting the elbow to the correct position, if needed. • Set up a mirror and have the student demonstrate the ready position.
2. Feet not in proper position in relation to the tee (or plate)	• Place tape on the floor and have the student stand on the tape. • Place a jump rope on the ground parallel to the plate. The student must stand behind the rope before hitting the ball.
3. Student not stepping forward on front foot	• Place a footprint or tape where the student should step. • Have the student practice the swing a set number of times while the partner counts the number of times the student does not step. The object is to get a score of zero. • Tie a pinny or scarf around the opposite leg. • Tape bubble wrap to the floor. Have the student step in opposition on that spot to create a noise.
4. Limited hip and shoulder rotation	• Have the student check the position of his belt buckle. After the ball is hit, the belt buckle should be pointing in the direction of the target. • The batter stands in the batting position with correct feet and hands but no bat. The batter holds rubber tubing or a stretch band in her hands while the partner holds the other end, adding resistance as the batter swings. This increases the batter's awareness of shoulder rotation.
5. Arms not coming through in an extended position	• Hang an object (small wind chimes, sheet, pie plates) from a net or rope suspended between two game standards. Have the student touch the object as the arms swing forward. • Have the student's partner hold an object (hula hoop, beanbag, plastic bottle). The student takes the object out of the partner's hand as she swings her arms forward.
6. Head moving during the swing or student not keeping eyes on the ball	• Place a baseball or softball glove on the student's head. The student swings the bat. The object is for the student to keep the head stationary, which will keep the glove on his head. • Color half of a 6-inch (15 cm) ball one color and the other half a different color (you can use markers or paint). After hitting a pitched or tossed ball, the student must be able to tell the teacher or a partner what color she hit.
7. Student not continuing the follow-through	• Have the student practice swinging an imaginary bat. The student should focus on keeping his head still and rotating his shoulders so that the rotation progresses from the front shoulder under the chin to the back shoulder under the chin.

TWO-HAND SIDEARM STRIKING LESSON PLAN

(SECOND LESSON)

AGE GROUP: Third grade.

FOCUS: Attaining a level swing.

SUBFOCUS: Proper step.

OBJECTIVE: To swing the bat in a horizontal plane three out of five times, as measured by teacher evaluation (**cue:** swing **through** the ball).

MATERIALS AND EQUIPMENT: One plastic bat or piece of PVC plastic pipe, two traffic cones, a hula hoop, and one small foam ball per child.

ADVANCE PREPARATION: If possible, set up a learning station for each child. Attach a construction paper target to the wall about 3 feet (1 m) above the floor. Balance a foam ball on an 26-inch (66 cm) traffic cone, and place the cone approximately 10 feet (3 m) from the wall. Place another cone against the wall for later use. To prepare for the warm-up, scatter hula hoops throughout the gymnasium. Place a plastic bat or piece of PVC pipe (1 inch [2.5 cm] in diameter and approximately 3 feet [1 m] long) inside each hoop.

ORGANIZATION AND MANAGEMENT: Students are in self-space for warm-up, instruction, and practice. Teaching stations are set up as described in the advance preparation section.

WARM-UP:

Today we're going to review two of our locomotor skills, galloping and skipping. Let's start with galloping. Who can show me a good gallop? (Choose two students to demonstrate galloping while stressing the key elements of keeping one lead foot and the irregular step-together pattern.)

Excellent. When I put the music on, I would like everyone to gallop in general space. The hula hoops will be used later, so just go around them now. Do you understand these directions? Go.

Watch the students gallop to determine whether they are performing the skill correctly and to make sure they are using the general space appropriately.

(Stop music.) *Freeze. Stand quietly where you are. Now, let's review skipping. It is a* **step, hop.** (Select two students to demonstrate skipping.) *When the music begins, I would like you to skip in general space. When the music stops, you will gallop. When it stops again, you will skip. Now, which locomotor skill will we begin with?* **(Skipping.)** *Good.* (Begin music. Stop the music several times for the students to change locomotor skills.)

Watch students for correct execution of the skills.

(Stop music.) *Freeze. I would like each of you to find the nearest hula hoop, place the equipment outside of the hoop, and sit inside the hoop. Go.*

INTRODUCTION:

Yesterday we learned how to hold a bat correctly. Who can tell me how I place my hands? **(Preferred hand is above the other hand and they are on the end of the bat.)**

Pretend I am the pitcher or your target. I would like each of you to stand up **inside** *your hula hoop, pick up the bat (or PVC pipe), hold it correctly, and turn your side toward me. Go.*

Watch for correct hand placement on the bat and correct side orientation.

How far back should I bring my hands? **(So they are even with the armpits.)** *Excellent. Everyone pull your bat back to where it should be.*

Walk around the gymnasium to make sure the students are holding their bats correctly. Point out correct student performance.

Everyone stand outside of your hoop. (Demonstrate as you give directions.) *Bring the bat back, even with your armpits. Swing the bat forward as you step. Remember, we use some of the same ideas we used with the overhand throw—we step with our stepping foot (stepping in opposition) and we make sure we squash the bug (pivot) on our back foot.*

As I repeat the cues **ready** *and* **step and swing,** *each of you show me your swing. Remember to stay* **near** *your hoop but not in it. This way we can really spread out and we won't trip on the hoops.*

Repeat the cues *ready* and *step and swing* as you watch for hand position, step, and swing.

Freeze. Now, this time when you swing, I want you to think about swinging so that your bat is level. You have to swing **through the ball.** *Watch as I show a level swing. (Demonstrate swinging level.) See how different that is than if I swing like this? (Demonstrate a swing that finishes upward.) If I strike the ball, where would it go?* **(Up.)** *That's right. I want to swing level. (Demonstrate again.) Now, if I chop down (demonstrate), where will the ball go?* **(Down.)** *That's right. I want to swing* **level.** *I need to* **swing through the ball.** *Everyone practice your swing on your own and think about swinging* **through the ball.** *Go.*

Watch for correct execution of the skill.

Freeze. I think you're ready to put your skills to use. When I call out a color you are wearing, I would like you to take your bat and sit beside one of the traffic cones away from the walls. (Dismiss children by color of clothing.)

This time you will be hitting off a batting tee or, for us, a traffic cone. Watch as I place the ball on the tee. I need to stand so that my side is toward the target. I bring my bat back, step, and swing. If I stand too far in front of the cone, can I have a level swing? (Demonstrate.) **(No.)** *I need to stand so that my front foot (the foot closest to the wall) is even with the cone. Everyone stand up, place the ball on the cone, and stand as if you were going to hit it but* **don't strike it yet.**

Walk around the space to make sure students are holding their bats correctly and are standing beside the cones properly. If necessary, painter's tape can be placed on the floor to assist students in finding their ready positions.

*Excellent. Now, as I repeat the cues, I would like you to say the cues with me—***ready, swing through the ball***—as you hit the ball off the cone.*

Repeat the cues with the students as they perform the skill. Students should repeat the activity at least five times with you telling them when to retrieve the balls and when to strike.

You're doing very well. I would like you to practice your swings by yourselves. Try to swing so that you can hit the construction paper in front of your cone. Go.

Students repeat this drill for about 3 minutes as you walk around making corrections. After 3 minutes instruct the students to stop, and then point out several children who are showing the correct form. Students then resume practice.

Freeze. This time, I am going to walk around the gymnasium and give each of you different things to do. So if you see someone doing something different from what you are doing, it's all right. Resume practicing.

Help each student with problem areas. If a student is coming under the ball, place a traffic cone behind the one with the ball. To strike the ball, the student will have to swing level. If a student is chopping down on the ball, place the cone in front of the other cone (nearer the wall). If the student is having no difficulty, place the other cone in front of the first cone and put a ball on top of it. Challenge the student to strike both balls.

Freeze. Everyone return your equipment to where you found it when class began— bats in hoops, extra cones and balls against the wall—and line up. (Line up students to leave.)

CLOSURE:

I am going to pretend to strike a ball with the bat. I will call on several students to tell me whether I am performing the skill correctly. (Use a reverse grip, step with wrong foot, hold the bat too low or too high, chop the ball, and so forth.) *How does it look?* (Students correct each problem.)

Now, tell me the cues we used today for two-hand sidearm striking. **(Ready, swing through the ball, hit, and follow through.)** *How do I swing through a ball?* **(Hit it in the middle, swing level).** *Excellent. Tomorrow we will move our cones farther back and continue to work on hitting the targets.*

8

Volleying

Many sports require accurate passes for successful play (e.g., basketball, football, soccer throw-ins). With these passes, the passer has the ball and then throws it to another person. In the skill of volleying, however, the ball originates with someone else. The passer must move to the ball and contact it briefly to pass it on to a teammate or over the net. As in catching and striking, the receiver's actions are very much affected by the oncoming ball.

In this chapter, we focus on the forearm pass and the overhead volley (pass) used in volleyball. While striking skills with balloons may begin in the primary grades, forearm and overhead volleying are more advanced and instruction should begin in the intermediate grades.

We have found that beach balls provide an excellent lead-in for mastering volleying skills. They are larger, move slower, do not sting, and are fairly inexpensive. If funding permits, volleyball trainers would be the next type of ball for students to use as they progress. These balls move a little faster than beach balls and are more durable. Foam balls, Gator Skin balls, or Super-Safe balls may serve as substitutes. Real volleyballs, however, should be reserved for middle school students.

National Standards & Grade-Level Outcomes for K-12 Physical Education (SHAPE America, 2014) does not address forearm passing, but it does include overhead volleying (S1.E23) as a skill for fourth and fifth graders. We believe forearm passing is also an upper-elementary skill.

FOREARM PASSING

Forearm passing is used exclusively in the sport of volleyball. Kindergarten students can begin the basics of forearm passing (hitting a ball with two hands at the same time) as they begin to learn striking skills. However, the skill is very complicated because it involves coordinating arms and legs and being able to react to a ball moving toward you. Mastery of most of the critical elements will not occur until fourth grade. Being able to forearm pass a ball to a specific location will occur later.

Critical Elements

Move to the Ball

Move so that the arms are below the ball.

Ready Position

Eyes on ball, knees bent, feet shoulder-width apart, one foot in front of the other, hands together, and arms parallel to thighs.

Extend to Hit

Wait until the ball is at a middle to low level. The ball contacts the lower half of the forearm. When the ball contacts the arm, it is below shoulder level. Legs extend as the ball is contacted to generate power.

Follow Through

Hands remain joined and arms do not go past shoulder level.

Cue Words

The cue words you select for each phase of the skill will depend on the age of the students you are teaching and your areas of emphasis. In usable sets are some of the cue words we use to teach forearm passing. You may use each set individually or mix and match the cue words as needed. We have found that it is beneficial to have the students say the words out loud as they practice the skill.

Move to the ball—move so that the arms are below the ball.

Ready—eyes on ball, knees bent, feet shoulder-width apart, one foot in front of the other, hands together, and arms parallel to thighs.

Get under the ball—move so that the arms are below the ball.

Extend to hit—wait until the ball is at a middle to low level. The ball contacts the lower half of the forearm. When the ball contacts the arm, it is below shoulder level. Legs extend as the ball is contacted to generate power.

Lift or bump—contact the ball on the lower half of the forearm and below the shoulder level. Legs extend to create power.

Follow through—hands remain joined and the arms do not go past shoulder level.

> *Cue set 1:* move to ball, ready, hit and extend, follow through
> *Cue set 2:* move, ready, lift
> *Cue set 3:* move, ready, bump
> *Cue set 4:* get under the ball, lift

Ways to Teach Correct Hand Positions

Since learning the correct way to hold the hands is essential to the forearm pass, the following are ways to learn correct hand placement:

1. **Fist method**—make a fist with one hand with the thumb on top. Take the other hand and wrap it around the fist with the thumb on top. The two thumbs are together. Extend arms downward to create a flat surface for contact.

2. **Traditional method**—place the nonpreferred hand on top of the preferred hand, making an X. Hands are rolled (or curled) to allow the thumbs to come together. Extend arms downward and roll wrists outward to create a flat surface for contact.

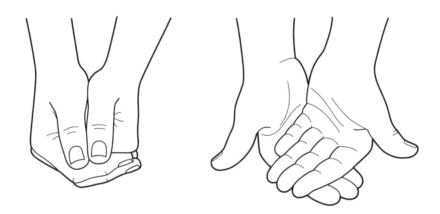

Suggested Activities for Reinforcing and Assessing the Critical Elements

In the learning process, it is essential that students know how a skill is supposed to look, what its critical elements are, and how to perform each critical element correctly. In the preceding section, we provided pictures and descriptions of forearm passing, divided it into its critical elements, and provided possible cue words. In addition to the material in chapter 1 that reinforces the concepts for all locomotor and manipulative skills, the following section provides specific activities for reinforcing the critical elements unique to forearm passing.

PARTNER SKILL CHECK

Objective

To allow partners to assess each other's progress in learning the skill.

Equipment

Partner skill check assessment, pencils, and one ball for each pair of partners. If the students cannot read or do not speak English, the picture version of the partner skill check assessment may be useful.

Activity

1. One partner observes the other to see if she has the correct form for the ready position.

2. If the ready position is correct, then the partner places a *Y* in the first box. If the ready position is incorrect, he places an *N* in the first box. Nonreaders can put a smiling face in the box if the ready position is correct or a frowning face if the ready position is incorrect.

3. This evaluation continues until each of the critical elements has been assessed five times.

4. A partner skill check assessment is used for each student.

Extensions

• You may use the partner skill check assessment to measure the skill development of each student.

• You may send the partner skill check assessment home with report cards or as individual skills develop.

SUCCESS BUILDERS

The success builder activities allow you to address individual needs. If students need additional help on individual critical elements, the activities listed here will help reinforce correct performance.

Objective

To allow partners to improve areas of deficiency as assessed by the partner skill check.

Equipment

See the following individual stations. We suggest using an unbreakable mirror and a poster of each critical element of forearm passing at each station. The mirror is particularly helpful in these activities because it allows the children to see what they are doing. The easiest way to make the posters is to print out the drawings from this book and enlarge them. Laminating the posters will ensure their use for many years.

Activity

1. Set up a station for each of the critical elements in the teaching area. Post a description or a picture of the specific element at the corresponding station.

2. The details for each station follow:

HAND POSITION

There are two primary ways to arrange the hands for forearm passing. The teacher should use the one most appropriate for her students. As a review, the two methods are as follows:

- The fist method is used with beginners. To perform this, make a fist with one hand with the thumb on top. Take the other hand and wrap it around the fist with the thumb on top. The two thumbs are together. Extend arms downward to create a flat surface for contact. As soon as possible, encourage the student to use the traditional method.

- For the traditional method, place the nonpreferred hand on top of the preferred hand, making an X. Hands are rolled (or curled) to allow the thumbs to come together. Extend arms downward and roll wrists outward to create a flat surface for contact.

Equipment

Poster of the fist method, mirror (if available), and partner evaluations

Activity

The student joins her hands to demonstrate the proper hand position. The partner checks to see if her position matches the poster. The student refers to the mirror for help. The student separates her hands and, on a signal from her partner, assumes the correct hand position again. Once the student can demonstrate the correct hand position to the partner, partners may return to practicing the entire skill.

MOVE TO THE BALL

Move so that the arms are below the ball.

Equipment

Poster of moving to the ball, partner evaluations, and a 10-foot (3 m) square box taped to the floor.

Activity

The student assumes a ready position. The partner tosses a ball approximately 10 feet (3 m) in the air. The student must catch it. After three catches, the partner begins to toss the ball so that the student has to move to catch it. None of these tosses should require the student to go outside of the 10-foot (3 m) square. Once the student can move to the ball, the partners may return to practicing the entire skill.

READY

Eyes on ball, knees bent, feet shoulder-width apart, one foot in front of the other, hands together, and arms parallel to thighs.

Equipment

Poster of the ready position, mirror (if available), and partner evaluations.

Activity

The student assumes the ready position. The partner checks to see if his position matches the poster. The student refers to the mirror for help. The student pretends to pass a ball and, on a signal from his partner, assumes the ready position again. Once the student can demonstrate the ready position to the partner, the partners may return to practicing the entire skill.

EXTEND TO HIT

Wait until ball is at a middle to low level. The ball contacts lower half of the forearm. When the ball contacts the arm, it is below shoulder level. The legs extend as the ball is contacted to generate power.

Equipment

Poster of the extend to hit, ball suspended from a basketball goal (child's waist height), beach balls, and partner evaluations.

Activity 1

The partner loosely holds a ball at waist level with arms fully extended. The student attempts to contact the ball and hit it out of her partner's hands.

Activity 2

Using the suspended ball, the student stands so that his arms are under the ball. He will use his legs to provide the majority of the power as he contacts the ball. The partner watches to see if most of the power comes from the legs and there is little arm swing. Once the student can follow through, the partners may return to practicing the entire skill.

FOLLOW THROUGH

Hands remain joined and arms do not go past shoulder level.

Equipment

Poster of the follow-through, projector, unbreakable mirror, and partner evaluations.

Activity 1

The student stands so that he is between the projector and a wall. It should be possible for the student to cast a shadow on the wall when he practices. Place a tape line on the wall slightly below the student's shoulder. The student practices the forearm pass, and his partner places a piece of tape on the wall showing how far his hand went after the pass. The partners continue the activity until the student consistently stops the follow-through before reaching shoulder level.

Activity 2

The student faces the mirror and practices the forearm pass without a ball. The student watches the mirror to determine where she ends the follow-through. The partner may also evaluate the student. Once the student can extend to hit, the partners may return to practicing the entire skill.

SUGGESTED CULMINATING ACTIVITIES TO REINFORCE THE ENTIRE SKILL

INDIVIDUAL ACTIVITIES

SELF-HIT

Objective
To improve forearm passing by repeatedly hitting the ball into the air.

Equipment
Beach ball or other soft-texture ball (e.g., volleyball trainer, Gator Skin ball, foam ball) for each student.

Activity
1. The student finds an open space.
2. The ball is tossed in the air.
3. The student attempts to repeatedly hit the ball without letting it touch the ground.

Extensions
- The ball may bounce once and the student may continue to hit it.
- The student must remain in a specific area (a 10-foot [3 m] square) when contacting the ball.

TARGET GAME

Objective
To improve forearm passing by hitting a specific target.

Equipment
Tape (to make large targets of triangles, squares, rectangles, or other shapes on the wall of the gymnasium or activity area) and a ball for each student (e.g., beach ball, foam ball, Gator Skin ball). These targets should be at least 9 feet above the floor to simulate the height of a volleyball net, approximately 1 to 1.5 feet (30-45 cm) higher than the net.

Activity
1. Students will use forearm passing to hit the ball against the wall and into the target.
2. Students attempt to hit the target five times in a row.

Extensions
- Instead of using different geometric shapes, students could attempt to hit specific colors.
- The ball can hit the ground once and then be hit again.
- Taped targets may be around the gymnasium. Students may be challenged to hit each target five times in a row and then move to a new target.
- Tape targets on the floor of the gymnasium. Challenge students to have the ball land in each target.

PARTNER ACTIVITIES

PARTNER PASS AND CATCH

Objective

To improve accuracy of forearm passing.

Equipment

One beach ball, foam ball, or volleyball trainer per pair of students.

Activity

1. Partners stand approximately 10 feet (3 m) apart.
2. One student tosses the ball to his partner.
3. The receiver uses a forearm pass to send it back so that the first student can catch it.

Extensions

- Have the partners count how many passes and catches they can complete in a row.
- Have the tosser stand in a hula hoop and toss the ball to the partner. The partner uses the forearm pass to hit the ball back to the tosser. If the tosser stays in the hula hoop with both feet and catches the ball, the pair receives five points. If one foot goes outside of the hoop, the pair earns three points. If the ball is caught but both feet are outside of the hoop, the pair earns one point. No points are earned if the ball is not caught. Students can keep score.

KEEP IT GOING

Objective

To improve forearm passing by hitting the ball back and forth with a partner.

Equipment

One beach ball, foam ball, or volleyball trainer per pair of students.

Activity

1. Partners stand approximately 10 feet (3 m) apart.
2. One partner tosses the ball to the other, and she uses a forearm pass to send it back.
3. The original tosser uses a forearm pass to send the ball back to her partner again in an attempt to keep the ball going.

Extensions

- Allow the ball to bounce once before it is hit again.
- Have the partners keep track of how many hits they are able to perform in a row.
- After each successful pass, each student moves back one step to increase the challenge.
- Add a volleyball net (or a rope placed between two game standards) and have the partners keep the ball going back and forth over the net.

WALL BALL

Objective

To develop forearm passing by hitting the ball against the wall.

Equipment

One foam ball or volleyball trainer per student pair and a line taped on the wall approximately 10 feet (3 m) above the floor.

Activity

1. Partners stand at least 10 feet (3 m) from the wall.
2. One partner uses the forearm pass to hit the ball against the wall.
3. Her partner has to catch the ball after it comes off the wall but before it hits the ground.
4. When the partner has caught the ball, she must use the forearm pass to send the ball back to the wall from the place she caught it.
5. Partners count how many passes and catches they have in a row.

Extensions

- Place a target on the wall and challenge the partners to strike it.
- Count the number of passes correctly performed in a row.

BACK IT UP

Objective

To develop passing skills while trying to increase the distance between partners.

Equipment

One beach ball, foam ball, or volleyball trainer for each set of partners.

Activity

1. Students face each other and use forearm passing to move the ball back and forth once between them.
2. If the ball is passed two times, then the students take one step back and perform the forearm pass again.
3. This continues until the students no longer perform the skill correctly or the distance between the two cannot be covered. When this occurs, the partners return to the starting point and begin again.

Extension

Introduce the concept of measurement and have the partners place a cone or other object to show the farthest distance they were able to attain. They may use a tape measure to determine the exact distance. This measurement can be recorded and compared to the totals for other groups. Class totals may be established, graphed, and displayed on the bulletin board.

Based on Bryant and McLean Oliver 1975.

GROUP ACTIVITIES

ON THE MOVE

Objective

To improve forearm passing by moving to intercept the ball.

Equipment

Two balls for each group of three students.

Activity

1. Divide the class into groups of three. Provide balls to two of the players in each group. Have these two players stand facing the third player (receiver). All group members should be approximately 10 feet (3 m) apart.
2. Using an underhand toss, player 1 tosses the ball to the receiver. The receiver uses a forearm pass to return the ball to player 1.

3. The receiver then slides to face player 2. Player 2 then tosses the ball to the receiver. The receiver uses a forearm pass to return the ball to player 2.

4. The activity continues until each player tosses the ball three times. Players rotate so they all have an opportunity to be the receiver.

Extensions

- Allow the ball to bounce once before it is hit again.
- Decrease the time between passes so that the receiver is in constant motion.
- Have the partners count the number of hits they are able to perform in a row.
- After each successful pass, have the players move back one step to increase the challenge.

Reprinted, by permission, 1989, from B.L. Viera and B.J. Ferguson, 1989, *Volleyball: Steps to success* (Champaign, IL: Human Kinetics).

CIRCLE UP

Objective

To improve the accuracy of forearm passing by striking balls to other students.

Equipment

One beach ball, foam ball or volleyball trainer per group of four to six students.

Activity

1. Divide the class into groups of four to six people. Group members form a circle with approximately 6 feet (1.8 m) between each student.

2. The students use a forearm pass to pass the ball around the circle. Every member of the group should contact the ball.

3. As a safety precaution, students should call out "I've got it" before striking the ball.

Extensions

- Students total the number of correct passes the entire group makes before the ball touches the ground.
- A preset order can be determined so the students pass to the same person each time.

TWO'S A CROWD

Objective

To practice using forearm passing while trying to score points.

Equipment

One ball for each group of four students and a marked play area that is 20 feet (6.1 m) square with a center line for each group.

Activity

1. Students form groups of four and then divide into partners.

2. Each set of partners stands on a side of the playing area.

3. One partner tosses the ball to the other, who uses the forearm pass to send the ball across the center line to the opposing team.

4. The opposing team must return the ball using one forearm pass.

5. A team scores one point when the other group hits the ball out of bounds or misses the ball.

6. Teams can exchange players and start a new game, or the partners can change playing areas and challenge a different team.

Extensions

- Increase the size of the playing area, which increases the challenge for the players.
- The game can be played with six players, three on each side.

SMALL-GROUP VOLLEYING

Objective

To practice using forearm passing while trying to score points.

Equipment

One beach ball, foam ball, or volleyball trainer; two 28-inch (71 cm) cones; and one 16-foot (4.9 m) jump rope for each group of four students.

Activity

1. Create a small court with the cones and rope. Place the rope in the tops of the cones and separate the cones until the rope is straight.
2. Students form groups of four and then divide into partners.
3. Each set of partners stands on a side of the playing area.
4. One partner uses an underhand strike to send the ball to the other, and this player uses a forearm pass to send the ball across the center line to the opposing team.
5. The opposing team must return the ball using a forearm pass.
6. A team scores one point when their opponents hit the ball out of bounds or a team misses the ball.
7. Teams can exchange players and start a new game, or the partners can change playing areas and challenge a different team after five points have been scored.

Extensions

- Increase the size of the playing area, which increases the challenge for the players.
- The game can be played with six players, three on each side.
- The six players may be used differently than previously. Two students hold a 10-foot (3 m) jump rope in the air. The other four students (two on each side) must perform forearm passes over the rope. After 10 forearm passes, rotate positions of the groups.
- Perform the previous extension, but have the rope holders walk in a circle during the volleying. This also will require the players to move. They should move so the fronts of their bodies always face the rope.

CREATE YOUR OWN ACTIVITY

Objective

To allow students to create their own activities to reinforce forearm passing.

Equipment

One piece of paper and a pencil per group and a predetermined list of equipment you will allow the students to use in their activities (e.g., bowling pins, cones, ropes, hula hoops, beach balls, foam balls).

Activity

1. Form groups of two to five students. You may select the groups, or the students may form their own.
2. Each group creates an activity using forearm passing as the basic skill. Students are required to have rules that encourage correct performance of the skill, include all players, and address all safety concerns.

3. The groups write their individual names, the rules of the activity, and the equipment needed on their papers and then show their activities to you.

4. After you approve their activities, the groups retrieve the necessary equipment and begin playing.

5. You must approve all changes to the activities.

Extensions

- Groups teach their activities to other groups.
- Groups teach their activities to the entire class.

Forearm Passing Troubleshooting Chart

If you see this	Then try this
1. Incorrect hand position	• Teach the fist method: Make a fist with one hand with thumb on top. Take the other hand and wrap it around the fist with thumbs on top. The two thumbs are parallel. Extend arms downward to create a flat surface for contact. • Place a piece of tape diagonally across the palm of the bottom hand and have the student place the other hand on top of it. Once the hands curl, the pinkie-finger side of the top hand will be along the tape line.
2. Elbows are bent (arms not extended or parallel)	• A partner stands beside the student. The student assumes the correct hand position and places his hands in his partner's hands. The partner tosses the ball for the student to forearm pass. • Suspend a beach ball from a basketball goal so the ball is at the student's waist level. The student extends her arms and tries to pass the ball while keeping her arms straight.
3. Arms swing up past shoulder level	• Place a piece of paper on the wall in front of the student and draw a line parallel to the floor slightly below the student's shoulder level. Have the student hold a marker in his outstretched hands and draw a line up the paper to the parallel line. • Suspend a rope between two game standards slightly lower than the student's shoulders. Toss the ball to the student, who will hit the ball and stop her arm swing when she touches the rope.
4. Feet are not in a stride position	• Place two tape marks on the floor to indicate where the student should place his feet. • Have the student walk around. When you say *now,* the student assumes a stride position with her feet in the proper position for the forearm pass.
5. Student does not lift with the legs	• Student assumes a stride position with his knees bent and his arms in the proper position. On your signal, he extends his legs and lifts his arms slightly. • Suspend a rope between two game standards slightly higher than the student's head. As the student contacts the ball, she must extend her legs and touch the rope with the top of her head.
6. Student does not get under the ball	• Student holds his arms in the proper position and moves to catch a tossed ball on his outstretched arms. • Student places baby powder on her forearms. She moves under the ball and tries to contact the ball so powder sticks to the ball.

SUMMARY

Since forearm passing is used only in the game of volleyball, this manipulative skill is not taught at an early age. When initiating instruction, emphasize mastery of the proper hand alignment. Allowing children to interlock the fingers or cross the thumbs will encourage bad habits. If students are unable to grasp the traditional hand placement, then encourage use of the fist method until they can master the traditional method.

Another challenge to mastering this skill is using the legs for power. Students have previously practiced many striking skills in which the arms provided the bulk of the power for the movement. Therefore, the teacher will have to emphasize leg extension to generate force instead of swinging the arms to generate force.

We do not encourage playing a real game of volleyball; limit instruction to activities in which students master the critical elements of the skill in small-sided tasks. Proper instruction and many practice opportunities while working alone or with a partner will ensure improved mechanics and better participation later.

FOREARM PASSING LESSON PLAN

(FIRST LESSON)

AGE GROUP: Fourth grade.

FOCUS: Correct hand placement in preparation for forearm passing.

SUBFOCUS: Contacting the ball on the middle of the forearm and extending the legs to generate force.

OBJECTIVE: To assume the correct hand position for forearm passing, contact the ball on the middle of the forearm and extend the legs to generate force four out of five times, as measured by teacher observation (**cues:** *make an X, roll your hands, use your forearms, lift with your legs*).

MATERIALS AND EQUIPMENT: One foam ball or beach ball (or similar ball) per student and two lines that are approximately 10 feet (3 m) apart. The lines should be the entire length of the gymnasium. Posters of the critical elements of the forearm pass should be placed around the gymnasium.

ORGANIZATION AND MANAGEMENT: Students are in self-space for warm-up, instruction, and practice.

WARM-UP:

Today we're going to warm up with music. When the music starts, I would like you to jog in general space. When the music stops, you will freeze in your self-space.

Watch for students moving safely.

(Stop music.) *Everyone stand where you are and look toward me. I would like to make your warm-up more challenging by reviewing the concept of bending and extending. Watch as I bend my arm. Now I extend the arm to make it straight. Can you bend at the knees? Can you extend your legs to make them straight? Can you bend your wrist? Can you extend your wrist? Excellent. This time, I'm going to use the words we just talked about to make our warm-up more challenging. Use the locomotor movement that I call out, and when the music stops, freeze in a position where you will either bend or extend the body part I name. Do you understand what you are to do? Go.*

Watch for students performing the locomotor skills correctly and using the bending and extension commands correctly. Stop the children several times to change the locomotor movement and the limb they will bend or extend.

FORMATION: Students find self-space in the gymnasium and face you.

INTRODUCTION:

Today, we will be putting the extend *and* bend *words to use with forearm passing. This is a skill used only in the sport of volleyball. The word* volley *means that the ball does not hit the ground. It is just hit repeatedly without touching the ground. Forearm passing has a lot in common with catching a ball that comes below the waist. Stand up in your self-space, and let's review what catching below the waist looks like.*

Ready position—face the target, feet shoulder-width apart, knees bent, eyes on approaching ball, elbows bent near sides, and hands in front of the body.

Step and reach—step toward the thrower and extend the arms and hands to meet the ball with pinkies together. (Watch for step and reach with pinkies together.) *Excellent. You remember the catch well.*

Since we're learning about forearm passing, what part of the body do you think will contact the ball? That's right: the forearms. Everyone point to your forearms. We won't catch the ball with the forearms; we want the ball to hit the forearms and rebound (or bounce) off. To do this correctly, the arms need to be together. To do that, the hands must be together.

Place the hand you write with in front of you. Take your other hand and place it on top, making an X. (Walk around and make sure each student can do this.) *Now roll your hands so that your thumbs are together.* (Check each student again.) *If it feels very strange, change your hands so that the other one is on the bottom. Notice that this provides a nice flat platform on your forearms for the ball to hit. Can you think of a way to make your arms even flatter? You can make sure your elbows point toward the floor. This is the basic hand position. Okay, unhook your hands. Can you put them back the correct way? Unhook again and then reconnect. Ask a partner to see if your hands are correct.*

To have your body ready, place one foot in front of the other. You want your arms to make the platform, so your arms are extended and you will keep your back straight but keep your bottom down by bending the knees.

Watch for straight arms extended in front of the body.

Pretend a ball is coming toward you. Make an X, roll your hands, let the ball hit your forearms, and extend your legs. Repeat several times. (Always have students begin with arms apart.) *Freeze. You are doing very well. Help me remember: How do I hold my hands?* **(Make an X and roll the hands.)** *Excellent. Now you are ready to work with a ball. Select a student to toss a beach ball to you. Watch as I strike the ball.* (Demonstrate several times.) *Who can tell me where I strike the ball?* **(Lower part of the forearm.)** *Excellent! What can you tell me about my feet?* **(One is in front of the other.)** *Is the force coming from my arms or my legs?* **(Legs.)** *You want your legs to provide the force. If I swing with my arms, the ball won't go where I want it to go. My arms should never go above my shoulders. They begin close to my thighs but end at my shoulders. It's time to practice with a partner. There are balls placed against the walls and there are lines marked off. When I tell you to go, you will find a partner and stand back to back. Go.*

Excellent. One of you should stand on the line in the middle of the gymnasium. The other should select a ball and then stand on the line closest to the door but directly across from your partner. Go. The partners who are on the center line will practice forearm passing first. When I say go, your partner will toss you the ball and you will forearm pass it back to him. We would like the ball to go about as high as a basketball goal—no lower, no higher. The tosser will have time to practice later. Right now, only those on the center line will pass. Remember to have your hands ready and to use your legs for power. Go.

Watch for correct hand placement and use of legs for power. Partners practice for 3 to 5 minutes and then change places. If possible, pinpoint several students who are able to control the ball and use their legs for power.

Freeze. Sit down where you are. Review the hand placement and correct passing techniques. This time we will make it a little more challenging. Select a student to assist you. My partner will stand in a hula hoop and she will be about 10 feet (3 m) *away from me. She will toss me the ball and I will forearm pass it back to her. If she can catch it without either foot leaving the hoop, we earn five points. If only one foot leaves the hoop, we earn three points. If both feet leave the hoop, but she still catches it, we earn one point. After five tosses and passes, we change duties. Remember, you want the ball to go about as high as a basketball goal.* (Demonstrate several times.) *Partners with the ball, find a large space for you and your partner. Partners without the ball, take one of the hula hoops and place it about 10 feet* (3 m) *from your partner. Let's set this up now.* (When everyone is organized, permit them to go.)

Watch for hand placement, ball height, and use of legs for power. Students practice for 2 to 3 minutes. If any problems performing the skill occur, stop the class and reteach the appropriate critical elements of forearm passing.

Freeze. All of you are doing very well. This time, I'm going to rearrange your groups so that you are in groups of three. (Arrange students and return extra hoops and balls.) *There are posters on the wall that show the parts of a good forearm pass. You will continue to forearm pass the tossed ball back to your partner, but now the third person sees if you have all of the parts of the skill. Each person passes three times. Then the watcher tells you one thing you are doing well with the skill and one thing to work on. You then work on that problem area three more times. Then everyone changes jobs: passing, tossing or catching, and watching. Do you understand these directions? Go.*

Watch for correct hand position, arm extension, and use of legs for force. Students practice for 5 to 7 minutes.

CLOSURE: Line up the students to leave.

*Girls and boys, show me how my hands should be joined for the forearm pass. Where do I strike the ball? **(On the forearms.)** Which part of my body provides most of the power? **(The legs.)** Next time, we'll practice passing the ball back and forth with a partner.*

OVERHEAD VOLLEYING

As with forearm passing, overhead volleying is more like a striking skill than a throwing skill. The ball is contacted briefly on the fingers and directed to another teammate or over the net. Overhead volleying focuses on height and accuracy.

Generally, overhead volleying is the second hit when receiving a ball in volleyball. Since the serve involves a great deal of force, it is not advisable to use the fingers to contact the ball on the first contact. The forearm pass, however, can absorb that force and then direct the ball for the second hit. The objective of that second hit, the overhead volley (or *set*), is to pass the ball to a teammate in preparation for the attack (*spike* or *dink*). *National Standards & Grade-Level Outcomes for K-12 Physical Education* (SHAPE America, 2014) does not address this skill until the fourth grade. In that grade, students should be able to use overhead volleying to send a ball upward and demonstrate four of the five critical elements of a mature pattern (S1.E23.4). In the fifth grade, students should be able to volley a ball and send it upward to a target (S1.E23.5). See table 8.1.

Table 8.1   Outcomes for Overhead Volleying

	Kindergarten–grade 3	Grade 4	Grade 5
S1.E23 Overhead volleying	Developmentally appropriate and emerging outcomes first appear in grade 4.	Volleys a ball with a two-hand overhead pattern, sending it upward, demonstrating 4 of the 5 critical elements of a mature pattern. (S1.E23.4)	Volleys a ball using a two-hand pattern, sending it upward to a target. (S1.E23.5)

Reprinted, by permission, from SHAPE America – Society of Health and Physical Educators, 2014, *National standards & grade-level outcomes for K-12 physical education* (Champaign, IL: Human Kinetics).

Critical Elements

Move to the Ball	**Ready Position**	**Hands**	**Extend to Hit**	**Follow Through**
Move so that the body is under the ball.	Feet shoulder-width apart, knees bent, and head back.	Hands are in front of the forehead with index fingers and thumbs forming a window. Look through the window for the ball.	Contact the lower back of the ball with the fingers and thumbs and extend arms and legs for force. Wrists are snapped at contact.	Palms are facing away from each other, thumbs are pointing toward the target, and arms and legs are extended.

Cue Words

The cue words you select for each phase of the skill will depend on the age of the students you are teaching and your areas of emphasis. In usable sets are some of the cue words we use to teach overhead passing. You may use each set individually or mix and match the cue words as needed. We have found that it is beneficial to have the students say the cue words out loud as they practice the skill.

Move to the ball—move so that the body is under the ball.

Get under the ball—move to the ball so that the head is *under* the ball.

Ready—feet shoulder-width apart, knees bent, head back. Hands are in front of the forehead with index fingers and thumbs forming a window. Look through the window for the ball.

Extend to hit—contact the lower back of the ball with the fingers and thumbs. Extend arms and legs for force. Wrists are snapped at contact.

Follow through—palms are facing away from each other, thumbs are pointing toward target, and arms and legs are extended.

Bend—elbows are bent as arms are above head with index fingers and thumbs forming a window. The knees are also bent in anticipation of the ball.

Use your viewfinder—elbows are bent as arms are above head with index fingers and thumbs forming a window.

Push hands away—palms are facing away from each other, thumbs are pointing toward target, and arms and legs are extended.

Extend—as the ball is contacted, the arms and legs extend to provide force to propel the ball.

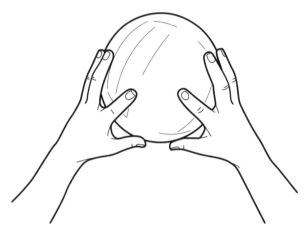

Use your viewfinder.

Cue set 1: move to the ball, ready, extend to hit, follow through
Cue set 2: get under the ball, use your viewfinder, extend to hit, push hands away
Cue set 3: bend and extend
Cue set 4: get under the ball, extend to hit

SUGGESTED ACTIVITIES FOR REINFORCING AND ASSESSING THE CRITICAL ELEMENTS OF OVERHEAD VOLLEYING

In the learning process, it is essential that students know how a skill looks, what its critical elements are, and how to perform each individual critical element correctly. In the preceding section, we provided pictures and descriptions of overhead volleying, divided it into its critical elements, and provided possible cue words. In addition to the material in chapter 1 that reinforces the concepts for all locomotor and manipulative skills, the following section provides specific activities for reinforcing the critical elements unique to overhead volleying.

SKILL CHECK

Objective

To allow partners to assess each other's progress in learning the skill.

Equipment

Partner skill check assessment, pencils, and one ball for each pair of partners. If the students cannot read or do not speak English, the picture version of the partner skill check assessment may be useful.

Activity

1. One partner observes the other to see if she has the correct form for the ready position.
2. If the ready position is correct, then the partner places a *Y* in the first box. If the ready position is incorrect, he places an *N* in the first box. Nonreaders can put a smiling face if the ready position is correct or a frowning face if the ready position is incorrect.
3. This evaluation continues until each of the critical elements has been assessed five times.
4. A partner skill check assessment is used for each student.

Extensions

- You may use the partner skill check assessment to measure the skill development of each student.
- You may send partner skill check assessments home with report cards or as individual skills develop.

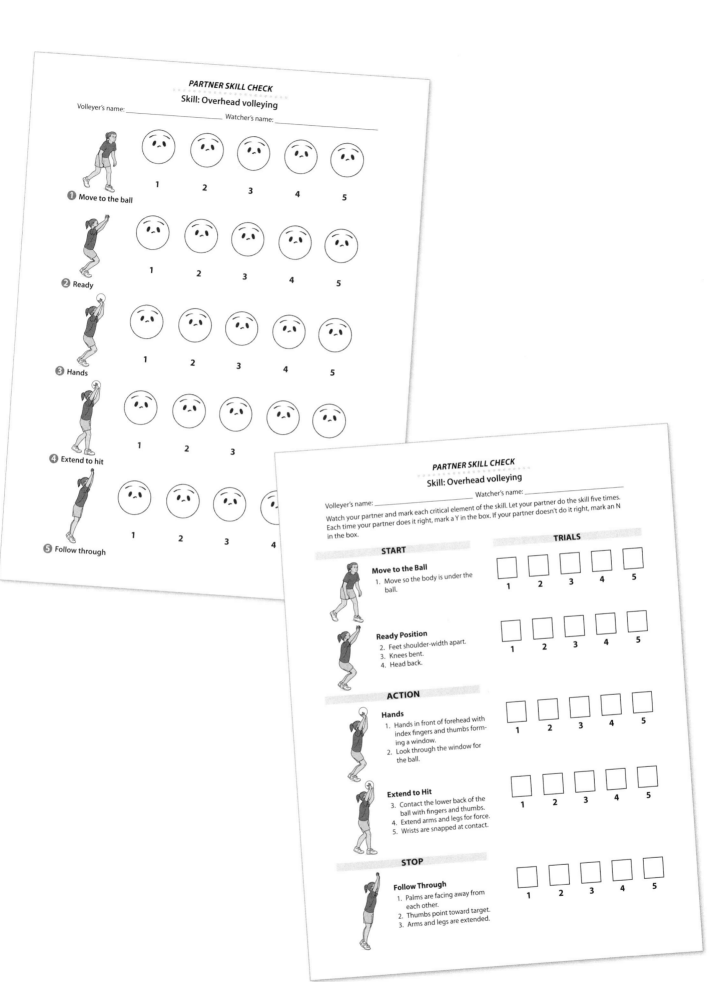

PARTNER SKILL CHECK
Skill: Overhead volleying

Volleyer's name: _____

Watcher's name: _____

① Move to the ball

1 2 3 4 5

② Ready

1 2 3 4 5

③ Hands

1 2 3 4 5

④ Extend to hit

1 2 3

⑤ Follow through

1 2 3 4

PARTNER SKILL CHECK
Skill: Overhead volleying

Volleyer's name: _____

Watcher's name: _____

Watch your partner and mark each critical element of the skill. Let your partner do the skill five times. Each time your partner does it right, mark a Y in the box. If your partner doesn't do it right, mark an N in the box.

TRIALS

START

Move to the Ball
1. Move so the body is under the ball.

☐ ☐ ☐ ☐ ☐
1 2 3 4 5

Ready Position
2. Feet shoulder-width apart.
3. Knees bent.
4. Head back.

☐ ☐ ☐ ☐ ☐
1 2 3 4 5

ACTION

Hands
1. Hands in front of forehead with index fingers and thumbs forming a window.
2. Look through the window for the ball.

☐ ☐ ☐ ☐ ☐
1 2 3 4 5

Extend to Hit
3. Contact the lower back of the ball with fingers and thumbs.
4. Extend arms and legs for force.
5. Wrists are snapped at contact.

☐ ☐ ☐ ☐ ☐
1 2 3 4 5

STOP

Follow Through
1. Palms are facing away from each other.
2. Thumbs point toward target.
3. Arms and legs are extended.

☐ ☐ ☐ ☐
1 2 3 4 5

SUCCESS BUILDERS

The success builder activities allow you to address individual needs. If students need additional help on specific elements, the activities listed here will help reinforce correct performance.

Objective

To improve areas of deficiency as assessed by the partner skill check.

Equipment

See the following individual stations. We suggest using an unbreakable mirror and a poster of each critical element of overhead volleying at each station. The mirror is particularly helpful in these activities because it allows the children to see what they are doing. The easiest way to make the posters is to print out the drawings from this book and enlarge them. Laminating the posters will ensure their use for many years.

Activity

1. Set up a station for each of the five critical elements in the teaching area. Post a description or a picture of the specific element at the corresponding station.
2. The details for each station follow:

MOVE TO THE BALL

Move to the ball so that the body is under the ball.

Equipment

Mirror, poster of move to the ball, tape (floor or painter's) or circle on the floor, and partner evaluations.

Activity

The partner holds the ball high in the air. The student demonstrates the ability to move under the ball and look through the window at the ball. The partner checks to see if this position matches the poster. The student refers to the mirror for help. Once the student can demonstrate to the partner moving to the ball, the partners may return to practicing the entire skill.

READY

Feet shoulder-width apart, knees bent, head back.

Equipment

Poster of the ready position, mirror (if available), and partner evaluations.

Activity

The student assumes the ready position. The partner checks to see if her position matches the poster. The student refers to the mirror for help. The student then walks around and, on a signal from her partner, assumes the ready position again. Once the student can demonstrate proper body and hand positions, the partners may return to practicing the entire skill.

HANDS

With the head back, hands are in front of the forehead with index fingers and thumbs forming a window. Look through the window for the ball.

Equipment

Poster of the correct hand position, mirror (if available), and partner evaluations.

Activity

The student demonstrates the proper hand position. The partner checks to see if his position matches the poster. The student refers to the mirror for help. The student then walks around and, on a signal from his partner, assumes the correct hand position again. Once the student can demonstrate the proper hand position, the partners may return to practicing the entire skill.

EXTEND TO HIT

Contact the lower back of the ball with the fingers and thumbs. Extend arms and legs for force. Wrists are snapped at contact.

Equipment

Poster of the extend to hit, mirror, projector (or some means of shining light onto the student), and partner evaluations

Activity

The student demonstrates the extend to hit element in front of the mirror or light. The partner looks for the wrist snap as the student demonstrates this element. The partner checks to see if her position matches the poster. The student refers to the mirror for help. Once the student can demonstrate to the partner a good extend to hit, the partners may return to practicing the entire skill.

FOLLOW THROUGH

Palms are facing away from each other, thumbs are pointing toward the target, and arms and legs are extended.

Equipment

Poster of the follow-through, mirror, projector (or some means of shining a light onto the student), and partner evaluations

Activity

The student demonstrates the follow-through in front of the mirror or light. The partner checks to see if his position matches the poster. The student refers to the mirror for help. Once the student can demonstrate to the partner a good follow-through, the partners may return to practicing the entire skill.

SUGGESTED CULMINATING ACTIVITIES TO REINFORCE THE ENTIRE OVERHEAD VOLLEYING SKILL

INDIVIDUAL ACTIVITIES

SELF-VOLLEY

Objective

To improve overhead volleying by hitting the ball in the air.

Equipment

One ball per student (beach ball, foam ball, volleyball trainer).

Activity

1. Give each student a ball. Have each student find a self-space in the gymnasium.
2. Have each student toss the ball to herself and volley the ball in the air.
3. The student should catch the ball after each volley.

Extension

If the students are successful with the one volley and catch activity, have them try for two volleys, then three, and finally continuous volleys in the air.

WALL VOLLEYING

Objective

To practice overhead volleying against a wall.

Equipment

One ball per student (e.g., beach ball, foam ball, volleyball trainer).

Activity

1. Give each student a ball. Have each student find a space on the wall.
2. Have each student toss the ball to himself and volley the ball to the wall. He should aim at a spot approximately 10 feet (3 m) above the floor.
3. The student should catch the ball once it rebounds off the wall.

Extension

If the students are successful with the one volley and catch activity, have them try to volley twice in a row, then three, and finally continuous volleys against the wall.

PARTNER ACTIVITIES

PARTNER TOSS AND VOLLEY

Objective

To improve the overhead volleying skill.

Equipment

One beach ball, foam ball, or volleyball trainer per student pair.

Activity

1. Partners stand at least 10 feet (3 m) from one another.
2. One partner tosses the ball to the other at a high level.
3. The receiver uses an overhead volley to send the ball back to the tosser so that he does not have to move. After five correct volleys, the partners exchange roles.

Extensions

- Partners count how many successful volleys and catches they have in a row.
- Have the tosser stand in a hula hoop. If the ball is caught while the tosser has both feet in the hoop, award five points. If the tosser takes one step out of the hoop, award three points. If the tosser has to leave the hoop to catch the ball, award one point.

COUNT IT!

Objective

To improve overhead volleying while volleying the ball continuously with a partner.

Equipment

One ball (beach ball, foam ball, volleyball trainer) for each set of partners.

Activity

1. Partners stand facing each other.
2. The first partner tosses the ball into the air to the second partner, who must hit it using an overhead volley.

3. The partners continue to volley the ball to each other and count each correct pass.

4. The activity continues until the partners either fail to use the correct technique or miss the ball.

5. The partners begin again and try to score more hits.

Extension

Increase the challenge by using a rope or net for the partners to volley over.

WALL BALL

Objective

To develop overhead volleying by hitting the ball against the wall.

Equipment

One beach ball, foam ball, or volleyball trainer per student pair and a line taped on the wall approximately 10 feet (3 m) above the floor.

Activity

1. Partners stand at least 10 feet (3 m) from the wall.

2. One partner uses an overhead volley to hit the ball against the wall.

3. The second partner has to catch the ball after it comes off the wall but before it hits the ground.

4. When the partner has caught the ball, he must use an overhead volley to send the ball back to the wall from the place it was caught.

5. Partners count how many successful volleys and catches they have in a row.

Extension

Place a large target on the wall and challenge the partners to strike it.

BACK IT UP

Objective

To develop volleying skills while trying to increase the distance between partners.

Equipment

One ball (beach ball, foam ball, volleyball trainer) for each set of partners.

Activity

1. Students face each other and use overhead volleying to move the ball back and forth once between them.

2. If the ball is hit two times, then the students take one step back and perform the overhead volleying again.

3. After each successful volley between the partners, the partners take a step back.

4. This continues until they no longer perform the skill correctly or the distance between the two cannot be covered. When this occurs, the partners return to the starting point and begin again.

Extension

Introduce the concept of measurement and have the partners place a cone or other object to show the farthest distance they were able to attain. They may use a tape measure to determine the exact distance. This measurement can be recorded and compared to other groups' totals. Class totals may be established, graphed, and displayed on the bulletin board.

Based on Bryant and McLean Oliver 1975.

CHALLENGES

Objective

To practice overhead volleying in a variety of situations.

Equipment

One beach ball, foam ball, or volleyball trainer per pair of students and laminated challenge cards. Different types of challenges may require additional equipment.

Activity

1. One partner chooses a challenge card and reads the challenge.
2. Students must correctly perform the volleying skill while meeting the challenge.
3. Possible challenges might include the following:
   - Partners see if they can volley the ball back and forth 4, 8, or 10 times without missing.
   - Partners see how high they can volley the ball to each other without hitting an overhead object.
   - One partner tosses the ball into the air, and the other partner tries to get under the ball and volley it back to the partner.

Extensions

- Place multicolored targets, hoops, cones, or buckets in the play area or on the wall (approximately 10 feet [3 m] above the floor) and have the partner tell the volleyer which target to hit.
- Set up game poles or volleyball standards and tie a rope or net between them. Have the students play a mini-volleyball game between them.
- Have the partners count the number of correct volleys. Establish a total for the class. In a follow-up lesson, challenge the class to increase the total number of correct volleys.

GROUP ACTIVITIES

NET BALL

Objective

To use overhead volleying in a modified game.

Equipment

One beach ball or lightweight ball and one 10-foot [3 m] rope per group of four to six students.

Activity

1. Divide the class into groups of six.
2. Two students hold each end of the rope. This becomes their net. They hold the net as high as they can reach.
3. The other students are the volleyers.
4. Two students are on each side of the net.
5. The game begins with one student performing an overhead volley. Students volley the ball back and forth over the rope using the overhead volley.
6. After the ball hits the floor or leaves the playing area, a point is awarded and the next student performs the overhead volley to begin play.
7. After five total points have been scored, the partners on one side move to be net holders, the net holders go to the other side, and the last group moves to the other side of

the net. This allows each pair to have the opportunity to play twice and hold the net once during each rotation, Rotate the net holders after each student has begun play.

Extensions

- Have the net holders walk slowly in a circle while the volleyers are playing. This forces the volleyers to move.
- Use more players on each side.

SQUARE BALL

Objective

To use overhead volleying to hit the inside area of the opposing team's squares.

Equipment

Eight to 10 beach balls or lightweight balls, volleyball net or rope, and floor tape.

Activity

1. Divide the class into two equal groups and place the groups on either side of the net.
2. Create three 5-foot [1.5 m] squares with floor tape on both sides of the net.
3. Provide each student with a ball to begin the game. On the teacher's signal, students begin volleying over the net.
4. When the ball is volleyed over the net, the receiving side must let the ball hit the ground. The student closest to the ball may retrieve it and volley it back over the net. Students do not cross the net to retrieve a ball.
5. A team scores one point each time they volley the ball and it lands inside a square on the opposing team's side.

Extension

The game stops when one team scores 10 points.

IT'S YOURS, NOT MINE!

Objective

To use overhead volleying to get all objects onto the opponent's side.

Equipment

Eight to 10 beach balls or lightweight balls and a volleyball net or rope.

Activity

1. Divide the class into two equal groups and place the groups on either side of the net.
2. Place four or five balls on each side to begin the game.
3. When a student has a ball, he tosses it into the air and uses an overhead volley to get the ball to the opposing team's area.
4. Students are encouraged to move and volley any ball.
5. The game continues until you use a signal to stop the action.
6. Each team counts the number of balls on their side.
7. The team with the greatest number of balls will lead an exercise or activity, and then a new game is started.

Extension

Set up two courts and use fewer balls.

Adapted, by permission, from J. A. Wessel, 1974, *Project I Can* (Northbrook, IL: Hubbard).

TARGET BALL

Objective

To improve accuracy of overhead volleying by hitting a specific target.

Equipment

Select a target 10 to 15 feet (3-4.5 m) above the floor. It may be a basketball backboard, a poster, or a line painted on the wall. Each student needs a ball (e.g., beach ball, foam ball, volleyball trainer).

Activity

1. Create a color box in which samples from each color of construction paper have been placed.
2. There will be large targets on the wall that are the same colors as those in the color box.
3. Select a student to draw a color from the color box.
4. The students must hit the selected target with an overhead volley.
5. Students continue to hit toward the targets of the selected color until you give a stop signal.

Extensions

- Students work with partners. The partner chooses the target. The volleyer must then try to hit the selected target. Partners take turns selecting targets and volleying.
- Targets may be spread throughout the activity area. The partner may catch the volley.

CREATE YOUR OWN ACTIVITY

Objective

To allow students to create their own activities to reinforce overhead volleying skills.

Equipment

One piece of paper and pencil per group and a predetermined list of equipment you will allow students to use in their activities (e.g., hula hoops, cones, ropes, beach balls, foam balls).

Activity

1. Form groups of two to six students each. You may select the groups, or the students may form their own.
2. Each group creates an activity using overhead volleying as the basic skill. Students are required to have rules that encourage correct performance of the skill, include all players, and address safety concerns.
3. The groups write their individual names, the rules of the activity, and the equipment needed on their papers, and then they show their activities to you.
4. After you approve their activities, the groups retrieve the necessary equipment and begin playing.
5. You must approve all changes to the activities.

Extensions

- Groups may teach their activities to other groups.
- Groups may teach their activities to the entire class.

Overhead Volleying Troubleshooting Chart

If you see this	Then try this
1. Student is not forming a window with fingers held above the head	• Play a game of I Spy, where the student must look up through a window formed with the fingers and thumbs to find the object mentioned. These items can be permanent overhead fixtures in the gymnasium (e.g., basketball baskets, specific ceiling tiles).
2. Student is not moving under the ball	• Shine a flashlight on the ceiling and have the student move to get under the light. • Toss a ball to the student, who must get under the ball and catch it directly over her head.
3. Student loses balance after performing the overhead volley	• Place a tape line on the floor. Have the student stand just behind the line. He should volley the ball to a partner. Neither student should move over the line on the follow-through.
4. Student hits the ball with the palm instead of the fingers	• Put the ball on the student's fingers as she looks through the window. • Toss the ball to the student and have him try to hit the ball without making a sound.
5. Student pushes the ball down instead of hitting it up and out	• Have the student volley the ball and then look at her finger and hand positions. • Have the student try to make the ball go through the basketball hoop using the overhead volley.
6. Student does not extend the arms and legs when striking the ball	• Have the student practice going from the ready position to the extend to hit position without the ball. • Have the student try to volley the ball close to, but not touching, the ceiling.

SUMMARY

Volleyball is a very popular recreational sport. Learning to properly volley a ball to a partner or teammate becomes very important to students' overall success in the game. Students and recreational players can use overhead volleying effectively once they understand how and when to execute this important skill. Maintaining the proper body position, getting under the ball, and extending the body at the point of contact are critical elements the students must perform before they have repeated success with this skill.

OVERHEAD VOLLEYING LESSON PLAN

(FIRST LESSON)

AGE GROUP: Fourth grade.

FOCUS: Moving under the ball for contact.

SUBFOCUS: Movement concept of under.

OBJECTIVES: To perform forearm volleying by moving under the ball and limiting the amount of time the ball is in contact with the fingers four out of five times, as measured by teacher observation (**cues:** *get under the ball* and *push hands away*).

MATERIALS AND EQUIPMENT: One beach ball or foam ball per student pair.

ORGANIZATION AND MANAGEMENT: Students are in self-space for warm-up, instruction, and practice.

WARM-UP: Students enter gymnasium and find their own self-space.

Today we're going to review the movement concept of location, specifically over and under. When I put the music on, I would like you to gallop in general space. When the music stops, you will wait for further directions. Do you understand? (Begin music.)

Watch for lead foot and step-together pattern. Stop music.

*Freeze. Can you move so you are standing **under** a basketball goal? Go. Make your hands into a triangle and look up through your viewfinder.* (Demonstrate hand position for overhead volleying.) *Are you **under** the goal? Your head will have to be back and your thumbs and forefingers should be close to touching each other. Good.*

When I put on the music, I would like you to slide in general space. When the music stops, you will freeze where you are and wait for more directions. Do you understand? (Begin music.)

Watch for eyes forward and not crossing the feet. Stop music.

*Freeze. Move so you are directly **under** a light. Go. Look through your viewfinder again to make sure you are **under** the light. Your galloping and sliding are wonderful. This time we will jog in general space. When the music stops, you will freeze where you are and wait for more directions. Go.* (Begin music.)

Watch for maintaining space. Stop music.

*Freeze. Move so you are directly **under** an overhead object. Look through your viewfinder again to make sure you are **under** the object.*

INTRODUCTION:

Freeze. Everyone find their self-space and sit down.

*Last time we learned to use the forearms to hit a volleyball. Today we are going to learn how to perform an overhead volley. To do this, use your fingers and you need to get **under** the ball, just as we practiced earlier. In fact, the hardest part is getting **under** the ball and looking through the viewfinder. You already know how to do that. Watch as I demonstrate the entire skill. Move so you are under the ball. Have your arms above your head and bend your elbows as you look through your viewfinder. Extend your arms and contact the ball briefly with your fingers and thumbs, then push your hands away. The ball is not carried in the hands, but rather struck with the fingers and thumbs.* (Demonstrate several times. Stress the concept of getting under the ball.)

SKILL DEVELOPMENT:

Stand up in your self-space. Let's practice this several times without a ball. Get under the ball, use your viewfinder, extend to hit, push hands away. (Stress the concept of pushing hands away after contact.)

Freeze. You are doing very well. When we use the overhead volley, we are trying to get it high in the air. Why would height be important? **(This allows a teammate time to get to the ball.)** *So distance is not as important as height. How could we create the* *force for that height?* **(By extending arms and legs to contact the ball and having a follow-through.)**

So let's practice the cue words without the ball a few more times: Get under the ball, use your viewfinder, hit and extend, push hands away. (Stress the concept of using arm and leg extension as well as following through to generate force.)

Now you are ready to try this with a ball. Find a partner and stand toe to toe before I count to five: one, two, three, four, five. If you do not have a partner, come stand beside me. (Finish pairing students.)

One of you go pick up a beach ball while the other finds an open space. Go.

You should be three giant steps apart from one another. Excellent. The student who picked up the ball is the tosser. The other is the volleyer. I would like the tosser to toss the ball at a high level so that it goes right above the volleyer's head. The volleyer will use the overhead volley to hit the ball back to the tosser. What are the cue words again? **(Get under the ball, use your viewfinder, extend to hit, push hands away.)** *The same people will toss and volley until I tell you to stop. Do you have any questions? Go.*

Walk around the teaching area and watch for proper execution of the skill. If two students are performing particularly well, stop the class and point out the correct performance. After 3 to 4 minutes, stop the students and ask them to exchange roles.

Freeze. Place the ball on the floor. In the game of volleyball, the ball does not always come to the exact place where we are. We have to move to the ball. This time, I would like for the original tosser to toss the ball so that the volleyer has to move a little to get the ball. How could you make this easier for your partner? **(You help your partner if you toss the ball higher to allow more time for her to get under the ball.)** *What are the cue words again?* **(Get under the ball, use your viewfinder, extend to hit, push hands away.)** *The same people will toss and volley until I tell you to stop. Do you have any questions? Go.* (After 3 to 4 minutes, ask the students to exchange roles. If a pair of students is performing particularly well, allow them to use a Super-Safe ball.)

Freeze. Place the ball on the floor. This time you and your partner will attempt to keep the ball going. One will toss it and then the two of you will continue to volley it back and forth using the overhead volley. Watch as (student) and I demonstrate. Notice that we do not move a great deal. You want height, not distance. Do you have any questions? Go.

Watch students for correct form. Praise those students with control. Allow this practice to continue for 2 to 3 minutes. Again, allow students to use Super-Safe balls when they are ready.

Freeze. Place the ball at your feet. This time I want you and your partner to count to see how many successful overhead volleys you can execute in a row. If the form is incorrect, then the volley does not count. What are the cue words again? **(Get under the ball, use your viewfinder, hit and extend, push hands away.)** *Are there any questions? Go.* (Allow students to practice for 3 to 4 minutes.)

Freeze. I need one of you to return the ball to the proper place. Everyone line up.

CLOSURE: Children are lined up to leave.

(Student), tell me one thing I should do to get ready to overhead volley a ball. (Do as the child instructs. Call on other students, and continue to do *exactly* what the children explain. Keep modifying the movement and asking questions until your overhead volley is performed correctly.)

Now, help me remember some of the cues we have used. **(Get under the ball, use your viewfinder, hit and extend, push hands away.)** *Excellent. Next time, we will work on hitting a target with the overhead volley.*

9

Kicking and Punting

Soon after children begin walking, they begin propelling objects with their feet either by kicking them from the ground or holding the object and trying to kick (a punt). Later, the skills of kicking and punting are found in such diverse activities as kick the can, kickball, football, and soccer. Without proper instruction, children often learn to kick and punt with the wrong part of the foot, or they develop such poor mechanics that a mature pattern is impossible to attain.

Although *National Standards & Grade-Level Outcomes for K-12 Physical Education* (SHAPE America, 2014) addresses kicking beginning in kindergarten, it does not address punting until the fourth and fifth grades.

KICKING

Children begin kicking by standing still and kicking a nonmoving object. The outcomes provide a logical skill progression. A kindergartener should be able to kick a stationary ball while standing still, demonstrating two of the five elements of a mature kicking pattern (S1.E21.K). The first grader should be able to kick a stationary ball after moving toward it, demonstrating two of the five elements of a mature kicking pattern (S1.E21.1). Finally, second graders advance to the last phase, in which they move toward and kick a moving ball, demonstrating three of the five elements of a mature kicking pattern (S1.E21.2). Once these tasks are accomplished, third graders should be able to kick a ball on the ground and in the air, demonstrating four of the five elements of a mature kicking pattern (S1.E21.3), and then they begin kicking for accuracy. (S1.E21.3). Unfortunately, educators sometimes attempt to teach this last skill (accuracy) before their students have mastered the earlier skills (technique). See table 9.1.

Table 9.1 Outcomes for Kicking

	Kindergarten	Grade 1	Grade 2	Grade 3	Grade 4	Grade 5
S1.E21 Kicking	Kicks a stationary ball from a stationary position demonstrating 2 of the 5 elements of a mature kicking pattern. (S1.E21.K)	Approaches a stationary ball and kicks it forward demonstrating 2 of the 5 critical elements of a mature pattern. (S1.E21.1)	Uses a continuous running approach and kicks a moving ball demonstrating 3 of the 5 critical elements of a mature pattern. (S1E21.2)	Uses a continuous running approach and intentionally performs a kick along the ground and a kick in the air demonstrating 4 of the 5 critical elements of a mature pattern for each. (S1.E21.3a) Uses a continuous running approach and kicks a stationary ball for accuracy. (S1.E21.3b)	Kicks along the ground and in the air and punts using mature patterns. (S1.E21.4)	Demonstrates mature patterns of kicking and punting in small-sided practice task environments. (S1.E21.5)

In this chapter, we emphasize the critical elements of kicking when the ball is stationary, and the child's movement is limited to his approach steps. We have included extensions for the child and the ball in motion where appropriate.

To increase practice time and promote safety, we recommend using one of the following suggestions for each activity:

- Use partially deflated balls so that students do not spend a lot of time chasing the balls they kick.
- Have students work with partners, but be sure they are a safe distance apart in case one child kicks a ball with excessive force.
- Use a wall or fence as the partner.

Of course, physical education catalogs today are filled with softer balls that are safer for kicking. Other options include inexpensive plastic balls and foam balls found in discount stores. Your equipment budget and facilities will dictate what precautions you use.

Critical Elements

 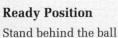   

Ready Position	**Step**	**Leap**	**Kick**	**Follow Through**
Stand behind the ball and focus eyes on the ball.	Step forward on the kicking foot to generate power for the kick.	Leap forward on the nonkicking foot, placing that foot beside the ball, and lean forward with the kicking foot off the ground.	Contact the ball at or slightly below the center with either the laces of the shoe or the inside of the foot.	The arm opposite the kicking leg swings forward, and the kicking foot continues forward in the direction of the kick. There is a backward lean on the follow-through.

Text is from Albemarle County Physical Education Curriculum Revision Committee, 2008.

Cue Words

The cue words you select for each phase of the skill will depend on the age of the students you are teaching and your areas of emphasis. In usable sets are some of the cue words that we use to teach kicking. You may use each set individually or mix and match the cue words as needed. We have found that it is beneficial to have the students say the cue words out loud as they practice.

Ready—focus eyes on the stationary ball.

Step—step forward with the kicking foot.

Approach—watch the ball and step forward with the kicking foot.

Leap—leap onto the nonkicking foot.

Plant—plant the nonkicking foot beside the ball while bringing the kicking leg forward.

And—step forward with nonkicking foot and place it beside the ball.

Leg back—bring the kicking leg back.

Kick—contact the ball below its center with either the inside of the foot (for balls that will stay on the ground) or shoe laces (for balls that will go into the air).

Boom—swing the kicking leg forward and contact the ball below the center with either the shoelaces (for balls that will go into the air) or the inside of the foot (for balls that will stay on the ground.

Follow through or high—kicking foot continues in the direction of the kick with the opposing arm stretched forward for balance.

> *Cue set 1:* ready, step, leap, kick, follow through
> *Cue set 2:* approach, leap, plant, kick, follow through
> *Cue set 3:* ready, leap, kick, high
> *Cue set 4:* ready, and, kick
> *Cue set 5:* leg back, boom

SUGGESTED ACTIVITIES FOR REINFORCING AND ASSESSING THE CRITICAL ELEMENTS

In the learning process, it is essential that students know how a skill is supposed to look, what its critical elements are, and how to perform each critical element correctly. In the preceding section, we provided pictures and descriptions of kicking, divided it into its critical elements, and provided possible cue words. In addition to the material found in chapter 1 that reinforces the concepts for all locomotor and manipulative skills, the following section provides specific activities for reinforcing the elements unique to kicking.

PARTNER SKILL CHECK

Objective

To allow partners to assess each other's progress in learning the kick.

Equipment

Partner skill check assessments, pencils, and one ball for each set of partners. If the students cannot read or do not speak English, use the picture version of the partner skill check assessment. If the assessment is to be performed inside, appropriate safety considerations should be made; for example, everyone should kick in the same direction, kick on the teacher's command, and use softer balls.

Activity

1. One partner observes the other to see if she has the correct form for the ready position.
2. If the ready position is correct, the partner places a *Y* in the first box. If the ready position is incorrect, he places an *N* in the first box. Nonreaders may put a smiling face if the ready position is correct or a frowning face if the ready position is incorrect.
3. This evaluation continues until each of the elements has been assessed five times.
4. A partner skill check assessment is used for each student.

Extensions

- You can use the partner skill check assessment to measure the skill development of each student.
- You can send partner skill check assessments home with report cards or as individual skills develop.

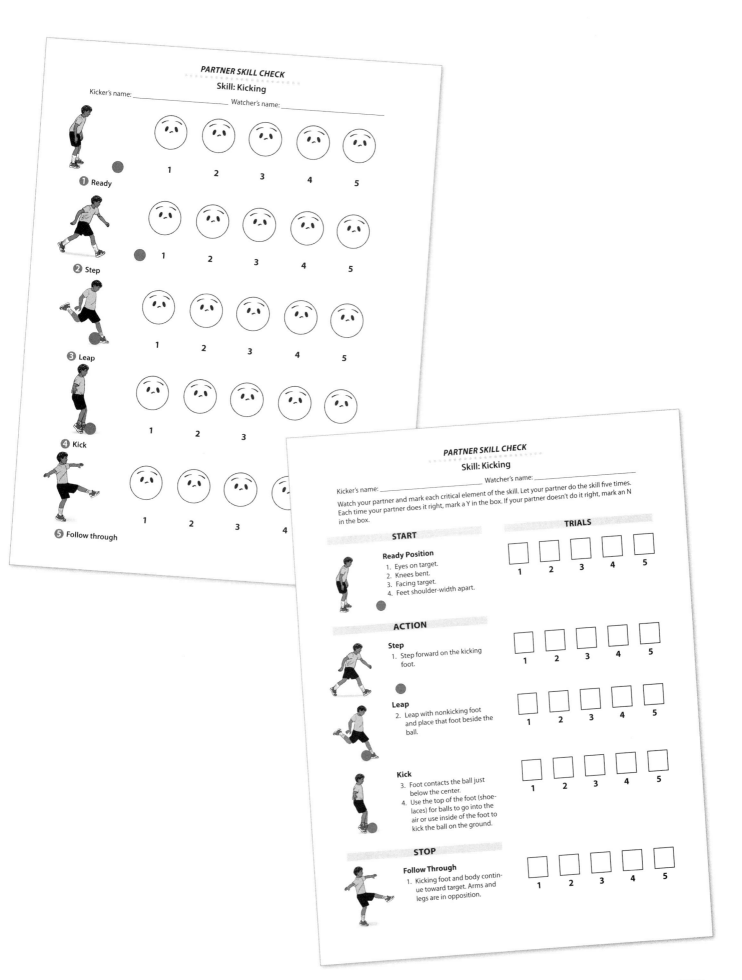

PARTNER SKILL CHECK

Skill: Kicking

Kicker's name: _____

Watcher's name: _____

① Ready
1 2 3 4 5

② Step
1 2 3 4 5

③ Leap
1 2 3

④ Kick

⑤ Follow through
1 2 3 4

PARTNER SKILL CHECK

Skill: Kicking

Kicker's name: _____

Watcher's name: _____

Watch your partner and mark each critical element of the skill. Let your partner do the skill five times. Each time your partner does it right, mark a Y in the box. If your partner doesn't do it right, mark an N in the box.

START

Ready Position
1. Eyes on target.
2. Knees bent.
3. Facing target.
4. Feet shoulder-width apart.

TRIALS

1 2 3 4 5

ACTION

Step
1. Step forward on the kicking foot.

1 2 3 4 5

Leap
2. Leap with nonkicking foot and place that foot beside the ball.

1 2 3 4 5

Kick
3. Foot contacts the ball just below the center.
4. Use the top of the foot (shoelaces) for balls to go into the air or use inside of the foot to kick the ball on the ground.

1 2 3 4 5

STOP

Follow Through
1. Kicking foot and body continue toward target. Arms and legs are in opposition.

1 2 3 4 5

SUCCESS BUILDERS

The success builder activities allow you to address individual needs. If students need additional help on individual critical elements, the activities listed here will reinforce correct performance.

Objective

To allow partners to improve areas of deficiency as assessed by the partner skill check.

Equipment

See the following individual stations. We suggest using an unbreakable mirror and a poster of each element of kicking at each station. The mirror is particularly helpful in these activities because it allows the children to see what they are doing. The easiest way to make the posters is to print out the drawings from this book and enlarge them. Laminating the posters will ensure their use for many years.

Activity

1. Set up a station for each of the five critical elements in the teaching area. Post a description or a picture of the specific elements at the corresponding station.
2. The details for each station follow:

READY

Focus eyes on the ball.

Equipment

Poster of the ready position, mirror (if available), and partner evaluations.

Activity

The student assumes the ready position. The partner checks to see if her position matches the poster. The student then walks around and, on a signal from her partner, assumes the ready position again. When she has had several successful trials, the partners may return to working on the entire skill.

STEP AND LEAP

Step forward with the kicking foot. Then leap forward on the nonkicking foot, placing that foot beside the ball. Lean forward with the kicking foot behind and off the ground.

Equipment

Poster of the step and leap, mirror (if available), floor or painter's tape, and partner evaluations. Use the tape to mark on the floor where the student's feet should be to start and where they should be on the step and leap.

Activity

The student starts in the ready position with both feet on the tape. The student steps forward onto the stepping tape and leaps onto the leaping tape. The partner watches and gives feedback. Once the student can do this three times in a row, he goes to another area and attempts the skill without the tape. When he has had several successful trials, the partners may return to working on the entire skill.

KICK

The foot contacts the ball at or below its center.

Equipment

Poster of the kick, mirror (if available), partially deflated ball (this limits how far the ball will travel) with a line drawn around the middle of the ball, partially deflated ball without any markings, and partner evaluations.

Activity

The student works with a partner. The partner stands to the side and slightly in front of the student's starting position. The student leaps onto the nonkicking foot and brings the kicking foot forward to contact the ball. The student should contact the ball below the marked center line. Once the student is successful three times, she tries the kick with a partially deflated ball that has no markings. When she has completed several successful trials, the partners may return to working on the entire skill.

FOLLOW THROUGH

The arm opposite the kicking leg swings forward, and the kicking foot continues forward in the direction of the kick.

Equipment

Poster of the follow-through, mirror (if available), partially deflated ball, and partner evaluations.

Activity

The student may work with a partner. The student practices swinging the kicking leg forward and bringing the opposite arm forward at the same time. The mirror and partner evaluations should give essential feedback. When the student has had several successful trials, he attempts to kick a partially deflated ball placed on the floor. The partner checks again to make sure the follow-through is correct. When the student is successful on several trials, the partners may return to working on the entire skill.

SUGGESTED CULMINATING ACTIVITIES TO REINFORCE THE ENTIRE SKILL

As stated earlier, students should master the mechanics of kicking before you emphasize accuracy. Kicking is very complicated because it can be performed four ways: ball stationary and child stationary, ball stationary and child moving, ball moving and child stationary, and ball and child both moving. When the challenge of hitting a target is added, correct performance of the critical elements can be compromised. As the outcomes report, accuracy should not be emphasized until the third grade, and even then a stationary ball should be used. Begin with large targets.

INDIVIDUAL ACTIVITIES

HIT THE CORNERS

Objective

To improve kicking accuracy by hitting a specific target.

Equipment

One playground or soccer ball per student.

Activity

1. Students stand 30 feet (~9 m) from a soccer goal (or other well-defined four-corner area).
2. Students practice kicking the ball into each of the four corners of the goal. Students take turns kicking and retrieving balls only on your instruction (see figure).

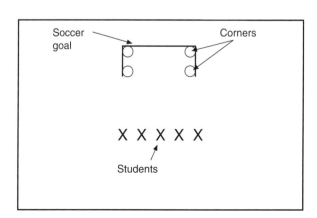

Setup for Hit the Corners activity.

Extensions

- The student must call out which corner he will hit on each kick.
- The second person in line tells the student which corner to hit. If successful, she is given another challenge. If unsuccessful, the second student gets to kick.
- You may challenge each group to hit a specific area.

HIT THE WALL

Objective

To improve kicking distance by kicking a ball so that it hits a wall 25 feet (7.6 m) away before it touches any other surface.

Equipment

One playground or soccer ball per student.

Activity

1. Have students form lines of three approximately 35 feet (10.7 m) from one wall of the gymnasium or play area.

2. Place a playground ball approximately 10 feet (3 m) in front of each line (see figure).

3. On your signal, the first student in each line attempts to kick the ball so that it hits the wall before it touches any other surface.

4. Due to safety concerns, students should be allowed to kick and retrieve the ball only on your signal.

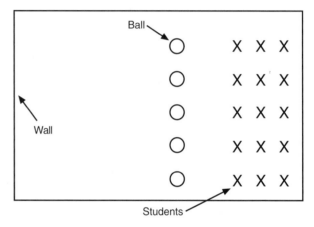

Setup for Hit the Wall activity.

Extensions

- When the students are first learning the skill, move the lines closer to the wall to ensure success. Move the start line back as the students' skills improve.
- The second student in line tells the first what she is doing well with the kick and what she needs to do to improve the kick.
- Use a baseball or softball backstop or fence as the wall if playing outside.

MAGIC FENCE

Objective

To practice the kicking action while emphasizing the leap.

Equipment

Twenty-four 6-inch (15.2 cm) cones and 12 jump ropes. You can also use weighted 2-liter bottles to raise the jump ropes off the floor.

Activity

1. Set up six magic fences. Each fence consists of four cones and two ropes. Place the handles of one rope in the tops of two cones. The handles should stick out of the bottom of the cones to anchor the rope. Place the cones as far apart as the rope allows. Do the same to the second rope, and then set the two sections of the rope fence parallel to each other and about 2 inches (5 cm) apart.

2. Scatter the magic fences throughout the play area (see figure).

3. Assign groups of students to each magic fence.

4. On your signal, the students leap over their fences.

5. Upon landing, the students perform the kicking action.

6. The students continue to leap over their fences until you give a stop signal.

Setup for Magic Fence activity.

Extensions

• The students travel around the gymnasium or play area leaping over all the fences.

• Change the widths of the magic fences by using longer ropes.

• Put all of the magic fences end to end, creating one long fence. Place a ball at each fence, but have the students leap over the fence without using the ball so they can judge the proper ball placement. (Ball placement is an important safety issue. The ball must be placed on the opposite side from the leaper. For other safety reasons, each fence should have only one student leaping at a time.) Upon landing, the leaper tries to kick the ball. The partner retrieves the ball and then takes his turn.

CONE KICK

Objective

To practice kicking while emphasizing the leap.

Equipment

One cone (6-inch [15.2 cm] or lightweight) and three laminated paper footprints per student. If this activity is performed inside, the footprints should be securely taped to the floor for safety.

Activity

1. Each student sets up her footprints and cone (see figure). Footprints 1 and 2 must be shoulder-width apart. Have the student leap, making sure she lands on her nonkicking foot, and place footprint 3 where she lands. Then place the cone to the side and slightly in front of footprint 3. The cone is now in place to be kicked.

2. When the equipment is appropriately set, the student takes off (leaps) with the nonkicking foot and lands on footprint 3.

3. The kicking foot kicks the cone.

Setup for Cone Kick activity.

Extensions

• Use a foam ball or a slightly deflated ball.

• Use the footprints and add the Magic Fence activity.

PARTNER ACTIVITIES

CHALLENGES

Objective

To practice kicking in a variety of situations.

Equipment

One playground or soccer ball per pair of students and laminated challenge cards. Different types of challenges may require additional equipment.

Activity

1. Each student selects a challenge card.
2. Students perform the tasks as described on the cards.
3. Possible challenges may include the following:
   - Kick the ball using hard force (light force).
   - Kick the ball to a target at a middle level (low level, high level).
   - Kick the ball high in the air (low to the ground).
   - Kick a ball at the same time as your partner kicks one, and try to make them go the same height and land at the same time.

Extensions

- Attach multicolored targets, pictures, or hoops to a wall or fence in the play area and have the partner tell the kicker which target to hit.
- Set up standards and tie a rope between them. Suspend various objects from the rope (at various levels) and challenge the students to hit them. Possible targets could include hoops or large aluminum pans.

2-4-6-8

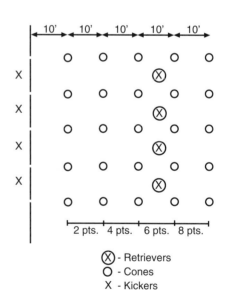

Setup for 2-4-6-8 activity.

Objective

To practice kicking by using different amounts of force.

Equipment

One playground ball or foam ball per pair of students and enough cones to set up the play area. The play area consists of a space defined by five rows of cones that are placed approximately 10 feet (3 m) apart. Jump ropes mark the start area and are placed 10 feet (3 m) in front of the first row of cones (see figure).

Activity

1. One partner (the retriever) enters the play area while the kicker stays in the start area behind the ropes. For safety, the retriever should position herself in the six-point area.
2. The kicker first tries to kick the ball only into the first area, which is worth two points. The retriever in the field kicks the ball back.
3. The kicker then tries to kick the ball into the second area (for four points), then into the third area (for six points), and finally into the last area (for eight points).

4. If the kick is executed correctly and lands in the targeted area, the partners may add the points to their score.

5. After four kicks, the partners change places.

Extensions

- The students try to score the highest number of points in their four kicks.
- The pairs count the number of points scored for each properly executed kick. Later, the class can use math skills (addition) to determine the total score for the class.
- The pairs count their correct kicks, and you keep a total for the class. In a follow-up lesson, challenge the class to increase the total number of correct kicks. You may choose to chart these numbers to motivate the students and to reinforce the skill.
- The kickers start in the eight-point area and kick back to their retrievers, who are standing behind the ropes. The kickers then move up and kick from the six-point, four-point, and two-point areas. Then the partners change areas.

GROUP ACTIVITIES

KEEP THE BALLS OUT OF THE MIDDLE

Objective
To practice kicking and trapping a ball.

Equipment
A very large play area and one to four foam balls (8 inches [20.3 cm] in diameter) or other soft balls. The number of balls needed will vary based on the skill level of the students.

Activity

1. Divide the class into two groups.
2. Place one group in the center of a large circle and the other group outside of the circle.
3. On your start signal, the students on the outside roll the balls into the circle. The students inside the circle must stop (trap) the balls and then kick them back outside of the circle.
4. The students on the outside retrieve the balls, return to their positions, and roll the balls into the circle again; then the activity continues.
5. Have the two groups change places after 1 to 2 minutes.

Extensions

- Tally the total number of correct kicks for each group. You may choose to chart these or record them to serve as a target to improve on in a later lesson.
- Tally the total number of correct kicks for the entire class. The class should try to increase their total correct kicks each time they play the activity.
- Observe the students while they are playing. Tell any student having trouble kicking correctly to go to the practice area and work with a partner.
- Have the students kick the balls without stopping them.

CREATE YOUR OWN ACTIVITY

Objective
To allow students to create their own activities to reinforce the skill of kicking.

Equipment

One piece of paper and pencil per group and a predetermined list of equipment you will allow the students to use in their activities (e.g., playground balls, cones, hoops).

Activity

1. Form groups of two to five students. You may select the groups, or the students may form their own.
2. Each group creates an activity using the kick as the basic skill. Students are required to have rules that encourage correct performance of the skill, include all players, and address all safety concerns.
3. The groups write their individual names, the rules of the activity, and the equipment needed on their papers, and then they give their activities to you.
4. After you approve their activities, the groups retrieve the necessary equipment and begin playing.
5. You must approve all changes to the activities.

Extensions

- Groups may teach their activities to other groups.
- Groups may teach their activities to the entire class.

KICK AND GO

Objective

To kick balls of various sizes.

Equipment

A variety of balls that can be kicked (e.g., playground balls of different colors, soccer balls of different sizes, foam balls). No two balls should be identical.

Activity

1. Place students in lines of three with a ball in front of each line (see figure).
2. On the start signal, the first student in each line stands up, approaches the ball, and kicks it as far as he can. For safety, a start command must be used for each rotation.
3. This student then runs to retrieve a kicked ball. He may *not* return with the same ball that he kicked.
4. The student hands the ball to the next student in line.
5. The activity continues through several rotations.

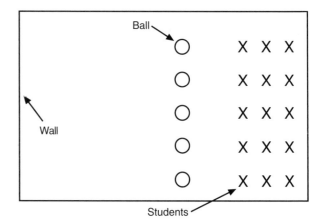

Setup for Kick and Go activity.

Extensions

- Students dribble the balls back to the line.
- The student must name the type of ball he retrieved. Other members of the line are allowed to help if needed.

Based on Bryant and McLean Oliver 1975.

SUMMARY

Children enjoy using their feet to move objects on the ground. As with all skills, logical progressions are necessary for skill mastery. When first learning to kick, the ball and the child should be stationary. Once the student has demonstrated an ability to perform kicking from a stationary position, the movement part of kicking can be introduced. The kicker's movement will eventually become running, leaping, and kicking. With proper instruction and logical progressions, your students can become skilled kickers.

Kicking Troubleshooting Chart

If you see this	Then try this
1. Eyes not looking at the ball	• Have the student draw a face on the ball or use any word already on the ball for a focal point. • Place three different types of balls in front of the student (playground, foam, and soccer). Call out the ball the student is to approach and touch (not kick).
2. Student not stepping forward on the kicking foot or not taking a large enough step	• Place an object (e.g., footprint, color spot) in front of the student for her to step on. • Place an object (e.g., jump rope) in front of the student for her to step over. • Tie a pinny or scarf around the opposite leg. • Tape bubble wrap to the floor. Have the student step in opposition on that spot to create a noise.
3. Student stepping onto the nonkicking foot instead of leaping	• Have the student practice the leap before he tries to use it with the kick. • Place two ropes parallel to each other on the ground for the student to leap over.
4. No forward lean	• Have the student check his shadow for the forward lean. • Have the student pretend to be a runner leaning forward to win a race. Once the student can lean forward, have her practice leaping and leaning.
5. Nonkicking foot not placed beside or diagonal to the ball	• Place a nonskid footprint next to the ball and have the student practice the leap and land on the footprint. • Have the student's partner check to see if part of the kicker's foot is hidden by the ball.
6. Knee of the kicking leg is straight as it swings behind the body, or the kicking leg is not off the ground behind the body	• Place a 6-inch (15 cm) cone so that the student must leap and the knee of the kicking leg travels over the top of the cone. No part of the student's foot or leg should touch the cone. • Have the student watch her shadow to check the position of the kicking leg. • Have the student's partner check the position of the kicking leg.
7. Foot is making contact above the center of the ball	• Draw a line on the ball and challenge the student to kick the ball below that line. • Set up two 6-inch (15 cm) cones with a strip of tape or string across the top of the cones. Have the student place the ball on the side opposite him and try to kick the ball while keeping the foot below the tape or string.
8. Arm opposite the kicking leg not continuing in the direction of the ball	• Have the student stand and practice swinging the kicking leg forward to touch the fingers of the outstretched opposite hand. • Set up a rope at the student's waist level and have him practice the kick without a ball. He must follow through on the kick so that the kicking foot and the opposite arm touch the bottom of the rope.

KICKING LESSON PLAN

(SECOND LESSON)

AGE GROUP: Third grade.

FOCUS: Leaping into the kick.

SUBFOCUS: Technique and power.

OBJECTIVES: To execute a correct leap four out of five times, as measured by teacher and partner observation (**cues:** *take off on one foot, get airborne, land on the other foot*), and to approach the ball, leap, plant the foot, and contact the ball four out of five times, as measured by teacher observation (**cues:** *approach, leap, kick*).

MATERIALS AND EQUIPMENT: One playground ball for each student.

ADVANCE PREPARATION: Tape a line to the floor that divides the gymnasium in half. In addition, place nonparallel lines throughout the teaching area. Floor tape or painter's tape is useful. The nonparallel lines should be of varying widths and lengths (see figure).

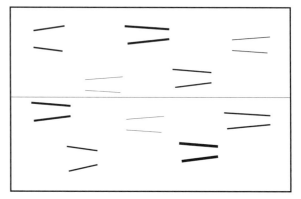

Setup for kicking lesson plan.

ORGANIZATION AND MANAGEMENT: Students are in self-space for instruction and warm-up. Later, students will find their own practice areas in the gymnasium.

WARM-UP: Music is playing as students enter the gymnasium. They move in general space according to your locomotor directions, for example, sliding, galloping, jogging, walking, and skipping. Later, challenge the students to freeze where they are and pretend to kick an imaginary ball. After warming up, students find their self-space and sit on the floor facing you.

INTRODUCTION:

*Today we are going to work on our kicking again. We need to really think about generating power, or kicking harder. Of course we will remember our safety rules while we learn. Now to generate power, we need to run up to the ball, leap, and kick. Watch how I approach the ball. I'm **not** going to kick it, just approach it.* (Approach the ball, leap onto your nonkicking foot, and stop.) *Girls and boys, who can tell me the type of locomotor movement I just did? (Leap.) Excellent. When we want to kick correctly and generate more power, we need to approach correctly, and the leap is **very** important.*

*Before we begin our kicking today, we're going to practice our leaping. Who can tell me the parts of a good leap? (**Take off on one foot and land on the other.**) That's correct. We do those same things—take off on one foot and land on the other—when we run. What are some differences between the leap and the run? (**In the air longer for the leap. The step or stride is longer for the leap.**) Great.* (Select two students.) *Can you demonstrate a leap for everyone? Use the lines next to you. Try to leap from one line to the other. Think of the cue words: take off on one foot, get airborne, and land on the other foot. Everyone watch to see how they take off and land. Excellent. Now everyone watch their arms. Notice that the arm opposite the leaping leg stretches out. This gives them balance.*

Girls and boys, when I say go, I would like you to find a set of lines and sit down. There may be no more than three people at each set of lines. Go.

Excellent. I would like you to take turns leaping across the lines. We are going to pretend that the area between the lines is water, and you really don't want to get your feet wet. You will take off behind one line and land across the other line. Before we begin, who can tell me some safety rules we should have? (Students generate ideas. They should include **take turns** and **watch where you are going**. You can also limit the distance the children may run.) *When I say go, you will begin. Go.*

When you are satisfied that the activity is being performed safely, watch for skill performance. Ensure that the students are taking off on one foot and landing on the other. Repeat the cue words *take off on one foot, get airborne,* and *land on the other foot* throughout. If students are not getting enough height, challenge them to move farther down the lines so that the distance they have to leap is greater.

Freeze. Excellent. You are doing well with your approach and leap. Now, I would like you to take turns helping each other. Two students will watch, while the third student performs the skill. The watchers must look for taking off on one foot, getting airborne, landing on the other foot, and using the arms to help. The arm opposite the leaping leg is stretched out for balance.

Can you remember those things? Great. When a member of your group leaps over the lines, you must be able to say what he or she is doing right and what he or she needs to work on. Then let that person practice it a few more times. I'll tell you when to change duties. Select your first leaper. Go.

Watch to make sure the leapers are performing the skill correctly and the watchers are giving good feedback. Repeat the cue words out loud. After several minutes, students rotate duties. Rotations continue until everyone has had an opportunity to work on the leap with feedback from peers.

*Freeze. Everyone sit down where you are. Your leaping is terrific. When I say go, I would like you to find your self-space and practice taking one step, leaping onto the foot you **don't** kick with, and pretending to kick. You should step with the foot you kick with first. Watch me as I demonstrate. I kick with my **right** foot, so I will step right, leap to my left, and then pretend to kick. Do you have any questions? Go.*

Watch for correct approach, leap, and kick.

*Excellent. We are ready to **really** kick a ball. When I call on each group, I would like those students to each pick up a playground ball and sit on the line in the middle of the gymnasium with the balls in your laps. Now, since it would be very dangerous to have balls bouncing all over the gymnasium, I have let some of the air out of them. They will still kick fine, but they won't bounce off the walls so hard.* (Dismiss groups individually.)

This time we are going to practice our approach and leap, and then we will really kick a ball. Watch me as I demonstrate: ready, step, leap, kick, and follow through. We have to watch the ball the entire time and then let our kicking foot follow in the direction of the kick. Notice that the arm opposite the kicking leg comes forward. This gives us balance. Have every other student kick toward an opposite wall (see figure).

*Here are the safety rules: You may kick only when given the **go** signal, and you will go get your playground ball only when told to do so. Do you understand these rules? Let's all kick together the first time: ready, step, leap, kick, follow through.*

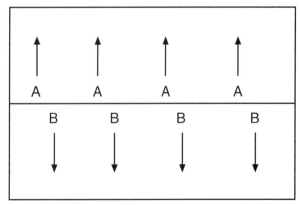

Students are kicking toward an opposite wall.

Students practice kicking while you repeat the cues out loud. Watch specifically for the approach and the leap. Encourage students to contact the ball below its center and to follow through.

Allow students to retrieve the balls and give the *go* command again. This continues for at least five repetitions. Reteach problem areas that arise and point out students who are using correct technique.

Freeze. Now I want to teach you a new activity. It's called Hit the Wall. First, we must put away the deflated balls and sit in five lines at the end of the gymnasium (see figure).

Place a properly inflated playground ball 10 feet (3 m) in front of each line of students.

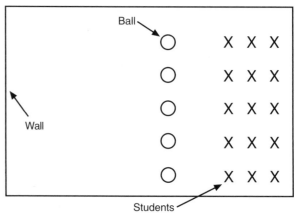

Setup for Hit the Wall activity.

When I say go, the first person in line will approach the ball, step, leap, kick, and follow through. The goal is to have the ball hit the wall before it hits the ground. After all of the students who are first in line have kicked, I will let those students retrieve the balls. You will return the ball to the next person in line and he will kick, while you go to the end of the line. Now you should talk to the person in front of you. That person must tell you what you did well and what you should work on next time. Now, watchers, you have to tell the kickers how to get better. What are some of the things we are looking for? **(Watching the ball, getting airborne, kicking the ball below its middle.)** *Does everyone understand? Go.*

Watch for proper performance and good feedback from the watchers. To decrease waiting time, add more lines if it can be done safely.

Freeze. We're out of time. Please put away your equipment and line up for your teacher.

CLOSURE: As students are lined up to leave, play teach the teacher:

1. *Who can tell me how to leap?* **(Take off on one foot, get airborne, and land on the other foot.)**

2. *How is a leap different from a run?* **(In the air longer, longer stride.)**

3. *So why is a leap so important to a kick?* **(Gives the kick more power.)**

4. *We talked a little bit about the follow-through today. Who remembers some important parts to the follow-through?* **(Arm opposite the kicking leg is extended for balance, watch the ball the entire time, let the leg continue toward the target after the kick.)**

Your approach, leap, and kick are great. Tomorrow we will work on improving your follow-through.

PUNTING

Punting is much more difficult to master than kicking because it involves two distinct but necessary skills: dropping the ball and kicking it as it falls. Because of the difficulty of coordinating these movements, *National Standards & Grade-Level Outcomes for K-12 Physical Education* (SHAPE America, 2014) does not address punting until the fourth grade. The outcomes state that fourth graders should be able to punt using a mature pattern (S1.E21.4) and fifth graders should be able to demonstrate a mature punting pattern in small-sided practice task environments (S1.E21.5). See table 9.2.

Table 9.2   Outcomes for Punting

	Kindergarten–grade 3	Grade 4	Grade 5
S1.E21 **Kicking (Includes punting)**	Punting not addressed for kindergarten through grade 3.	Kicks along the ground and in the air, and punts using mature patterns. (S1.E21.4)	Demonstrates mature patterns of kicking and punting in small-sided practice task environments. (S1.E21.5)

Reprinted, by permission, from SHAPE America – Society of Health and Physical Educators, 2014, *National standards & grade-level outcomes for K-12 physical education* (Champaign, IL: Human Kinetics).

As with kicking, we recommend using one of the following suggestions for each punting activity:

- If students are working with partners, be sure they are a safe distance apart in case one child punts the ball excessively hard.
- Use a wall or fence as the partner.
- Make sure all students are punting in the same direction.
- Initially, require all students to punt only on your command.

You should practice this skill outside unless you have softer balls that are safer for indoor punting, such as inexpensive plastic balls found in discount stores, foam balls, Gator Skin balls, or Super-Safe balls. Your equipment budget and facilities will dictate what types of balls you use.

Critical Elements

Ready Position

Stand in a stride position with the nonpunting foot slightly in front of the punting foot, feet shoulder-width apart. Distribute weight equally on both feet, bend knees, and hold the ball with both hands in front of the body at waist level.

Leap

Leap onto the nonpunting foot in the direction of the punt, lifting the punting foot off the ground behind the body.

Drop and Punt

Drop the ball from outstretched hands. Bring the punting leg forward, and contact the ball on top of the punting foot (shoelaces). There is a backward lean at contact, and the leg and foot should be at full extension on contact.

Follow Through

The leg continues in the direction of the punt as the opposite arm comes forward for balance.

Cue Words

The cue words you select for each phase of the skill will depend on the age of the students you are teaching and your areas of emphasis. In usable sets are some of the cue words we use to teach punting. You may use each set individually or mix and match the cue words as needed. We have found that it is beneficial to have the students say the cue words out loud as they practice.

Ready—stand in a stride position with the nonpunting foot slightly in front of the punting foot, feet shoulder-width apart. Distribute weight equally on both feet, bend knees, and hold the ball in front of the body at waist level with both hands.

Leap—leap onto the nonpunting foot in the direction of the punt, lifting the punting foot off the ground behind the body.

Drop and punt—drop the ball from outstretched hands. Bring the kicking leg forward and contact the ball on top of the punting foot (shoelaces). The leg should be at full extension on contact.

Drop—drop it from waist level.

Punt and **pow**—contact the ball on the shoelaces. The leg should be at full extension on contact.

Follow through—the leg continues in the direction of the punt as the opposite arm comes forward for balance.

> *Cue set 1:* ready, leap, drop and punt, follow through
>
> *Cue set 2:* ready, drop, punt
>
> *Cue set 3:* ready, drop, pow

SUGGESTED ACTIVITIES FOR REINFORCING AND ASSESSING THE CRITICAL ELEMENTS

In the learning process, it is essential that students know how a skill is supposed to look, what its critical elements are, and how to perform each individual element correctly. In the preceding section, we provided pictures and descriptions of punting, divided it into its critical elements, and provided possible cue words. In addition to the material in chapter 1 that reinforces the concepts for all locomotor and manipulative skills, the following section provides specific activities for reinforcing the critical elements unique to punting.

PARTNER SKILL CHECK

Objective

To allow partners to assess each other's progress learning the skill of punting.

Equipment

Partner skill check assessments, pencils, and one ball for each set of partners. If the students cannot read or do not speak English, the picture version of the partner skill check sheet may be useful. If the assessment will be performed inside, appropriate safety considerations should be made; for example, everyone should punt in the same direction on the teacher's command, softer balls should be used, and so forth.

Activity

1. One partner observes the other to see if she has the correct form for the ready position.

2. If the ready position is correct, the partner places a Y in the first box. If the ready position is incorrect, he places an N in the first box. Nonreaders can put a smiling face if the ready position is correct or a frowning face if the ready position is incorrect.

3. This evaluation continues until each of the elements has been assessed five times.
4. A partner skill check assessment is used for each student.

Extensions

- You can use the partner skill check assessment to measure the skill development of each student.
- You can send partner skill check assessments home with report cards or as individual skills develop.

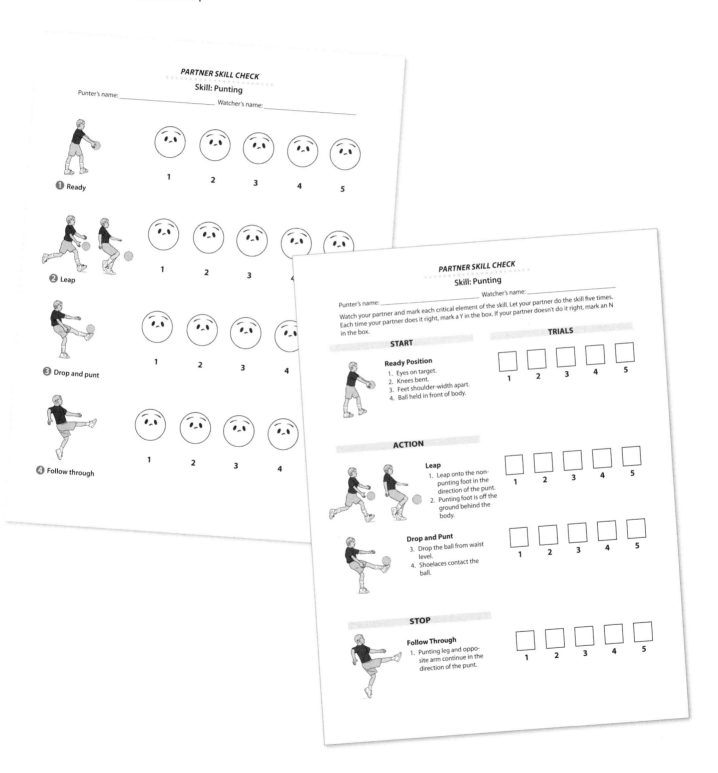

SUCCESS BUILDERS

The success builder activities allow you to address individual needs. If students need additional help on individual critical elements, the activities listed here will help reinforce correct performance.

Objective

To allow partners to improve areas of deficiency as assessed by the partner skill check.

Equipment

See the following individual stations. We suggest using an unbreakable mirror and a poster of each critical element of the punt at each station. The mirror is particularly helpful in these activities because it allows the children to see what they are doing. The easiest way to make the posters is to print out the drawings from this book and enlarge them. Laminating the posters will ensure their use for many years.

Activity

1. Set up a station for each of the four critical elements in the teaching area. Post a description or a picture of the element at the corresponding station.

2. The details for each station follow:

READY

Stand in a stride position with the nonpunting foot slightly in front of the punting foot. Distribute weight equally on both feet. Hold the ball with both hands in front of the body at waist level.

Equipment

Poster of the ready position, mirror (if available), and partner evaluations.

Activity

The student assumes the ready position. The partner checks to see if her position matches the poster. The student then walks around and, on a signal from her partner, assumes the ready position again. When she has had several successful trials, the partners may return to working on the entire skill.

LEAP

Leap onto the nonpunting foot in the direction of the punt, lifting the punting foot off the ground behind the body.

Equipment

Poster of the leap, mirror (if available), floor or painter's tape, and partner evaluations. Use the tape to mark on the floor where the student's feet should start and where they should be on the step and leap. The distance between the start and step lines is approximately half the distance as the step and leap lines.

Activity

The student starts in the ready position with both feet on the tape. The student steps forward onto the stepping tape and leaps onto the leaping tape. The partner watches and gives feedback. Once the student can do this three times in a row, he goes to another area and attempts the skill without the tape. When he has had several successful trials, the partners may return to working on the entire skill.

DROP AND PUNT

Extend arms forward at waist level. Step forward on the nonpunting foot, lean forward with the punting foot off the ground, and contact the ball below the center with the top of the foot (shoelaces).

Equipment

Poster of the drop and punt, mirror (if available), a variety of slow-moving balls (e.g., large beach balls, smaller beach balls, volleyball trainers), and partner evaluations.

Activity

The student practices extending her arms and dropping the ball. She should begin with the large beach ball and attempt to punt it. When she is successful at contacting the ball on the top of her foot with the leg extended five times in a row, she may attempt a smaller beach ball. Later, a volleyball trainer is used, then a Super-Safe ball (or its equivalent). In each instance, the partner provides feedback. When the student has had several successful trials, the partners may return to working on the entire skill.

FOLLOW THROUGH

The punting foot continues forward in the direction of the punt.

Equipment

Poster of the follow-through, mirror (if available), and partner evaluations.

Activity

The student practices swinging the punting leg forward and bringing the opposite arm forward at the same time. The mirror and partner evaluations should give essential feedback. When the student has had several successful trials, she attempts to punt a beach ball. The partner checks again to make sure the follow-through is correct. When the student is successful on several trials, the partners may return to working on the entire skill.

SUGGESTED CULMINATING ACTIVITIES TO REINFORCE THE ENTIRE SKILL

INDIVIDUAL ACTIVITIES

OVER THE NET

Objective

To practice punting over a target.

Equipment

Large play area, one ball (playground ball, foam ball, foam football) per student, two or more volleyball nets, and two clipboards with paper and pencils.

Activity

1. Divide the class into two groups with one group on each side of the net. Set up a start line approximately 10 to 15 feet (3-4.5 m) away from the net. On your start signal, students attempt to punt the balls over the net from behind the start line.

2. When a ball goes over the net, the student who punted the ball goes to a designated area and records a tally mark.

3. The student continues punting from their side.

Extensions

- Perform the activity inside with a volleyball net if you have slow-moving soft balls (e.g., beach balls, volleyball trainers).
- The student changes sides every time the ball goes over the net. (You may choose to use a backstop if there is enough space on the other side to play). The student must change sides by going around the end of the net.

PARTNER ACTIVITIES

CHALLENGES

Objective

To practice punting in a variety of situations.

Equipment

One playground ball per pair of students and laminated challenge cards. Different types of challenges may require additional equipment.

Activity

1. Each student selects a challenge card.
2. Students perform the tasks as described on the cards.
3. Possible challenges may include the following:
   - Punt the ball using hard force (light force).
   - Punt the ball to a target at the middle level (high level).
   - Punt the ball high in the air.
   - Punt the ball as far as you can.
   - Punt the ball into a target (e.g., into the enclosed tennis courts).
   - Punt a ball at the same time as your partner does and try to make them go the same height and land at the same time.

Extensions

- Attach multicolored targets, pictures, or hoops to a wall or fence in the play area and have the partner tell the punter which target to hit. Being within five feet of the target will count as a hit.
- Have the students punt over a volleyball net, soccer goal, or fence from approximately 30 feet (~9 m) away.

KEEP IT GOING

This activity should be played outside in an open area.

Objective

To improve punting accuracy by punting to a partner.

Equipment

One playground ball (or other appropriate ball), paper, and pencil per pair of students.

Activity

1. Partners spread out in an open space.
2. Partners punt the ball back and forth and tally how many successful punts and catches they make in a row

Extensions

- Use groups of three and form triangles for punting.
- The punter attempts to punt the ball so that her partner can catch it easily. The catcher attempts to catch the ball before it hits the ground.
- Partners tally how many successful punts and catches they make.
- Challenge the students to improve the number of successful punts and catches they can perform in a row.

2-4-6-8

Objective

To practice punting using different amounts of force.

Equipment

One playground ball per pair of students and enough cones to set up the play area. The play area consists of a space defined by five rows of cones that are approximately 10 feet (3 m) apart. Place jump ropes 10 feet (3 m) in front of the first row of cones to mark the start area (see figure).

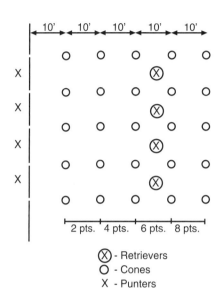

Setup for 2-4-6-8 activity.

Activity

1. One partner goes in the play area and the punter stays in the start area behind the ropes.

2. The punter tries to punt the ball into the first area, which is worth two points. The partner in the field punts the ball back to his partner.

3. The punter then tries to punt the ball into the second area (for four points), then into the third area (for six points), and finally into the last area (for eight points).

4. If the ball lands in the targeted area and the punt is executed correctly, the partners add the points to their score.

5. After four punts, the partners change places.

Extensions

- Students try to score the most points in their four punts.
- The pairs keep track of the points scored for each properly executed punt. Later, the class uses math skills (addition) to determine the total score for the class.
- The pairs keep track of their number of correct punts, and you keep a total for the class. In a follow-up lesson, challenge the class to increase the total number of correct punts. You may choose to chart these numbers to motivate the students and to reinforce the skill.
- The punters begin at the maximum distance (the eight-point area) and punt back to their partners behind the ropes. The punters then move up and punt from the six-point area, the four-point area, and the two-point area. Then the partners change places. The idea is to get the ball to your partner so he can catch it.

GROUP ACTIVITIES

OVER THE FENCE

This activity should be played outside.

Objective

To practice punting over a target from various distances.

Equipment

One playground ball per student.

Activity

1. Divide the class into two groups, and place the groups on either side of a fence (or wall or volleyball net).
2. On your start signal, students attempt to punt the playground balls over the fence.
3. When a ball comes over the fence, another student must try to catch it and then stand still.
4. On your signal, the students who have caught balls will punt the balls back over the fence from the spot where they were caught. Be sure that the students closest to the fence are out of the way of those punting behind them. Students *must* call for balls before attempting to catch them.

Extensions

- Have a definite line for students to stand on when punting and to return to after each catch.
- Allow the students to punt immediately after the ball is caught.
- You may perform the activity inside with a volleyball net if you have sufficient slow-moving soft balls (e.g., beach balls, volleyball trainers). You may want to have the students remove their shoes when punting these softer balls.

Adapted, by permission, from J.A. Wessel, PhD, 1974, *Project I CAN* (Northbrook, IL: Hubbard).

CREATE YOUR OWN ACTIVITY

Objective

To allow students to create their own activities to reinforce the skill of punting.

Equipment

One piece of paper and pencil per group and a predetermined list of equipment you will allow students to use in their activities (e.g., playground balls, cones, foam footballs).

Activity

1. Form groups of two to five students. You may select the groups, or the students may form their own.
2. Each group creates an activity using punting as the basic skill. Students are required to have rules that encourage correct performance of the skill, include all players, and address all safety concerns.
3. The groups write their individual names, the rules of the activity, and the equipment needed on their papers, and they then show their activities to you.
4. After you approve their activities, they retrieve the necessary equipment and begin playing.
5. You must approve all changes to the activities.

Extensions

- Groups may teach their activities to other groups.
- Groups may teach their activities to the entire class.

PUNT AND GO

This activity is best played outside.

Objective

To punt balls of various sizes.

Equipment

A variety of balls that may be punted (e.g., playground balls of different colors, soccer balls of different sizes, foam footballs). No two balls should be identical.

Activity

1. Place students in lines of three with a ball in front of each line (see figure).
2. On the start signal, the first student punts it as far as she can. For safety, a start command must be used for each rotation.
3. The student then runs to retrieve a punted ball. She may *not* return with the same ball that she punted.
4. The student hands the ball to the next student in line.
5. The activity continues for several rotations.

Extensions

- The student must name the type of ball he retrieves. Other members of the line are allowed to help if needed.
- Students are in lines of three. Make a very large circle out of cones, using one cone for each group. Have each group stand behind one of the cones. The groups now look like the spokes of a wagon wheel. Have the students do the activity as previously described. Students are punting into the center of the circle.

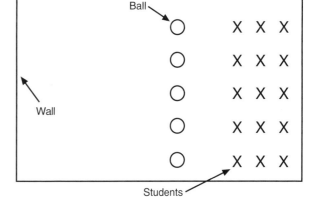

Setup for Punt and Go activity.

- Divide the class into two groups. Each group stands behind a restraining line. The lines are approximately 30 feet (~9 m) apart. Each student in group A starts with a ball and punts the ball toward group B's restraining line. On a signal from the teacher, each student in group B finds a ball she has not punted and returns to the group B restraining line to wait for the signal to punt. Students may not punt the same type of ball twice in a row.

Based on Bryant and McLean Oliver 1975.

SUMMARY

When children are punting, they are again demonstrating that they enjoy using their feet to move objects. As with all skills, logical progressions are necessary for skill mastery; therefore, punting movement should be limited to just a ball dropping during initial instruction. As with kicking, once the student has demonstrated an ability to punt from a stationary position, the movement part of punting can be introduced. The punter will leap, plant her foot, and punt. With proper instruction and logical progressions, your students can become skillful punters.

Punting Troubleshooting Chart

If you see this	Then try this
1. Arms not extended	• Have the punting student take a step forward, extend the ball out, and give it to her partner. The partner takes the ball. • Have the student watch his shadow to check for the arm extension.
2. Student not stepping forward on the punting foot or not taking a large enough step	• Place an object (e.g., footprint, color spot) in front of the student for her to step on. • Place a jump rope in front of the student for him to step over. • Tie a pinny or scarf around the opposite leg. • Tape bubble wrap to the floor. Have the student step in opposition on that spot to create a noise.
3. Student stepping onto the nonpunting foot instead of leaping	• Have the student practice the leap before she tries to use it with the punt. • Place two ropes parallel to each other on the ground for the student to leap over.
4. No forward lean before contact	• Have the student watch his shadow to check for the forward lean.
5. Knee of the punting leg remains straight as it swings behind the body, or the punting leg is not off the ground	• Place a 6-inch (15 cm) cone so that the student must leap and the knee of the punting leg travels over the top of the cone. No part of the student's foot or leg should touch the cone. • Have the student look at her shadow to check the position of the punting leg. • Have the student's partner check the position of the student's punting leg.
6. Student tossing the ball into the air	• Have the student stand and practice dropping the ball. • Have the student step and leap and then drop the ball into a box or hula hoop. • Have the student's partner watch to see if the ball is dropped or tossed.
7. Top of the punting foot (shoelaces) not contacting the ball	• Place baby powder on the ball. Have the student punt the ball and then check the ball and the foot to see which part of the foot contacted which part of the ball. • Suspend a beanbag, foam ball, or other object from a rope strung between two game standards. Have the student practice touching the top of her foot to the suspended object.
8. Arm opposite the punting leg not swinging forward or the punting foot not continuing in the direction of the ball	• Have the student stand and practice swinging her punting leg forward to touch the fingers of her outstretched opposite hand. • Set up a rope at the student's waist level and have him practice the punt without a ball. He must follow through on the punt so that the punting foot and opposite arm touch the bottom of the rope.

PUNTING LESSON PLAN

(FIRST LESSON)

AGE GROUP: Fourth grade.

FOCUS: Executing a proper drop and punt.

SUBFOCUS: Keeping your own space.

OBJECTIVES: To say the cue words for the punt every time (**cues:** *ready, drop and punt, follow through*) and to execute a correct drop and punt of a small beach ball four out of five times, as measured by teacher observation (**cue:** *let it drop from your hands*).

MATERIALS AND EQUIPMENT: One small beach ball per student.

ADVANCE PREPARATION: Place a line down the center of your teaching area (use floor or painter's tape).

ORGANIZATION AND MANAGEMENT: Students are in self-space for instruction and warm-up. Later, students will find their own space on the center line of the gymnasium for practice.

WARM-UP:

Today, we are going to learn a different type of kick. It is called a punt. To practice this skill, we have to really warm up the muscles in our legs. When I put on the music, I would like you to begin moving in general space with a locomotor skill of your choice. Who can name a locomotor skill? (Repeat the question several times until skip, slide, gallop, run, and walk are all mentioned.)

FORMATION: Students find their own self-space and sit down.

INTRODUCTION:

The special kick we will be doing today, the punt, is used in soccer and football and just for fun. We are going to practice three parts today. They are ready, drop and punt, and follow through. I am going to demonstrate how to punt. (Call on a student to retrieve the balls you punt. Punt several balls while repeating the cue words *ready, drop and punt,* and *follow through* each time.)

The ball contacts the shoelaces when dropped.

*Now this is **very** important. The hardest part of the punt is dropping the ball to kick it. You have to stretch your arms in front and hold the ball with **both** hands. The foot you don't punt with is in front. You drop the ball and punt it with the same foot you kick with. The ball is dropped, not thrown. Contact the ball on your shoelaces and really stretch your leg out in front.*

You will be able to practice this today. Since we are inside, it would be very dangerous to have footballs or soccer balls or even playground balls punted all over the gymnasium. Today we are going to practice punting small beach balls. Watch me as I punt the beach ball. Notice that I drop the ball and contact it where my shoelaces are on my shoes (see figure).

When I call on each group, I would like those students to each pick up a small beach ball and sit on the line in the middle of the gymnasium with the balls in your laps. (Have every other student face an opposite wall, as in the kicking lesson plan.)

Here are the safety rules: You may punt only when given the go signal, and you will go get your beach ball only when told to. Do you understand these rules?

*Let's all punt together the first time. Ready—hold the ball in front of you. The next parts come together quickly. Remember, they are drop and punt and follow through. Okay, let's say them out loud together: **Ready, drop and punt, and follow through.***

Students continue practicing and the teacher repeats the cues out loud. Watch specifically for dropping the ball and contacting it on the top of the foot. After students retrieve their balls, give the go command again. This continues for at least 10 repetitions. Reteach problem areas that arise, and point out which students have the correct technique so the other students can watch and learn.

Freeze. Sit down where you are. Now you will be able to practice your punting again. This time, you may retrieve the ball after you punt it and then punt it again without me telling you to go. Of course, I expect you to watch where you are punting and where you are running. Do you understand these rules? Remember to let the ball drop from your hands; don't throw it. Go.

Watch the students for safety and correct performance, especially on dropping the ball to punt it. Repeat the cue words *let it drop* often.

Freeze. Please sit down. Now, who can tell me differences between the beach balls we were punting and soccer balls or footballs? **(The beach ball is lighter.)** *Right. Does a lighter ball drop faster or slower than a heavier ball?* **(Slower.)** *That's right. Using the beach ball gives us time to react and punt the ball. What other kind of ball can you think of that would drop or travel more slowly than a soccer ball?* **(Gator Skin balls, balloons, volleyball trainers.)** *Great.*

This time when you are punting, I will be watching for the drop of the ball and to make sure that you contact the ball on the top of your foot. If you can do this correctly five times in a row, you may exchange your beach ball for a Gator Skin ball. You should not make this change until you are ready; in other words, you need five successful punts in a row. Do you understand? Go.

Walk around as students are punting and encourage students who are ready to change to Gator Skin balls. Correct performance is required. The activity continues for 5 minutes.

Freeze. I would like you to find a partner who is using a ball that is the same as yours (Gator Skin ball or beach ball) and sit back to back. Go. Now, one of you return your ball and your partner keeps his or hers. Go.

We are going to use the entire length of the gymnasium. You will be on one side of the gym and your partner will be on the other. (Choose a student who has performed very well on the punt.) *(Student), would you be my partner to demonstrate? (Student), you stand on the other side of the gymnasium. When I say go, I will punt to my partner. (Student) will try to catch it, then return to the end line. When I say go again, (student) will punt it back to me. Really watch how your partner is performing the punt. After a few minutes, you will need to talk to your partner and say something he or she is doing right and something he or she should work on. Watch my partner and me practice punting.*

Tell students to watch for step, drop and punt, using the top of the punting foot, and follow-through, emphasizing the drop and using the top of the foot. After you and the student have each demonstrated twice, stop the demonstration and perform the skill correctly.

Girls and boys, do you have any questions? Now, one of you line up on the baseline that has the posters (or the national flag or drawings) on it. The ball should be with that partner. The other partner lines up across from the first partner. (Make sure students are spread out.) *Again, you may punt only when I say go. Go.*

Watch students for step, drop and punt, using the top of the punting foot, and follow-through, emphasizing the drop and using the top of the foot. After each partner has performed twice, stop the practice and have the partners meet to discuss problem areas.

Have the students practice again for three repetitions and give feedback to each other again.

Freeze. Girls and boys, we are out of time. Those of you holding a ball should walk over, put it away, and line up for your teacher. Go. The rest of you may walk over and line up, too. Go.

CLOSURE: As students are lined up to leave, play teach the teacher:

1. *Who can tell me the cue words for the punt?* **(Ready, drop and punt, follow through.)**

2. *Why do you think we drop the ball rather than throw it for a punt?* **(More likely to contact it, more control, and so on.)**

3. *Tell me about the foot and leg of your punting leg when you contact the ball.* **(Leg is extended and the top of the foot contacts the ball.)**

4. *What are some of the safety precautions we used today to make our punting lesson safe?* **(Softer balls, punt only when told to.)**

Great job. Next time we will work on punting for accuracy and on the follow-through.

10

Dribbling

The manipulative skill of dribbling, which is used in both soccer and basketball, is designed for controlling *and* moving objects. The basketball and soccer dribbles, however, are two very distinct actions. One skill involves the hands (basketball dribble) and the other involves the feet (soccer dribble), but they will be combined in this chapter. They share the unique combination of movement and manipulation. *National Standards & Grade-Level Outcomes for K-12 Physical Education* (SHAPE America, 2014) addresses the two types of dribbling alone (see individual sections) and in combination with other skills when students are older. According to these outcomes, students should be able to dribble with hands or feet in combination with other skills (e.g., passing, receiving, shooting) by the fourth grade (S1.E20.4). By the fifth grade, students should be able to dribble with the hands or feet demonstrating a mature pattern in a variety of small-sided game situations (S1.E20.5). See table 10.1.

Table 10.1   Outcomes for Dribbling With Hands or Feet in Combination

	Kindergarten–grade 3	Grade 4	Grade 5
S1.E20 Dribbling in combination	Developmentally appropriate and emerging outcomes first appear in grade 4.	Dribbles with hands or feet in combination with other skills (e.g., passing, receiving, shooting). (S1.E20.4)	Dribbles with hands or feet with mature patterns in a variety of small-sided game forms. (S1.E20.5)

Reprinted, by permission, from SHAPE America – Society of Health and Physical Educators, 2014, *National standards & grade-level outcomes for K-12 physical education* (Champaign, IL: Human Kinetics).

DRIBBLING WITH HANDS

Young children begin bouncing balls soon after they discover that balls can bounce. The obvious connection between the bounce and the basketball dribble is very motivating for young children. Unfortunately, their enthusiasm for the skill often takes precedence over learning correct technique.

While children gravitate toward using a real basketball for dribbling, their small hands are not large enough to dribble a large ball correctly. We suggest using playground balls or smaller (junior or intermediate) basketballs when practicing. The regulation-size basketball might be appropriate in high school for some students when their skills improve and their hands are larger.

One of the most challenging aspects of dribbling with hands is the transition from standing in one location and controlling the ball to methodically adding more challenging situations (e.g., changing speeds, directions). Students often have difficulty controlling the ball and themselves. By having students perform many repetitions and slowly increasing the challenge of the skill, you can help them master these critical elements smoothly. While total mastery of dribbling with the hand can take many years, students should begin instruction in the primary grades. *National Standards & Grade-Level Outcomes for K-12 Physical Education* (SHAPE America, 2014) provides a very specific sequence of skill development (table 10.2). In kindergarten, the students should be able to dribble a ball with one hand and attempt the second contact (S1. E17.K). In first grade, students should be able to dribble continuously in self-space using the preferred hand (S1.E17.1). By the second grade, students should be able to dribble in self-space with the preferred hand and demonstrate a mature pattern (S1.E17.2a). The skill becomes more challenging in the second grade, when students should be able to dribble using the preferred hand while walking in general space (S1.E17.2b). By third grade, students should be able to dribble and travel in general space at a slow to moderate jog and control both the ball and the body (S1.E17.3). In the intermediate grades, the skill becomes more open as students dribble in self-space with either hand using a mature pattern (S1.E17.4a) and should be able to control the ball and body while dribbling in general space and at varying speeds (S1.E17.4b). In the fifth grade, students should be able to combine dribbling with other skills during one-versus-one practice tasks (S1.E17.5).

Table 10.2 Outcomes for Dribbling With Hands

	Kindergarten	Grade 1	Grade 2	Grade 3	Grade 4	Grade 5
S1.E17 Dribbling and ball control with hands	Dribbles a ball with 1 hand, attempting the second contact. (S1.E17.K)	Dribbles continuously in self-space using the preferred hand. (S1.E17.1)	Dribbles in self-space with the preferred hand demonstrating a mature pattern. (S1.E17.2a) Dribbles using the preferred hand while walking in general space. (S1.E17.2b)	Dribbles and travels in general space at slow to moderate jogging speed with control of ball and body. (S1.E17.3)	Dribbles in self-space with both the preferred and the nonpreferred hands using a mature pattern. (S1.E17.4a) Dribbles in general space with control of ball and body while increasing and decreasing speed. (S1.E17.4b)	Combines hand dribbling with other skills during 1-versus-1 practice tasks. (S1.E17.5)

Reprinted, by permission, from SHAPE America – Society of Health and Physical Educators, 2014, *National standards & grade-level outcomes for K-12 physical education* (Champaign, IL: Human Kinetics).

Critical Elements

Ready Position	Arm Motion	Fingers	Eyes Forward	Moving
Knees are bent, and the foot opposite the dribbling hand is forward. The ball is held in both hands in front of the body.	One hand contacts the ball at waist level or below and pushes downward on top of the ball (when stationary). The wrist flexes and the elbow extends in the direction of travel as the ball is pushed.	Use the pads of all four fingers and the thumb for contact. (Note: If students are told to use their fingertips to dribble, the fingertips become so rigid at ball contact that they are unable to develop a feel for the ball.)	As the ball is contacted, the eyes are focused looking over, not down at, the ball.	The pads of the fingers firmly contact the ball on top when stationary. When moving, contact is slightly behind the ball and to the side and away from the feet.

Cue Words

The cue words you select for each phase of the skill will depend on the age of the students you are teaching and your areas of emphasis. In usable sets are some of the cue words we use to teach dribbling with the hands. You may use each set individually or mix and match the cue words as needed. It is beneficial to have the students say the words out loud as they practice the skill.

Ready—knees are bent, and the foot opposite the dribbling hand is forward. The ball is held in both hands in front of the body.

Wave good-bye—one hand contacts the ball at waist level or below and pushes the ball downward using only the pads of the fingers. The wrist flexes and the elbow extends in the direction of travel as the ball is pushed.

Hello—the wrist and elbow flex upward to waist level as the ball rebounds off the floor.

Use your tickle fingers—students are asked which part of their hands they use to tickle someone. Those same parts of the hands (or tickle fingers) are used to dribble. Make sure the students are using the pads of all four fingers and the thumb. One hand contacts the ball at waist level or below and pushes the ball downward using only the pads of the fingers. The wrist flexes and the elbow extends in the direction of travel as the ball is pushed.

Push—at contact, the ball is pushed toward the floor as the arm extends.

> *Cue set 1:* ready, wave good-bye, hello
>
> *Cue set 2:* use your tickle fingers, push

SUGGESTED ACTIVITIES FOR REINFORCING AND ASSESSING THE CRITICAL ELEMENTS

In the learning process, it is essential that students know how a skill is supposed to look, what its critical elements are, and how to perform each element correctly. In the preceding section, we provided pictures and descriptions of dribbling, divided the skill into its critical elements, and provided possible cue words. Since the basketball dribble is a movement skill, it may be difficult to isolate its elements completely. You may find it necessary to combine several elements when using the activities in chapter 1 that reinforce the concepts for all locomotor and manipulative skills. In addition to the material in chapter 1, the following section provides specific activities for reinforcing the critical elements unique to dribbling with hands.

PARTNER SKILL CHECK

Objective

To allow partners to assess each other's progress learning the skill.

Equipment

Partner skill check assessments and one ball for each set of partners. If the students cannot read or do not speak English, the picture version of the partner skill check assessment may be useful.

Activity

1. One partner observes the other to see if he has the correct form for the ready position.
2. If the ready position is correct, then the partner places a *Y* in the first box. If the ready position is incorrect, she places an *N* in the first box. Nonreaders may put a smiling face if the ready position is correct or a frowning face if the ready position is incorrect.
3. This evaluation continues until each of the elements has been assessed five times.
4. A partner skill check assessment is used for each student.

Extensions

- You may use the partner skill check assessment to measure the skill development of each student.
- You may send partner skill check assessments home with report cards or as individual skills develop.

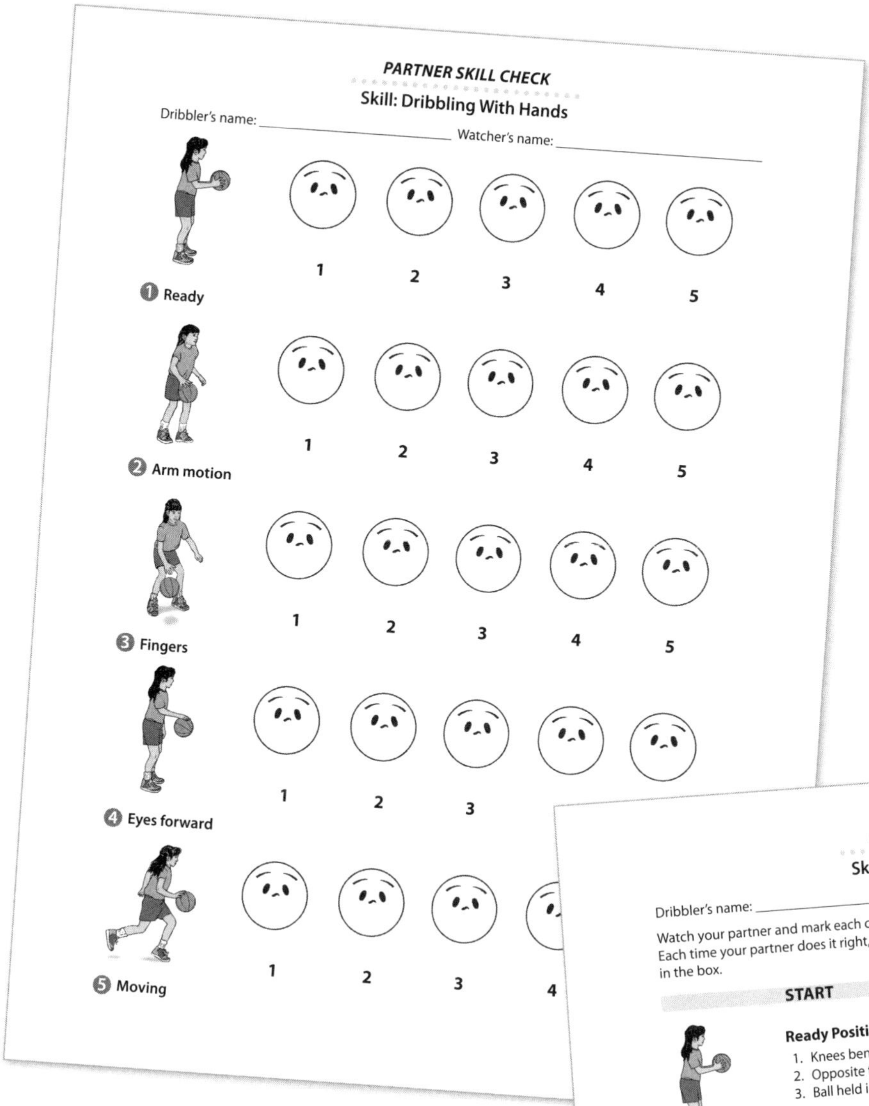

First worksheet (back):

PARTNER SKILL CHECK

Skill: Dribbling With Hands

Dribbler's name: _____

Watcher's name: _____

1 Ready
1 2 3 4 5

2 Arm motion
1 2 3 4 5

3 Fingers
1 2 3 4 5

4 Eyes forward
1 2 3

5 Moving
1 2 3 4

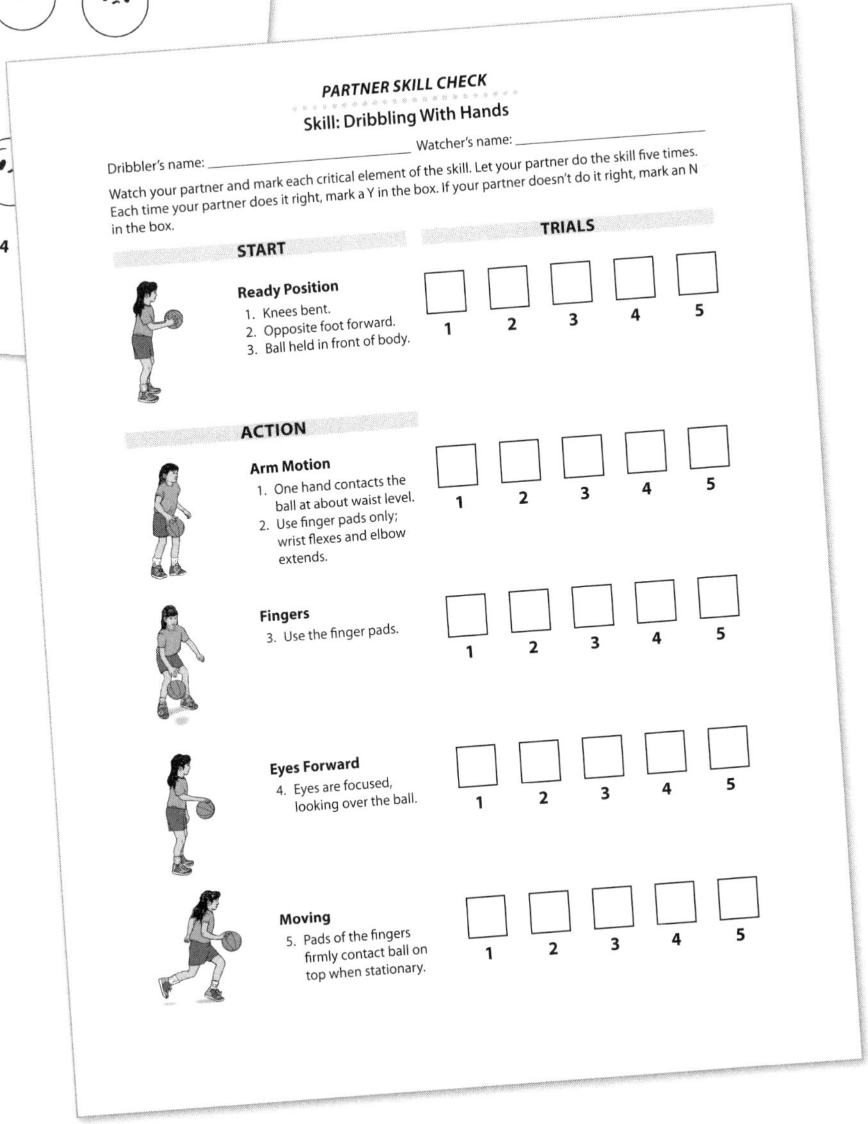

Second worksheet (front):

PARTNER SKILL CHECK

Skill: Dribbling With Hands

Dribbler's name: _____

Watcher's name: _____

Watch your partner and mark each critical element of the skill. Let your partner do the skill five times. Each time your partner does it right, mark a Y in the box. If your partner doesn't do it right, mark an N in the box.

START	TRIALS

Ready Position
1. Knees bent.
2. Opposite foot forward.
3. Ball held in front of body.

1 2 3 4 5

ACTION

Arm Motion
1. One hand contacts the ball at about waist level.
2. Use finger pads only; wrist flexes and elbow extends.

1 2 3 4 5

Fingers
3. Use the finger pads.

1 2 3 4 5

Eyes Forward
4. Eyes are focused, looking over the ball.

1 2 3 4 5

Moving
5. Pads of the fingers firmly contact ball on top when stationary.

1 2 3 4 5

267

SUCCESS BUILDERS

The success builder activities allow you to address individual needs. If students need additional help on specific critical elements, the activities listed here will help reinforce correct performance.

Objective

To allow partners to improve areas of deficiency as measured by the partner skill check assessment.

Equipment

See the individual stations listed next. We suggest using an unbreakable mirror and a poster of each critical element of dribbling at each station. The mirror is particularly helpful in these activities because it allows the students to see what they are doing. The easiest way to make the posters is to print out the drawings from this book and enlarge them. Laminating the posters will ensure their use for many years.

Activity

1. Set up a station for each of the critical elements in the teaching area. Post a description or a picture of the specific element at the corresponding station.
2. The details for each station follow:

READY

Knees are bent, and the foot opposite dribbling hand is forward. The ball is held in both hands in front of the body.

Equipment

Poster showing the ready position, mirror (if available), a ball, and partner evaluations.

Activity

The student assumes the ready position. The partner checks to see if her position matches the poster. The student refers to the mirror for help. The student then dribbles the ball and, on a signal from her partner, assumes the ready position again. Once the student can demonstrate the ready position to the partner, the partners may return to practicing the entire skill.

ARM MOTION AND FINGERS

One hand contacts the ball at waist level or below and pushes the ball down using the finger pads only. The wrist flexes and the elbow extends in the direction of travel as the ball is pushed.

Equipment

Poster showing the push, mirror (if available), a ball, and partner evaluations.

Activity 1

The student demonstrates the push motion with his hand without the ball. The fingers are slightly bent to show that the ball contacts the finger pads and not the palm. The partner checks to see if the student's position matches the poster. The student refers to the mirror for help. If the push is correct, the student is allowed to use a ball. Once the student can demonstrate a good push (with proper use of the finger pads) to the partner, the partners may return to practicing the entire skill.

Activity 2

The student demonstrates the push motion while sitting or kneeling. Often, decreasing the distance of the ball from the floor can increase the student's control of the dribble. Once the student can demonstrate a good push (with proper use of the finger pads) to the partner, the partners may return to practicing the entire skill.

Activity 3

With the partner's help, the student starts from the ready position and pushes his hand down without the ball. The partner checks to see if his position matches the poster. The student refers to the mirror for help. If the wrist flexion and elbow extension are correct, the student is allowed to use a ball. Once the student can demonstrate good wrist flexion and elbow extension to the partner, the partners may return to practicing the entire skill.

MOVING

The ball should be bounced diagonally in front of the body and away from the feet.

Equipment

Poster showing the ball being kept in front of the body, mirror (if available), a ball, and partner evaluations.

Activity 1

The student kneels on the knee that is on the same side as the preferred hand. The other leg is bent at the knee with the foot on the floor. The student practices dribbling the ball. Since one knee is bent, it will be easier to keep the ball bouncing in front of the body.

Activity 2

The student assumes a short stride position with the leg opposite the dribbling hand forward. The student should practice from this position, then progress to moving at a slow speed while keeping the ball in front of the body and away from the feet.

EYES FORWARD

As the ball is contacted, the head is up and the eyes are focused over the ball.

Equipment

Poster showing the correct position of the student as he is dribbling while moving, mirror (if available), a ball, and partner evaluations.

Activity 1

The student dribbles the ball while the partner watches. The partner raises one, two, three, four, five, or no fingers. The dribbler has to keep his head up and be able to tell the partner how many fingers are raised.

Activity 2

Partners each have a ball and face each other. One student (the leader) performs various movements while the other student mirrors the movements without looking at the ball or losing control.

SUGGESTED CULMINATING ACTIVITIES TO REINFORCE THE ENTIRE SKILL

National Standards & Grade-Level Outcomes for K-12 Physical Education (SHAPE America, 2014) provides an excellent sequence for mastering dribbling with the hand. The logical progression from dribbling in self-space, dribbling while walking in general space, becoming proficient with either hand, and changing dribbling speeds should be used in the following activities. Students enjoy performing the skills quickly, but control and form are often compromised. The correct performance of the skill at the most appropriate speed should be emphasized during the next activities.

INDIVIDUAL ACTIVITIES

COLOR TARGETS

Objective

To improve dribbling skills by dribbling on specific targets.

Equipment

Construction paper of different colors and sizes (about 8 to 12 targets of each color) taped to the floor of the gymnasium or activity area and a ball for each student (e.g., basketball, playground ball).

Activity

1. Create a color box in which samples from each color of construction paper have been placed. You will need more samples than you have students.
2. Select a student to draw a sample color from the color box.
3. The sample color chosen is the color target all students must locate and dribble toward.
4. Students continue to dribble in front of the targets of the selected color until you give a stop signal.
5. The activity continues until all students have been given an opportunity to draw from the color box.

Extensions

- Instead of using different colors, students could select different shapes from the shape box, letters from the alphabet box, or words from the word box.
- Students work with partners. One partner chooses the color, shape, letter, or word that will be used for a target. The other student must dribble toward the selected target. Partners take turns selecting targets and dribbling.

CREATE A WORD

Objective

To create words by dribbling on the letters.

Equipment

One ball (e.g., basketball, playground ball) per student and four complete sets of laminated alphabet letters scattered and *securely taped* to the floor of the gymnasium or activity area. It would be advantageous to have extra copies of vowels and selected consonants (e.g., N, R, S, T). You will also need paper and pencils or markers and a dry-erase board to serve as a word bank.

Activity

1. On your start signal, students begin to spell words by dribbling on different letters of the alphabet.
2. The ball must bounce on the letter three times in a row in order for that letter to be used. Students must dribble the ball continuously. If the dribble stops, the last letter collected does not count.
3. Students should continue to dribble the ball on the floor while moving to the next letter.
4. Once a student has created a word, he goes to the word bank (paper or dry-erase board) and writes the word. It will be helpful to have several word banks so students will not have to wait in line to write their words.
5. A word may be written only once on the paper or dry-erase board.

6. If a student dribbles on a letter that cannot be used to form the word being created, she must dribble on the letter three times to delete it.

Extensions

- Students work with partners. One student dribbles on letters to spell a word while the partner records the word and evaluates the dribbling performance. If the dribbler has not performed the skill correctly, he must make a correction before the letter can be used. When the first partner has spelled a word, the other partner is then given an opportunity to dribble.

- Students work with partners. Partners are given paper and pencil to record the letters they contact and to write down the words they create. Each partner must dribble and hit a vowel and two consonants. The pair now has six letters to use to create words. The partners attempt to create six words using one or more of the letters they have contacted. Once the partners have created six words and written them down, they attempt to spell the words by dribbling the ball three times on each letter. Once a word is spelled, it may be checked off the list. If the students are unable to use a letter they have contacted, they must dribble on that letter three times to delete it and select another letter.

MUSICAL HOOPS

Objective

To improve control of the dribble while moving.

Equipment

One ball per student, music, stopwatch, and 15 or more hula hoops scattered around the gymnasium.

Activity

1. While the music is playing, students dribble around the gymnasium and avoid the hula hoops.
2. When the music stops, students must dribble to find the first available hoop, place one foot in the hoop, and continue to dribble.
3. Time the class to determine how long it takes for everyone to find a hoop.

Extensions

- You may use a variety of colors of hoops and require that students go to a specific color when the music stops.
- You may require the students to use their preferred hand while dribbling to the hoop and to use their nonpreferred hand when they have one foot in the hoop.

CROSS THE LINE

Objective

To improve dribbling skills using either hand.

Equipment

One ball per student.

Activity

1. Each student begins moving in general space while dribbling a ball with one hand.
2. When the student crosses a line marked on the gymnasium floor (basketball, volleyball, or badminton court line), she must change hands and dribble with the other hand.
3. The student continues to move and change hands each time she crosses a line.

Extensions

- Use music. When the music stops, students must stop and maintain control of the ball. If a student has trouble, he retrieves the ball and continues.
- Use music that varies in tempo and challenge the students to move with the beat of the music.
- Challenge the students to move the ball at different levels and at different speeds and still change hands when crossing the lines, all the while maintaining control.

TO THE BEAT

Objective

To improve students' ability to control the ball while changing directions and dribbling with either hand.

Equipment

One ball per student and music.

Activity

1. Students stand in their self-space and face a leader.
2. Everyone has a ball. When the music begins, the leader performs actions while dribbling in place and the students mirror the actions. For example, the teacher might wave one hand while dribbling and the students have to copy her movements.

Extensions

- Add movements to the activity. If the leader moves backward, the students move forward. If the leader moves to the right, the students move to the left.
- Select a line dance that the students know and see if they can dribble the ball while performing the steps.

IT'S CROWDED

Objective

To improve students' abilities to keep their eyes looking over the ball while dribbling.

Equipment

One ball per student.

Activity

1. Each student dribbles a ball in general space.
2. Begin to decrease the size of the space in which the students may dribble until their movement is limited.
3. Slowly increase the size of the play area.

Extensions

- As the space decreases, ask the students to place their bodies at a different level while continuing to dribble.
- Students begin from a standing position and slowly lower their bodies to the floor while maintaining the dribble. Once students are sitting, they dribble the ball around their bodies before returning to a standing position.

DOUBLE-TROUBLE DRIBBLE

Objective
To improve coordination by dribbling two balls at the same time.

Equipment
Two balls of the same size per student.

Activity
1. Students kneel on both knees and hold a ball in each hand.
2. Students attempt to dribble both balls at the same time. (Hint: The task is easier if the balls are pushed down at the same time and allowed to rebound at the same time.)

Extensions
- After the student can control the kneeling double-trouble dribble, he may stand and attempt to dribble both balls again while maintaining control.
- The student who can accomplish the first extension may be challenged to move slowly around the gymnasium while maintaining control of two balls.
- The following may be performed with partners, with each pair using a total of two balls:
  - Partners kneel and face each other. Partner A double-trouble dribbles the balls five times, and then partner B takes over. The two balls never stop bouncing. After partner B is successful, partner A dribbles again.
  - Once the students can complete the activity, they may be challenged to stand and face each other and repeat the same drill.
  - One partner may stand still while the partner double-trouble dribbles around her. Then they change positions.

PARTNER ACTIVITIES

CHALLENGES

Objective
To practice dribbling in a variety of settings.

Equipment
One ball per pair of students and laminated challenge cards.

Activity
1. Each student selects a challenge card.
2. Students perform the tasks described on the cards.
3. Possible challenges may include the following:
    - Dribble the ball using hard force (light force).
    - Dribble the ball while changing levels with your body.
    - Dribble the ball at different levels (high, low).
    - Dribble the ball while walking toward your partner, and then dribble backward to the starting spot.
    - Dribble the ball around your body, keeping your feet stationary.
    - Dribble with the hand you write with. Dribble with the other hand.
    - Dribble in a straight pathway, a curvy pathway, or a zigzag pathway.
    - Dribble two balls at the same time.

Extensions

- Place multicolored targets on a floor and have the partner tell the dribbler which target to dribble on.
- Use hula hoops, ropes, or carpet squares to create a maze for the dribbler to dribble through.
- Set up game poles or volleyball standards with a volleyball net or rope between them. The dribbler must dribble under the net or rope. Adjust the net or rope so that it is about 2 feet (0.6 m) off the ground at the low end and 5 feet (1.5 m) off the ground at the high end.

FOLLOW THE LEADER

Objective

To improve the dribbling skill while following the actions of a partner.

Equipment

One ball (basketball, playground ball) per student.

Activity

1. Everyone has a partner. One partner is the leader and the other is the follower.
2. The leader walks around dribbling his ball while the follower mirrors his movements.
3. After a short time, the leader becomes the follower and the follower becomes the leader.

Extensions

- The leader moves at different speeds (fast or slow).
- The leader uses different locomotor movements while dribbling.
- Make larger groups (e.g., groups of four, six, or eight) and take turns being the leader until everyone has a turn.

GROUP ACTIVITIES

CREATE YOUR OWN ACTIVITY

Objective

To allow students to create their own activities to reinforce dribbling skills.

Equipment

One piece of paper and pencil per group and a predetermined list of equipment you will allow students to use in their activities (e.g., bowling pins, cones, ropes, hula hoops, basketballs, foam balls).

Activity

1. Form groups of two to five students each. You may select the groups, or the students may form their own.
2. Each group creates an activity using dribbling as the basic skill. Students are required to have rules that encourage correct performance of the skill, include all players, and address all safety concerns.
3. The groups write their individual names, the rules of the activity, and the equipment needed on their papers, and then they show their activities to you.
4. After you approve their activities, the groups retrieve the necessary equipment and begin playing.
5. You must approve all changes to the activities.

Extensions

- Groups may teach their activities to other groups.
- Groups may teach their activities to the entire class.

RIP AND ROAR

Objective

To dribble the ball while avoiding being tagged.

Equipment

One ball and one pinny for each student dribbler. (Neckties or flagbelts and flags can be used instead of pinnies.) The two taggers do not need pinnies.

Activity

1. Select two taggers.
2. Give everyone else a tail (pinny). The tails are placed in the back of the students' pants at the waistline.
3. The taggers start in the center of the gymnasium or play area. Everyone else is scattered throughout the area.
4. The taggers count to five while the other students dribble around the gym. After counting to five, the taggers run around and try to pull the tails of the other students.
5. If a student's tail is pulled or her dribble is out of control, she must go to a designated area and dribble five times while saying the cue words out loud. The student may then return to the activity.

Extensions

- Give the taggers balls to dribble.
- Set a time limit for each group of taggers and rotate after that time has expired.

MINEFIELD

Objective

To practice dribbling while avoiding obstacles.

Equipment

One ball (basketball, playground ball) per student and approximately 20 traffic cones or other objects (e.g., empty 2-liter bottles, dome cones, Poly Spots, jump ropes).

Activity

1. Scatter the cones throughout the gymnasium or play area.
2. Students each take a ball to self-space.
3. On the start signal, students begin to dribble around the mines (cones).
4. If a student hits a mine with his ball, he must go to the designated practice area. He must dribble five times while saying the cue words out loud. The student may then return to the activity.

Extensions

- Play dribble tag. Choose a student or several students to be taggers. Once a student is tagged, he goes to a designated practice area and has a peer evaluate the critical elements of the dribble. You may select a student to go to the designated area as the first watcher when the game begins. When the tagged student finishes demonstrating the dribble, the first watcher returns to the game and the student who was tagged stays in the area and becomes the new watcher. After he observes the next tagged student perform the skill, the watcher returns to the game. This rotation continues as long as the activity is played.

- If several students are waiting, they may double up and be observed by the same person. Every effort should be made to minimize waiting time.

HOOP BALL

Objective

To improve students' ability to keep the ball away from an opponent while keeping their eyes forward.

Equipment

Hula hoops and balls (enough of each so that half of the students each have a hula hoop and the other half each have a ball).

Activity

1. Scatter the hula hoops in the play area and have half of the students stand inside their own hoops.
2. The other half of the students dribble through the play area and try to avoid the hoops.
3. The students in the hoops try to touch a ball as students dribble past them.
4. If a ball is touched, the two students trade places.

Extensions

- Hoops may be more spread out for lower-skilled students. As students improve, hoops may be moved closer together.
- Students in the hoops may be permitted to step one foot out of the hoop and reach to touch a ball.

Dribbling With Hands Troubleshooting Chart

If you see this	Then try this
1. Ball bouncing lower and lower	• Review the concept of force with the student. • Hold the ball on the bottom while the student pushes on the top of the ball. You give with the ball and then push it back up. It is a continuous movement. • Have the student work with a partner. The student pushes the partner's hand down while the partner offers slight resistance.
2. Student using a part of the hand other than the fingers	• Have the student practice spider push-ups (finger pads of each hand push against each other so the palms of each hand come close to one another and then move away). Finger pads stay in contact at all times. Perform this several times. • Hold the ball on the bottom as the student pushes with his finger pads on the top of the ball. You give with the ball and then push it back up while watching the student's finger pads. This is a continuous movement.
3. Student keeping the wrist straight or locked	• Have the student practice waving good-bye to the floor. • Hold the ball on the bottom as the student pushes on the top of the ball. You control the movement of the ball while watching the student's wrist. • Place a piece of paper on the wall that extends from knee to chest level. Have the student face the paper with a marker in her hand. The student marks the paper using an up-and-down movement of the wrist.
4. Arm not fully extended while pushing the ball	• Have the student practice the arm motion without the ball. • Place a piece of paper on the wall that extends from knee to chest level. Have the student face the paper with a marker in his hand. The student marks the paper using an up-and-down movement of the wrist and arm.
5. Student watching the ball instead of looking forward	• The student places one hand above her mouth and parallel to the ground. This will block her view of the ball. • Have the students work in pairs. One partner dribbles a ball while following the locomotor movements of the other partner. The leading partner should begin with a walk and then increase the speed as the dribbler becomes more proficient. • Have the student dribble a ball while you hold up a picture or a number of fingers for a couple of seconds. The student must be able to tell you what he saw. • Place a softball glove (or deflated ball) on the student's head. The student must dribble without letting the glove (or ball) fall off.
6. Ball bouncing off the student's feet	• Have the student stand on a specific spot on the floor. Place a piece of tape next to the student and have the student dribble the ball on the tape. • Put a hula hoop on the floor and have the student dribble the ball inside the hoop. (Or the student may stand in the hoop and dribble the ball outside of the hoop.) • Have the student try to dribble while on her knees. Once this is accomplished, have the student kneel on one knee and dribble.
7. Student is unable to control the ball when moving	• Allow the student to dribble only three times in a row while moving; then he must stop. As he becomes more proficient, increase the number of dribbles allowed. • Play music as the student dribbles. When the music stops, the student must freeze and maintain control of the ball while dribbling in place. Students unable to maintain control must decrease their speed.

SUMMARY

Children are motivated at an early age to imitate the dribbling patterns of basketball players. Unfortunately, they are often allowed to continue practicing their self-taught dribbling without receiving proper instruction. Correcting improper dribbling techniques can take a great deal of effort. To minimize this situation, instruction in proper dribbling techniques should begin in kindergarten. If you avoid the slapping that usually occurs with young dribblers by stressing the use of the finger pads and the smooth pushing motion, your students will succeed on the courts.

DRIBBLING WITH HANDS LESSON PLAN

(SECOND LESSON)

AGE GROUP: Second grade.

FOCUS: Keeping the head up when dribbling.

SUBFOCUS: Keeping eyes focused looking over, not down at, the ball during dribbling.

OBJECTIVE: To keep the head up (not watching the ball) on four out of five dribbling attempts, as measured by teacher observation (**cue:** *eyes forward*).

MATERIALS AND EQUIPMENT: One playground ball for each child.

ORGANIZATION AND MANAGEMENT: Students are in self-space for warm-up, instruction, and practice.

WARM-UP:

Today we're going to warm up with music again. When the music starts, I would like you to jog in general space. When the music stops, you will freeze in your own self-space. What are some of the safety ideas we need to remember when moving in general space? **(Watch where you're going. Keep space between each person.)** (Begin music.)

Watch for students moving safely. Stop the music and remind students about moving safely.

*This time, I'm going to make it more challenging for you to move. You may use only the locomotor movement of skipping **and** you must stay on this half of the gymnasium.* (Select two students to demonstrate skipping.) *Do you understand what you are to do? Go.*

Watch for students moving safely and performing the skip correctly. Stop the students several times to change the locomotor movement and to decrease the size of the space in which they can move.

FORMATION: After the freeze command, tell the students to find self-space in the gymnasium and face you.

INTRODUCTION:

When we did our warm-ups today, I kept making the space smaller. How did this smaller space affect your movement? **(Had to move slower and really look where we were going.)** *That's right. Today we are going to work on dribbling again. This is also a skill that requires you to start slowly and to really look where you are going.*

First, we need to review what we learned about dribbling last time. Who can tell me the parts of the dribble? **(Ready, push, eyes forward, and keep the ball in front.)** *That's right.*

Which part of the hand do we dribble with? **(Finger pads.)** (Avoid using the term *fingertips* because students will literally push with their fingertips. Encourage the use of the finger *pads*.)

*When I call your birth month (the month you were born), you will get a ball and then return to your space. Make sure you select a ball you can dribble easily; it should **not** be too big for you.*

Dismiss students by month of the year to obtain balls.

We are going to play Follow the Leader. Using your fingers pads to push the ball, keep your eyes on me. I want you to do everything I do. If your ball gets away from you, go get it and return to your spot.

Have the students mirror your movements. Your movements may include the following:

- Kneeling on both knees: (1) Dribble the ball with the preferred hand and then the nonpreferred hand; (2) dribble the ball from the right hand to the left hand, forming a V shape in front of the body.
- With your left foot on the floor and kneeling on your right knee: (1) Dribble the ball with the right hand; (2) dribble the ball forward a few inches and then back.
- With your right foot on the floor and kneeling on your left knee: (1) Dribble the ball with the left hand; (2) dribble the ball forward a few inches and then back.
- Standing in a straddle position: Dribble the ball from the right hand to the left hand, forming a V shape in front of the body.
- Standing in a stride position (left foot forward): Dribble the ball with the right hand and raise a certain number of fingers on the left hand.
- Standing in a stride position (right foot forward): Dribble the ball with the left hand and raise a certain number of fingers on the right hand.

Watch for correct form. If the students have difficulty with the Follow the Leader activity, review the dribbling skill.

*Freeze and sit down in your space. Dribbling with your hand is not very difficult when you stay in one place. Moving around makes it harder. Just like with the warm-up we did today, you have to really watch where you're going. It's hard to watch where you're going and watch the ball at the same time, so you'll have to really **feel** for the ball so you know where it is.*

When the music starts, I would like you to stand up and begin dribbling the ball. You may move in general space, but you will have to really look where you are going. Of course, you will use your finger pads, push, and keep the ball in front of you. Also, you must move at a slow speed. When the music stops, you must freeze where you are until the music begins again. Do you understand these directions? (Begin music.)

Watch for keeping the head up, using finger pads, and maintaining ball control. Begin and stop the music at least five times.

Freeze. Terrific. You are all doing a wonderful job keeping your heads up and watching where you are going. Now I'm going to make it more challenging: You may move at a slow speed or at a medium speed, as long as you can control the ball. (Begin music.)

Watch for ball control, keeping the head up, and using finger pads. Begin and stop the music at least five times.

Freeze. Now let's make it a little harder. When the music stops, you will stop, face me, and do whatever I do while you continue to dribble the ball. Remember to keep your eyes forward and feel for the ball. Do you understand these directions? (Begin music.)

When you stop the music, perform actions with your nondribbling hand such as patting your head, raising one arm up and waving it, scratching your head, and giving a thumbs-up.

Freeze. That was wonderful. I think you're ready for something really hard. When I say go, each of you should find a partner, locate a space for the two of you, and sit back to back. Hold your ball in your lap. Go.

One of you should begin as the leader. The younger student will be the leader. Your partner will follow you. The two of you may move around the gymnasium at a slow speed, and the follower will do everything the leader does. However, if the leader loses control of the ball, the follower freezes and waits for the leader to retrieve the ball. Now the person who did not lose control of the ball becomes the leader. (Select a student to follow you and demonstrate moving safely, keeping eyes forward, and changing leaders.) *Do you understand? Go.*

Begin the music and watch for proper skill execution. Repeat the cue words *eyes forward* often. After several minutes, stop the music.

If you have not been the leader yet, you may be the leader until I stop the music again. Do you understand the directions? Go.

Begin the music, repeat the *eyes forward* cue, and watch for proper skill performance.

Freeze. Please sit down where you are and look at (student) and me. (Student) is younger than I am, so she will be the leader first. We are going to face each other and pretend that we are looking in a mirror. I want to do everything she does. (Examples of actions are patting head with nondribbling hand, changing hands.) We can move around a little, but really we should stay close. (Demonstrate with student.) *I will tell you when to change leaders. Do you understand the directions? Go.*

Begin music, repeat the *eyes forward* cue, and watch for proper skill performance. After several minutes, ask students to change duties.

Freeze. Please return your equipment to the storage bin and line up for your teacher.

CLOSURE: Students are lined up to leave.

Girls and boys, who can tell me some things I must remember when I dribble a ball with my hand? **(Keep eyes up or forward and watch where you're going.)** *Good. I can dribble with my fingers being very stiff* (demonstrate). *What's wrong with that?* **(Hard to have control over ball; you should use the pads of your fingers.)** *Excellent! You all are becoming wonderful dribblers. Next time we will concentrate on using either hand to dribble the ball.*

DRIBBLING WITH FEET

Elementary students enjoy soccer activities because of the continuous movement of dribbling with their feet. Practicing this skill not only provides a good cardiorespiratory workout, but it also promotes the development of eye–foot coordination. The size of the ball is crucial when learning this skill. Students need an appropriately sized ball so that they can control it. Few elementary students can control a regulation-sized soccer ball (size 5) but may perform well with smaller equipment: soccer balls size 1, 2, 3, or 4 (the smaller the number, the smaller the ball) or a 7-inch or smaller playground ball.

Initially, children spend as much time chasing the balls as controlling them. To reduce time spent chasing the balls, we recommend using partially deflated balls during the early learning period. Large beanbags are also acceptable replacements for balls when practicing on a wood or tile gymnasium floor. In addition, we recommend stressing the idea of *light force* when introducing the skill.

Once students understand the concept of force, the variations that are possible with dribbling with the feet make it motivating for elementary children. The children are not limited to using only one part of the foot. Both the inside and the outside of the foot can be used with the soccer dribble. The particular part of the foot used will depend on what the student wants to do with the ball.

Using either foot for the dribble is also essential to developing mastery. To promote this competency, the skill should be introduced in the primary grades before the students begin to form the habit of using only the preferred foot. *National Standards & Grade-Level Outcomes for K-12 Physical Education* (SHAPE America, 2014) addresses elements of dribbling with the foot in all of the elementary grades (table 10.3). In kindergarten, the students should be able to tap a ball using the inside of the foot and send the ball forward (S1.E18.K). In first grade, students should be able to tap or dribble a ball using the inside of the foot while walking in general space (S1.E18.1). In the second grade, students should be able to dribble with the feet in general space with control of the ball and their bodies (S1.E18.2). Additional speed is introduced in the third grade as students dribble at a slow to moderate jog with control of the ball and their bodies as they move through general space (S1.E18.3). Speed should increase and varies from slow to moderate speed in the fourth grade as students continue to maintain control of the ball and their bodies (S1.E18.4). By the fifth grade, students should be able to combine foot dribbling with other skills in one-versus-one practice tasks (S1.E18.5).

Table 10.3   Outcomes for Dribbling With Feet

	Kindergarten	Grade 1	Grade 2	Grade 3	Grade 4	Grade 5
S1.E18 Dribbling and ball control with feet	Taps a ball using the inside of the foot, sending it forward. (S1.E18.K)	Taps or dribbles a ball using the inside of the foot while walking in general space. (S1.E18.1)	Dribbles with the feet in general space with control of ball and body. (S1.E18.2)	Dribbles with the feet in general space at a slow to moderate jogging speed with control of ball and body. (S1.E18.3)	Dribbles with the feet in general space with control of ball and body while increasing and decreasing speed. (S1.E18.4)	Combines foot dribbling with other skills during 1-versus-1 practice tasks. (S1.E18.5)

Reprinted, by permission, from SHAPE America – Society of Health and Physical Educators, 2014, *National standards & grade-level outcomes for K-12 physical education* (Champaign, IL: Human Kinetics).

Critical Elements

Ready Position

Ball is on the ground directly below the head, feet are shoulder-width apart, and knees are bent.

Foot Taps Ball

Perform a short series of taps with the inside or outside of the foot (not the toe). Use of the nonpreferred foot should be practiced and encouraged.

Keep Ball Close

The ball should be on the ground directly below the head as it is contacted, with eyes looking forward. Keep the ball within 2 to 4 feet (0.6-1.2 m) while dribbling.

Move With the Ball

The foot dribble is a movement activity, and it should be performed at a speed that is faster than a walk.

Text is from Albemarle County Physical Education Curriculum Revision Committee, 2008.

Cue Words

The cue words you select for each phase of the skill will depend on the age of the students you are teaching and your areas of emphasis. In usable sets are some of the cue words we use to teach dribbling with the feet. You may use each set individually or mix and match the cue words as needed. It is beneficial to have the students say the words out loud as they practice the skill.

Eyes up—ball is on the ground directly below the head, feet are shoulder-width apart, knees are bent, and eyes are up.

Tap—perform a short series of taps with the inside or outside of the foot (not the toe). Use the nonpreferred foot when appropriate.

Use the flat part of your foot—the ball is tapped with either the inside or the outside of the foot.

Easy taps—use light force.

Go—the ball should be directly below the head on the ground as the ball is contacted, and eyes look forward. Keep the ball within 2 to 4 feet (0.6-1.2 m) while dribbling. The dribble must be faster than a walk.

Keep it close—tap the ball lightly so that it goes only 2 to 4 feet (0.6-1.2 m) from the body.

Cue set 1: eyes up, tap, go
Cue set 2: use the flat part of your foot, easy taps, keep it close

SUGGESTED ACTIVITIES FOR REINFORCING AND ASSESSING THE CRITICAL ELEMENTS

In the learning process, it is essential that students know how a skill is supposed to look, what its critical elements are, and how to perform each element correctly. In the preceding section, we provided pictures and descriptions of foot dribbling, divided it into its critical elements, and provided possible cue words. Since the dribbling with the feet is a movement skill, it may be difficult to isolate its elements completely. You may find it necessary to combine several elements when using the activities. In addition to the material in chapter 1 that reinforces the concepts for all locomotor and manipulative skills, the following section provides specific activities for reinforcing the critical elements unique to dribbling with feet.

PARTNER SKILL CHECK

Objective

To allow partners to assess each other's progress learning the skill.

Equipment

Partner skill check assessments and one ball for each set of partners. If the students cannot read or do not speak English, the picture version of the partner skill check assessment may be useful.

Activity

1. One partner observes the other to see if he has the correct form for the ready position.
2. If the ready position is correct, then the partner places a *Y* in the first box. If the ready position is incorrect, she places an *N* in the first box. Nonreaders may put a smiling face in the box if the ready position is correct or a frowning face if the ready position is incorrect.
3. This evaluation continues until each of the critical elements has been assessed five times.
4. A partner skill check assessment is used for each student.

Extensions

- You can use the partner skill check assessment to measure the skill development of each student.
- You can send partner skill check assessments home with report cards or as individual skills develop.

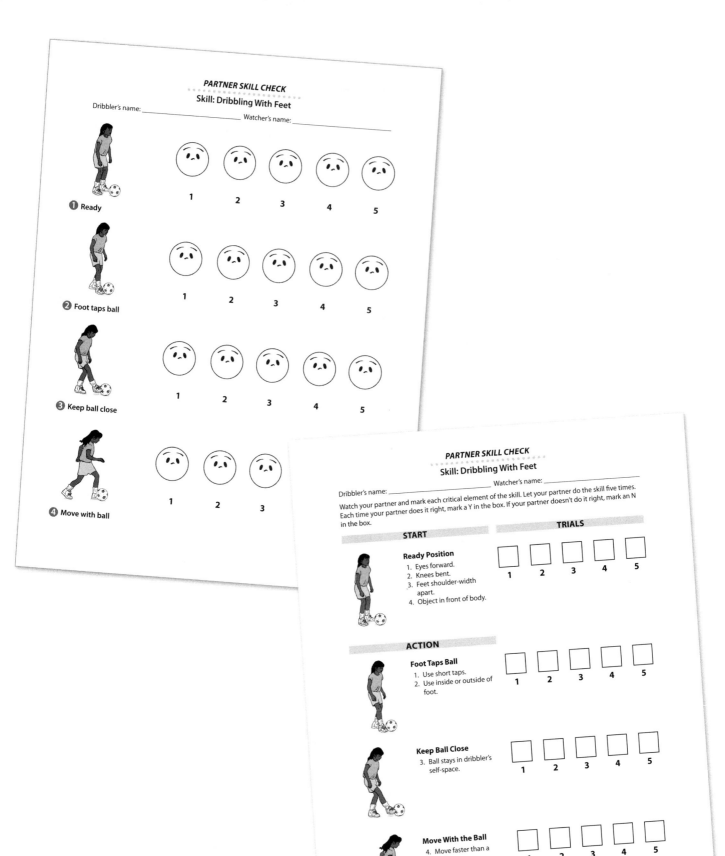

PARTNER SKILL CHECK

Skill: Dribbling With Feet

Dribbler's name: _____ Watcher's name: _____

1 Ready

1   2   3   4   5

2 Foot taps ball

1   2   3   4   5

3 Keep ball close

1   2   3   4   5

4 Move with ball

1   2   3

PARTNER SKILL CHECK

Skill: Dribbling With Feet

Dribbler's name: _____ Watcher's name: _____

Watch your partner and mark each critical element of the skill. Let your partner do the skill five times. Each time your partner does it right, mark a Y in the box. If your partner doesn't do it right, mark an N in the box.

START	TRIALS

Ready Position
1. Eyes forward.
2. Knees bent.
3. Feet shoulder-width apart.
4. Object in front of body.

1   2   3   4   5

ACTION

Foot Taps Ball
1. Use short taps.
2. Use inside or outside of foot.

1   2   3   4   5

Keep Ball Close
3. Ball stays in dribbler's self-space.

1   2   3   4   5

Move With the Ball
4. Move faster than a walk.

1   2   3   4   5

SUCCESS BUILDERS

The success builder activities allow you to address individual needs. If students need additional help on critical elements, the activities listed here will help reinforce correct performance.

Objective

To allow partners to improve areas of deficiency as measured by the partner skill check assessment.

Equipment

See the following individual stations. We suggest using an unbreakable mirror and a poster of each critical element for dribbling with the feet at each station. The mirror is particularly helpful in these activities because it allows the students to see what they are doing. The easiest way to make the posters is to print out the drawings from this book and enlarge them. Laminating the posters will ensure their use for many years.

Activity

1. Set up a station for each critical element in the teaching area. Post a description or a picture of the specific element at the corresponding station.
2. The details for each station follow:

READY

Ball is on the ground directly below head, feet are shoulder-width apart, and knees are bent.

Equipment

Poster of the ready position, mirror (if available), and partner evaluations.

Activity

The student assumes the ready position. The partner checks to see if his position matches the poster. The student refers to the mirror for help. The student then walks around and, on a signal from his partner, assumes the ready position again. When he has had several successful trials, the partners may return to working on the entire skill.

FOOT TAPS BALL

Using the inside or outside of the foot (not the toe), strike the ball with a short series of taps. Use the nonpreferred foot when appropriate.

Equipment

Poster showing the correct way the foot taps the ball, mirror (if available), ball, and partner evaluations.

Activity

The student demonstrates dribbling while moving in the designated area. The partner checks to see if her position matches the poster. The student refers to the mirror for help. Once the student can demonstrate for her partner the correct part of the foot that taps the ball, the partners may return to practicing the entire skill.

KEEP IT CLOSE

The ball should be on the ground and directly below the head as the ball is dribbled; eyes look forward. Keep the ball within 2 to 4 feet (0.6-1.2 m) while dribbling.

Equipment

Poster showing the distance between the child and the ball, mirror (if available), soccer ball, and partner evaluations.

Activity

The student demonstrates the dribble while moving in the designated area. The partner checks to see if the student's body position matches the poster. The partner reminds the student to keep his eyes up. The student looks at the partner's eyes while dribbling. The student can also look at the mirror for help. Once the student can demonstrate to his partner a good dribble with the ball kept close and the eyes looking forward, the partners may return to practicing the entire skill.

MOVE WITH THE BALL

The dribble must be done faster than a walk.

Equipment

Poster of student–ball relationship while dribbling, mirror (if available), and partner evaluations.

Activity

The student demonstrates the dribble while moving in the designated area. The partner checks to see if her position matches the poster. Once the student can demonstrate to her partner a jog while dribbling, the partners may return to practicing the entire skill.

SUGGESTED CULMINATING ACTIVITIES TO REINFORCE THE ENTIRE SKILL

National Standards & Grade-Level Outcomes for K-12 Physical Education (SHAPE America, 2014) provides an excellent sequence for mastery of foot (soon to be soccer) dribbling. The logical progression from tapping the ball with the inside of the foot sending it forward, then dribbling while walking in general space, and finally changing dribbling speeds should be used in the following activities. Students enjoy performing the skills quickly, but often control and form are often compromised. The correct performance of the skill at the most appropriate speed should be emphasized throughout all of these activities. In addition, it is essential that children use balls that are the appropriate size for them. Partially deflated balls (or larger beanbags on tile or wood floors) also assist the students as they learn this challenging manipulative skill that requires movement.

INDIVIDUAL ACTIVITIES

COLOR TARGETS

Objective

To improve control by dribbling over specified targets.

Equipment

Construction paper of different colors and sizes (about 8 to 12 targets of each color) securely taped to the floor or placed in the activity area and a ball for each student (e.g., soccer ball, playground ball).

Activity

1. Create a color box in which samples from each color of construction paper have been placed. You will need more samples than you have students.
2. Choose a student to select a sample color from the color box.
3. The sample color drawn is the color target that all students must find and try to dribble across.

4. Students continue to dribble across the targets of the color selected until you give a stop signal.

5. Designate another student to draw from the color box. The activity continues until all students have been given a chance to draw from the box.

Extensions

- Instead of using different colors, students can choose different shapes from the shape box, letters from the alphabet box, or words from the word box.

- Students work with partners. The partner chooses the color, shape, letter, or word that will be used for a target. Partners take turns selecting targets and dribbling.

CREATE A WORD

Objective

To create words by stopping the ball on top of letters while dribbling.

Equipment

One ball per student and four complete sets of laminated alphabet letters scattered and taped to the floor of the gym or play area. It would be advantageous to have extra copies of vowels and selected consonants (e.g., N, R, S, T). You will also need paper and pencils or a dry-erase board and markers to serve as a word bank.

Activity

1. On your signal, students begin to spell words by dribbling with their feet to different letters of the alphabet. They must stop the ball on top of the letter they intend to use.

2. The students must have the dribble under control. If the ball is out of control, the student must start the dribble from the point at which he lost control.

3. Once a student has created a word, she goes to the word bank (paper or dry-erase board) and writes the word. It will be helpful to have several word banks around the play area so students do not have to wait to record their words.

4. A word may be written only once on the paper or dry-erase board.

5. If a student dribbles over a letter that he cannot use to form the word being created, he must dribble over that letter again to delete it. Students should be encouraged to dribble *around* the letters they don't need.

Extensions

- Students work with partners. The dribbler tells her partner the word she will attempt to spell. The dribbler stops the ball on letters to spell a word while the partner records the letters and evaluates the dribble. If the dribbler does not perform the skill correctly, then she may not use the letter until the dribble is performed properly. When the first partner has spelled a word, the second partner is given a chance to perform the activity.

- Students work with partners. The partners are given paper and pencil to record the letters they stop the ball on and to write down the words they create. Each partner must dribble over to and stop the ball on top of a vowel and two consonants until the pair has six letters to use to create words. The partners attempt to create six words using one or more of the letters they have collected. Once the partners have created six words and written them down, they attempt to spell the words by dribbling over the letters with the ball. Once a word is spelled, it may be checked off the list. If the students are unable to use a letter they have collected, they must dribble over that letter again to delete it and select another letter.

PARTNER ACTIVITIES

CHALLENGES

Objective

To practice dribbling in a variety of situations.

Equipment

One ball (e.g., soccer ball, playground ball, foam ball, yarn ball) per pair of students and laminated challenge cards. On a tile or wood floor, large beanbags may be used instead of balls.

Activity

1. Each student selects a challenge card.

2. Students perform the tasks described on the cards.

3. Possible challenges could include the following:

   - Dribble the ball using fast speed (slow speed, middle speed) and keep the ball under control.

   - Dribble the ball with the outside of your feet (inside of your feet, inside and outside of your feet).

   - Dribble the ball around cones, dome cones, empty 2-liter bottles, chairs, or other objects.

   - Dribble the ball and change direction every time you get to a yellow cone (blue cone, green cone).

Extensions

- Partners count their number of correct dribbles, and you keep a total for the class. A correct dribble occurs when the correct part of the foot is used and the ball stays within 2 to 4 feet (0.6-1.2 m) of the student. Each contact counts as one point. In a follow-up lesson, challenge the class to increase the total number of correct dribbles.

- Place multicolored targets, hoops, cones, or buckets on the floor of the play area and have the partner tell the dribbler which target to dribble around.

- Time partners to determine how long they are able to move and keep the ball under control. In a future class, challenge the partners to improve their times.

- Challenge students to dribble for a specific time (e.g., 15 seconds). The challenges may be for everyone in the class, or students and their partners may take turns.

- Time partners as they dribble through a set course. Challenge the partners to improve their times on each attempt.

FOLLOW THE LEADER

Objective

To improve dribbling with feet by working with a partner.

Equipment

One ball (e.g., soccer ball, playground ball, foam ball) per student.

Activity

1. Everyone has a partner.

2. One partner is the leader and the other is the follower.

3. The leader dribbles his ball in open space while the follower follows and dribbles her ball.

4. After a short time, the leader becomes the follower and the follower becomes the leader.

Extensions

- The leader moves at different speeds (fast, slow).
- Make larger groups (e.g., groups of four, six, or eight) and each student takes turns being the leader.

GROUP ACTIVITIES

CREATE YOUR OWN ACTIVITY

Objective

To allow students to create their own activities to reinforce dribbling with feet.

Equipment

One piece of paper and pencil per group and a predetermined list of equipment you will allow the students to use in their activities (e.g., playground balls, soccer balls, foam balls, bowling pins, cones, hula hoops, jump ropes).

Activity

1. Form groups of two to five students. You may select the groups, or the students may form their own.
2. Each group creates an activity using dribbling as the basic skill. Students are required to have rules that encourage correct performance of the skill, include all players, and address all safety concerns.
3. The groups write their individual names, the rules of the activity, and the equipment needed on their papers, and then they show their activities to you.
4. After you approve their activities, the groups retrieve the necessary equipment and begin playing.
5. You must approve all changes to the activities.

Extensions

- Groups may teach their activities to other groups.
- Groups may teach their activities to the entire class.

RIP AND ROAR

Objective

To dribble the ball with the feet while avoiding being tagged.

Equipment

One ball and one pinny for each student dribbler. (Neckties or flagbelts and flags can be used instead of pinnies.) The two taggers do not need pinnies.

Activity

1. Select two taggers.
2. Give everyone else a tail (pinny). The tails are placed in the back of the students' pants at the waistline.
3. The taggers start in the center of the gymnasium or play area. Everyone else is scattered throughout the area.

4. The taggers count to five while the other students are dribbling around the area. After counting to five, the taggers try to pull the tails off the other students.

5. If a student's tail is pulled or his dribble is out of control, he must go to a designated area and dribble for 15 seconds while saying the cue words out loud. The student may then return to the activity.

Extensions

- Give the taggers a ball to foot dribble.
- Set a time limit for each group of taggers and rotate after that time has expired.

MINEFIELD

Objective

To practice dribbling with the feet while avoiding obstacles.

Equipment

One ball (e.g., playground ball, soccer ball, foam ball, yarn ball) per student and approximately 20 traffic cones. Empty 2-liter bottles, Poly Spots, or dome cones may be substituted for the traffic cones.

Activity

1. Scatter the cones throughout the gymnasium or play area.

2. Students each take a ball and scatter themselves throughout the area.

3. On the start signal, students begin to dribble around the mines (cones).

4. If a student hits a mine with her ball, she must go to the designated practice area. Before returning to the activity, she must foot dribble for 15 seconds while saying the cue words out loud.

Extensions

- Play a game of dribble tag. Select a student or several students to be taggers. Once a student is tagged, he goes to a designated practice area and has a peer evaluate the critical elements of dribbling with the feet. You may select a student to go to the designated area as the first watcher when the game begins. When the tagged student finishes demonstrating how to dribble with his feet, the first watcher returns to the game and the student who was tagged stays in the area and becomes the new watcher. After she observes the next tagged student perform the skill, the watcher returns to the game. This rotation continues as long as the activity is played.

- If several students are waiting, they may double up and be observed by the same person. Every effort should be made to minimize waiting time.

- Place hoops in the minefield and have half of the students stand inside them. The remaining students dribble through the mine field and past the hoops, trying to control the ball. If a student in a hoop is able to touch a ball with one of her feet, she changes places with the dribbler.

SOCCER MADNESS

Objective

To practice dribbling with the feet while avoiding other players.

Equipment

One soccer ball or playground ball per student and a well-defined outdoor play area.

Activity

1. Select two taggers.
2. The taggers stand in the middle of the play area and the rest of the students stand at one end of the play area.
3. On the start signal, the students begin to dribble a ball with their feet to the opposite end of the play area.
4. Each tagger dribbles a ball toward the rest of the students.
5. The taggers try to dribble their balls into the other students' balls. (Taggers must be close to the students they tag.) If this happens before the students reach the opposite end of the play area, the tagged students become taggers and join the original group of taggers. Any student who avoids a tag by kicking the ball away is automatically tagged.
6. After all students have reached the opposite end, the taggers return to the middle of the area. On the start signal, the players not tagged attempt to return to the starting side while avoiding the taggers.
7. This rotation continues until all but two of the students have become taggers. Now a new activity is started with the two untagged students as the first taggers.

Extensions

- Start the activity with more than two taggers.
- If a student's ball is tagged, he must go to a designated area and dribble around five cones before returning to the activity as a tagger.

Based on North American Sports Camps, Fun and Games.

IT'S CROWDED

Objective

To improve students' ability to keep their eyes focused forward while dribbling with their feet.

Equipment

One ball per student.

Activity

1. Each student dribbles a ball in general space.
2. Begin to decrease the size of the space in which the students may dribble until movement is limited.
3. Slowly increase the size of the play area.

Extensions

- Students dribble balls of different sizes.
- On a signal, students must change directions with the ball.

Dribbling With Feet Troubleshooting Chart

If you see this	Then try this
1. Student using the toe to dribble the ball	• Suspend an empty 2-liter soda bottle from a net or rope suspended between two game standards. The bottle should be no more than 1 inch (2.5 cm) off the ground. The student must tap the bottle from side to side using the inside or outside of the foot. • Have students work in pairs. One partner dribbles the ball a specified distance. The other partner counts the number of times the toe touches the ball. The object is to get a score of zero.
2. Student not using short taps to dribble the ball	• Review the concept of force. • Give each student a ball to dribble. Walk through the playing area and try to take the ball away from any student who taps it too far away. The object is for the students to keep all balls away from you. • Set up cones approximately 2 to 4 feet (0.6-1.2 m) apart throughout the playing area. The student must dribble the ball through the cones and tap the ball at least once before passing any cone.
3. Student always using the same foot	• Have students work in pairs. One partner dribbles the ball a specified distance. The student dribbling must alternate his feet during the dribble. The other partner counts every time the feet do not alternate. The object is to get a score of zero. • Suspend an empty 2-liter soda bottle from a net or rope suspended between two game standards. The bottle should be no more than 1 inch (2.5 cm) off the ground. The student must tap the bottle from side to side using the inside or outside of the foot.
4. Student watching the ball instead of looking forward	• Students work in pairs. Using an empty milk jug, deflated ball, or foam ball, one student tries to move the object through the playing area while maintaining eye contact with his partner. • Have the student play keep-away with a partner. • Have the student dribble a ball while you hold up a picture or a number of fingers for a couple of seconds. The student must be able to tell you what she saw. • Have the students work in pairs. One partner dribbles a ball while following the movements of the other partner. The leading partner should begin with a walk and then increase his speed as the dribbler becomes more proficient.
5. Student walking while dribbling the ball	• Students work in pairs. One partner is a tagger. The tagger may walk fast to try to catch the dribbler and get the ball. The dribbler may walk fast or run to stay away from the tagger. The object is to keep the ball away from the tagger. • Alternatively, use several taggers for the previous exercise.

SUMMARY

Soccer is one of the most popular organized sports that children play. In recent years, professional soccer and the World Cup Soccer Championships have received a great deal of media attention. Because of this, children are becoming more and more interested in learning how to play. However, the most difficult soccer technique for students to master is probably dribbling with the feet. The dribble is both a manipulative and a locomotor skill.

When young children first learn to dribble with their feet, it is a classic case of the ball controlling the child, not the child controlling the ball. Children often mistake a kick, chase, and kick as dribbling; managing the ball has not yet become part of the skill for them. By teaching the mechanics of dribbling and emphasizing the idea of light taps, students begin to understand how to control the ball. With this new skill, soccer will be transformed from a kick-and-chase activity to a challenging and enjoyable sport that children can play for many years.

DRIBBLING WITH FEET LESSON PLAN

(FIRST LESSON)

AGE GROUP: Second grade.

FOCUS: Keeping control while dribbling with the feet.

SUBFOCUS: Using different parts of the foot to dribble, moving in general space, and applying the concept of force with a manipulative skill.

OBJECTIVE: To control the ball while performing the foot dribble on four out of five attempts, as measured by teacher observation (**cues:** *use the flat part of your foot, easy taps,* and *keep it close).*

MATERIALS AND EQUIPMENT: One partially deflated playground ball for each student. You will need one floor hockey stick and one tennis ball for a demonstration.

ORGANIZATION AND MANAGEMENT: Students are in self-space for warm-up, instruction, and practice.

WARM-UP: Students enter the gymnasium and begin moving to music. Call out the different locomotor movements the children should perform, including jogging, skipping, galloping, and sliding.

Watch for students moving safely and performing the locomotor skills correctly. Modify the activity to include the movement concept of force. For example, challenge the children to jog with light force, skip with light force, gallop with light force, and so on.

Watch for students moving safely and performing the skills correctly.

FORMATION: Students find self-space in the gymnasium and face you.

INTRODUCTION:

Your locomotor skills are wonderful. Besides performing locomotor skills and using different amounts of force, you also had to do something else to be successful with the warm-up. What was it? **(Keeping self-space while moving in general space.)**

Great. Today we're going to work on a skill that also requires you to keep that self-space and use light force. This time you have to keep more than your body under control; you also have to keep an object under control. We're going to work on dribbling with the feet today.

To perform a dribble correctly, use the feet to **tap** *the ball forward, then move to it, and then* **tap** *it again. It takes a lot of practice to keep the ball from rolling too far. We're going to work with playground balls today that don't have as much air in them as they usually would. This way, they won't roll too far.*

When I call out the color that is on your shirt, you may go get a playground ball and return to your self-space and sit down.

*Great job. Everyone stand up where you are and place the ball on the floor. When I put the music on, I want you to move in general space at a slow speed and tap the ball with **light** force using only your feet. You must be able to keep the ball close to you, so you don't want to tap it too hard—use **light** force. (Begin music.)*

Watch for students moving safely and keeping the balls close to them by tapping lightly. Repeat the cue words *easy taps* and *keep it close.*

Freeze. You are doing very well. Now, if I want to really control a ball, should I tap it with a flat surface or a round surface? You think about that while I try an experiment.

Demonstrate using a hockey stick and a tennis ball. Place the ball on the ground. First, use the toe of the hockey stick and tap the ball several times. Next, use the flat side of the hockey stick to tap the ball several times.

When did I have the most control over where the ball went? That's right, when I used the flat part of the stick. When you dribble a soccer ball, you need to use the flat part of the foot, too. Everyone show me a flat part of your foot. That's right; you can use the inside or the outside. For control, you need that flat part of your foot. (Demonstrate a foot dribble using the inside and outside parts of your foot versus using the toe.)

*When the music begins, I would like you to move around the gymnasium and dribble the ball with the flat part of your foot. Again, you want to have **easy taps** and **keep it close.** (Begin music.)*

Watch for students using the insides and outsides of their feet to dribble. Repeat the cues *use the flat part of your foot, easy taps,* and *keep it close.*

Freeze. When I say go, I would like everyone to find a partner and sit down side by side with the two balls beside you. Go.

This time you will play Follow the Leader. The younger of the two of you will be the leader first. The other partner will follow the leader and keep control of the ball. I will clap my hands when it's time to switch. Now, see who is the younger. Stand up and place the balls on the floor. Do you understand the directions? Go. (Begin music.)

Watch for students using the insides and outsides of their feet to dribble, keeping control of the ball, and following the leader. Repeat the cues *use the flat part of your foot, easy taps,* and *keep it close.* After 2 to 3 minutes, clap your hands so the other partner becomes the leader.

Freeze. When I say go, I would like you and your partner to find another pair of students and sit near each other. Go.

*Now you have a group of four. I would like you to stand up in height order with the shortest person in front. Moving **slowly,** so as not to lose anyone, you will pretend that you are a train. The first person will be the locomotive and the rest of you will be cars on the train. You must dribble your ball and stay behind the locomotive. Do you understand these directions? Stand up with your group. When the music starts, you may begin. (Begin music.)*

Watch for control of the ball and following the leader. Repeat the cue words *easy taps* and *keep it close* often. (After 2 minutes, the locomotive is rotated so that everyone has a turn.)

Freeze. Please put your equipment away and line up.

CLOSURE: As students are lined up to leave, play teach the teacher.

Let's review the key ideas we learned today:

1. *What part of my foot do I use to dribble a ball? **(The flat part.)***
2. *What kind of force did we use today when foot dribbling a ball? **(Light force.)***
3. *Which foot do I use to dribble with? **(Either foot.)** That's right, and next time we will work on dribbling with the right foot and the left foot.*

References

Albemarle County Physical Education Curriculum Revision Committee. (2008). *Albemarle County physical education curriculum guide.* Unpublished manuscript, Albemarle County Public Schools, Charlottesville, VA.

Graham, G., Holt-Hale, S., & Parker, M. (2013). *Children moving: A reflective approach to teaching physical education.* Mountain View, CA: Mayfield Press.

NASPE (1992). Outcomes of quality physical education programs. Reston, VA: Author.

NASPE (1995). Moving into the future: National standards for physical education. Reston, VA: Author.

Pangrazi, B., Chomokos, N., & Massoney, D. (1981). From theory to practice: A summary. In A. Morrie (Ed.), *Motor development: Theory into practice* (pp. 65-71) [Monograph 3 of *Motor skills: Theory into practice*]. ERIC Document Reproduction Service No. ED 225 939.

Seefeldt, V. (1979). Developmental motor patterns: Implications for elementary school physical education. In C. Nadeau, W. Halliwell, K. Newell, & C. Roberts (Eds.), *Psychology of motor behavior and sport.* Champaign, IL: Human Kinetics.

SHAPE America. (2014). *National standards & grade-level outcomes for K-12 physical education.* Champaign, IL: Human Kinetics.

About the Authors

Vonnie Colvin, EdD, is a professor of physical education pedagogy in Longwood University's department of health, athletic training, recreation, and kinesiology. In addition to her teaching duties, she works with student teachers in the schools and is the program coordinator for the physical and health education teacher education program in her department. She was the 2013 recipient of the Virginia Association for Health, Physical Education, Recreation and Dance Outstanding University Physical Educator Award. Before coming to Longwood University in 2004, Colvin was a member of the department of kinesiology and health promotion at the University of Kentucky for 9 years. During her tenure in Kentucky, she received the Outstanding University Physical Educator Award and an Outstanding Service Award from the Kentucky Association for Health, Physical Education, Recreation and Dance in 2002.

Colvin is a member of both SHAPE America and the Virginia Association for Health, Physical Education, Recreation and Dance. She served as vice president of physical education for the Kentucky state organization in 1999, and she is currently vice president of the general division in the Virginia state association. In addition, Colvin served on the *Strategies* editorial board from 1999 to 2002 and was the chair in 2001.

Before moving to higher education in 1995, Colvin taught physical education in Louisa County, Virginia, for 21 years—8 years at the elementary level, 2 at the middle school level, and 11 at the high school level. During that time, she also worked with student teachers from Norfolk State University and Virginia Tech.

Colvin lives in Farmville, Virginia, and enjoys hiking, gardening, and reading.

Nancy Markos, MEd, is the 2002 National Elementary Physical Education Teacher of the Year for the National Association for Sport and Physical Education (NASPE) and the 2003 Outstanding Elementary School Teacher for the Curry School of Education at the University of Virginia. In 2011, Markos received the Golden Apple Award for the Albemarle County Public School Teachers.

Markos was an elementary physical education and health specialist for the Albemarle County school system in Charlottesville, Virginia, from 1984 until her retirement in 2011. At that time, Markos became the facilitator of health, physical education, and family life for the Albemarle County Public Schools until June 2014. Markos is now a consultant for Move, Live, Learn and a presenter for US Games.

She was also clinical instructor for the University of Virginia from 1985 until her retirement in 2011. She mentored students in the physical education and adapted physical education programs. Before coming to Virginia, Markos taught physical education at the elementary level for 3 years in Maryland and at the middle school level for 5 years in Maryland and Rhode Island.

Markos is a member of SHAPE America; the Virginia Association of Health, Physical Education, Recreation and Dance; and the education sorority Delta Kappa Gamma. She is past president of the Albemarle Education Association. Markos was a member of the writing and revision teams for the Standards of Learning for Physical Education and for the *Physical Education Resource Guide* for the Virginia Department of Education.

Markos lives in Earlysville, Virginia, and enjoys spending time with her family, playing golf, and working out.

Pam Walker, MEd, was named the 1995 Elementary Physical Education Teacher of the Year by the Virginia Association of Health, Physical Education, Recreation and Dance. In 2004, she received the Golden Apple Award for teachers in the Albemarle County Public Schools. She was an elementary physical education and health specialist in the Albemarle County school system in Charlottesville, Virginia, for 30 years until her retirement in 2008. She taught the last 25 years at Red Hill Elementary in North Garden, Virginia. Walker was a clinical instructor at the University of Virginia, where she worked with practicum students and student teachers for 18 years.

She has led a variety of workshops for physical educators and classroom teachers. Her workshops include teaching movement and fundamental skills, whole brain learning, classroom management skills, learning styles and strategies, stress management, and teaching for multiple intelligences. Walker has helped teachers incorporate teaching strategies and multiple intelligence learning into their classrooms. She received integrated thematic instruction (ITI) training and assisted teachers on her staff in implementing the ITI concepts.

Walker is a past member of VAHPERD, SHAPE America, the National Education Association, the education sorority Delta Kappa Gamma, and the professional education fraternity Phi Delta Kappa.

Walker lives in Schuyler, Virginia, and enjoys spending time with her family, swimming, golfing, hiking, and camping.

About SHAPE America

health. moves. minds.

SHAPE America—Society of Health and Physical Educators—is committed to ensuring that all children have the opportunity to lead healthy, physically active lives. As the nation's largest membership organization of health and physical education professionals, SHAPE America works with its 50 state affiliates and is a founding partner of national initiatives including the Presidential Youth Fitness Program, *Let's Move!* Active Schools and the Jump Rope for Heart and Hoops for Heart programs.

Since its founding in 1885, the organization has defined excellence in physical education, most recently creating *National Standards & Grade-Level Outcomes for K-12 Physical Education* (2014), *National Standards & Guidelines for Physical Education Teacher Education (2009)* and *National Standards for Sport Coaches* (2006), and participating as a member of the Joint Committee on National Health Education Standards, which published *National Health Education Standards, Second Edition: Achieving Excellence* (2007). Our programs, products and services provide the leadership, professional development and advocacy that support health and physical educators at every level, from preschool through university graduate programs.

Every spring, SHAPE America hosts its National Convention and Expo, the premier national professional-development event for health and physical educators.

Advocacy is an essential element in the fulfillment of our mission. By speaking out for the school health and physical education professions, SHAPE America strives to make an impact on the national policy landscape.

Our Vision: Healthy People—Physically Educated and Physically Active!

Our Mission: To advance professional practice and promote research related to health and physical education, physical activity, dance and sport.

Our Commitment: 50 Million Strong by 2029

Approximately 50 million students are currently enrolled in America's elementary and secondary schools (grades pre-K to 12). SHAPE America is leading the effort to ensure that by the time today's preschoolers graduate from high school in 2029, all of America's students will have developed the skills, knowledge and confidence to enjoy healthy, meaningful physical activity.

One step can start a national movement.

Membership does more than advance your career—it's also your first step in a national movement to help all children become healthy, physically educated adults.

Joining SHAPE America Is Your First Step Toward:

• **Improving your instructional practices.** Membership is your direct connection to the books and other classroom resources, webinars, workshops, and professional development you need. **Members save up to 30%!**

• **Staying current on trends in education.** We will deliver the news to you through our weekly e-newsletter *Et Cetera,* our quarterly member newsletter *Momentum,* and peer-reviewed journals like *Strategies: A Journal for Physical and Sport Educators,* the *American Journal of Health Education, Journal of Physical Education, Recreation & Dance,* and *Research Quarterly for Exercise and Sport.*

• **Earning recognition for you and your program.** Showcase your school's achievements and gain funding through grant and award opportunities.

• **Growing your professional network.** Whether it's a face-to-face event or online through the member-exclusive community—Exchange—you'll gain access to a diverse group of peers who can help you respond to daily challenges.

Join Today. www.shapeamerica.org/membership